ISBN-13: 978-1986143578 (CreateSpace-Assigned)
ISBN-10: 1986143570

V. J. Beanland

Journey to

Letters, Memoirs & Personal Diaries

1861–1951

Acknowledgements

A massive thank you to my father, Malcolm, for inspiring me to put together this wonderful collection. Also, to his cousin Peter for lending me Charles's diaries from 1888 and 1895 – I still have to return them!

My gratitude to The Gibraltar Heritage Journal for allowing me to publish my father's articles again, and to The Honourable Dr Joseph Garcia for adding a wonderful foreword.

By the power of the internet, this book now also has some bonus material, which explain a bit more about Emma Beanland (nee Saword) and her family – a side which my father knew little about. Thank you, Clare, for allowing me to give him even *more* family history!

To all my numerous cousins and family that supported me and encouraged me after the launch of the eBook last year. Your feedback really helped to keep me going. This paperback now includes many photographs that bring together the past and the future – thank you for letting me share them.

Finally, to my husband and children for patiently listening to me at times ramble on whilst staring at the screen and typing away in a hypnotic zombie-like manner! I couldn't do any of this without you.

V. J. Beanland (*or* Vanessa Wester)
2018

**For my father,
Malcolm Beanland**

*His love of history and the Beanland
heritage will never diminish.*

&

**For my mother,
Marie-Carmen Beanland**

*Who has patiently enjoyed listening to
him reminisce for over fifty years...*

Beanland/ Saword Family Tree

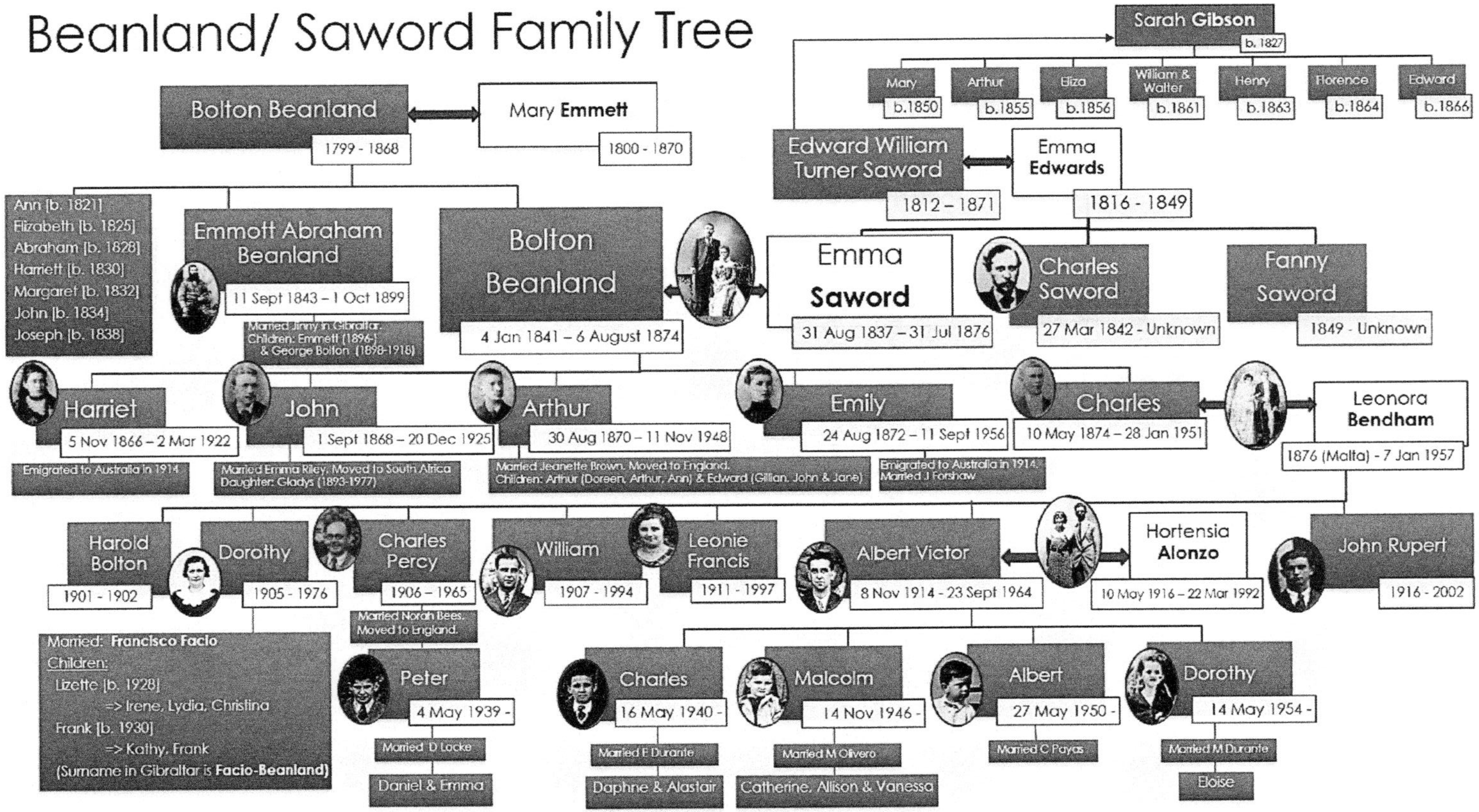

Contents

FOREWORD
By The Honourable Dr Joseph Garcia
Deputy Chief Minister of Gibraltar

FOREWORD

By The Honourable Dr Joseph Garcia
Deputy Chief Minister of Gibraltar

I am delighted, both as a historian and at a personal level, that Vanessa Wester, through her father Malcolm Beanland, has asked to me write a foreword for this book. I say that because Malcolm and I are related through his marriage to Marie-Carmen.

This book is as much a social history of Gibraltar as it is a family history which traces the origin of the Beanland family on the Rock. It covers an era where the widespread instant, electronic communications that we take for granted today, simply did not exist. This meant that people by and large relied on writing letters to their relatives. These communications were often phrased in flowery, colourful language and painted a real picture, not only of the immediate family situation that was described but also of the wider background which faced the author at that moment in time. The collection of letters is rightly described as a journey into the past. This is an added reason why the book is a fascinating read.

I was enthralled too with the story of the arrival of Bolton Beanland in Gibraltar in January 1867 on a military posting. This was an important part of life in Victorian Gibraltar and there are recollections of parades and marches with the pomp and ceremony that was customary and expected in a naval base which was a key staging post for the Empire.

The tragic story of Bolton and Emma's passing and the commendable decision on the part of his brother Abraham to raise their five children after they were orphaned cannot fail both to pull the heart-strings and to impress. A heroic decision indeed. The book covers these highs and lows as reflected in letters, papers and diaries and it spans the period through the Second World War up to 1951.

The Beanland story was one I had first heard from Malcolm and which was clearly spurred on by the almost accidental discovery in 1997 of a chest of letters, papers and old family photographs. It was a valuable find. I know that many readers will recall the Beanland stationery shop and printers, and for them this will be a trip down memory lane.

However, this is also an important contribution to the social history of Gibraltar seen through the eyes of different generations of Beanlands. I want to congratulate Vanessa and Malcolm for having taken the project forward and thoroughly recommend this fascinating work.

I wish them every success.

HOW BOLTON BEANLAND AND FAMILY CAME TO SETTLE IN GIBRALTAR IN VICTORIAN TIMES

By Malcolm Beanland

On the 4th August 2004, Gibraltar celebrated 300 years of British rule, since Admiral Sir George Rooke arrived with an Anglo Dutch fleet off Europa Point and took the Rock from Spain, eventually leading to the Treaty of Utrecht of 1713 when it was ceded in perpetuity to the British Crown.

Over three centuries, the Rock has withstood sieges and passed from being a fortress to the thriving Gibraltar that today welcomes over seven million tourists from all over the world who come to visit and enjoy the rich history and heritage that we have to offer.

But Gibraltar has another fascinating story to it and that lies in the rich culture and variety that is the Gibraltarian. Indeed, the story of the Gibraltarian has roots in different countries such as Genoa, Italy, Malta, Spain, and, of course, the United Kingdom. My story attempts to describe and portray the origins of my ancestors, the Beanland family, where the roots came from and why, how, and when they arrived in Gibraltar and their contribution towards Gibraltar society, small as it may be.

During my research, I have been extremely fortunate in that both my father, Albert Victor Beanland, 1914-1964, and my Grandfather, Charles Bolton Beanland, 1874-1951, kept valuable family letters and photos. These together with articles in Gibraltar newspapers, the use of the Garrison Library, the Gibraltar Archives, the Gibraltar Museum and, of course, the magic of the 21st Century, the Internet, have contributed to the article for which I am very grateful.

In 1997, with the passing of my aunt, Mrs. Leonia Bado, nee Beanland, the family had to hand over ownership of 74 Main Street, which had been our home since 1919, to Jyske Bank. This followed the sale of the business, Beanland Malin & Co, together with the freehold property, in 1979, to Galliano's Bank.

During the inevitable clearing up process, my wife came across a family chest containing some books and old photos that took me to the past and the story of how the posting of the 3rd Battalion, Royal Artillery was to have such repercussions for the BEANLAND family and Gibraltar.

The arrival of the Beanland family to Gibraltar is recorded in a little booklet that contains "The Letters of Bolton & Emma E Beanland and his brother Emmett Abram Beanland compiled by John Beanland, Urmston, Lancashire, England" and that were printed by Beanland Malin & Co, Printers & Lithographers at Gibraltar in 1916.

The letters, totalling 60, were written between 24th January 1861 and 12th July 1883.

The extracts are taken to illustrate the family history and at the same time Bolton Beanland's earliest experiences in the United Kingdom in 1861, his posting to Jamaica from 1862 – 1865, at Chester during 1866 and his delight to be posted to Gibraltar in 1867, letters from 1867 to 1873, when he paid to get discharged from the army to start a stationery shop at 5 Church Street, and his last letter in April 1874 before his premature death due to consumption on the 6th August 1874.

Extracts are also recorded from letters written by his brother Abraham Emmett Beanland from 4th July 1862 to 12th July 1883. These letters, as well as a diary kept by Harriett Beanland, Bolton's eldest daughter when only twelve years old do provide a very interesting background into the Beanland family and what life was in Gibraltar in the 1860's to 1870's on the Rock, then a major Military fortress. An article entitled, The Diary of Harriet Beanland as a girl 1874 – 1876 appeared in The Heritage Journal No 10 published in 2003.

Bolton Beanland was born on the 25th January 1841 at Reedyford Marsden, Lancashire. His birth certificate was registered in the district of Burnley, sub-district of Colne, in the county of Lancaster.

His father also called Bolton Beanland, was a boatman, and was born in 1804 in Colne, Lancashire and died aged 64 years old in Burnley, Lancashire. His mother was called Mary Beanland, formerly Emmett.

The Beanland family can be traced in direct descent to a certain Roberti Beanland who lived during the English Civil War and died on the 8 November 1672 during the reign of Charles II. (1660-1685). The Beanland family originally came from a small town called Kildwick in the West

Riding of Yorkshire and then moved to Lancashire around 1779 to the town of Colne where Abraham Beanland (b.1779 - d. about 1830) and Bolton Beanland (1804-1868) were born. They were my great grandfather's, own grandfather and father.

Bolton Beanland enlisted in the Army at Ashton, Lancashire, with the Royal Artillery on the 26th September 1859 at the age of eighteen years. He served with the Army for 13 years until he was just over 31 and a half years old having achieved the rank of Sergeant Major. In August 1873, whilst serving at Gibraltar, he bought himself out of the 3rd Battalion, 15th Brigade, 8th Battery, Royal Artillery for the princely sum, in those days, of 9 pounds sterling!

His Army Parchment Certificate dated 5 May 1873 at Gibraltar describes Bolton Beanland as 5ft 10" tall, having a sallow complexion, grey eyes and light brown hair. In it, his Commanding Officer, Colonel E. A. Williams CB described my great grandfather as:

"his conduct has been very good, and he was, when promoted in possession of four good conduct badges."

He started his own business, a stationery shop situated at 5 Church Street, today's Book Centre at 217 Main Street. Just as he was building up a life outside the Army, with his young wife, Emma Elizabeth nee Saword, and family, disaster struck, and he died prematurely on the 6th August 1874.

Aged 33 years old, he left behind a wife and five children: Harriett, aged 8; John, aged 6; Arthur, aged 4; Emily, aged 2; and baby Charles, my grandfather, just under three months old...

THE BEANLAND & GIBRALTAR LEGACY

By Vanessa Wester (V.J. Beanland)

The article my father, Malcolm Beanland, wrote for the Gibraltar Heritage Journal brought me to tears, I had no idea that my great grandfather was an orphan. My curiousity and interest in history culminated in this book, I just had to find out more about my ancestral past. The mystery box with old letters and diaries found by my mother held a treasure trove of information that was waiting to be unleashed.

There is no doubt in my mind that my great-great grandfather, Bolton, was a great man, yet it saddens me that he passed away at the early age of 33. However, what shocked me to the core was discovering that his wife, Emma, also died just two years later, aged just 38.

Five children were left orphaned, and had it not been for his brother, Emmett, who knows what would have happened to them. My great grandfather, Charles Beanland, continued on the Rock and thrived because of his Uncle Emmett – who must have truly sacrificed a lot for his brother's children.

The success of the Stationery business, started by Bolton in 1873, was also aided by the continuing relationship between Emmett and another Uncle, Charles Saword, Emma's brother – a merchant based in London, who I have found provided the initial investment for the shop and then helped to supply and stock the Beanland Stationer's Shop.

Charles Saword
Merchant's Agent
Married: Emma Read

Charles Saword

Further evidence of this relationship can be seen via the visit to London in 1895 by Charles Beanland, and the numerous communications between Charles and his uncle.

This paperback edition now includes, with great thanks to Clare Kirk, bonus material explaining a bit more about the Sawords and the double life Charles Saword actually led! Clare got in contact after she downloaded the kindle version of this book in 2017, to let me know she was a descendant linked to the Sawords mentioned in this book. I am thrilled to include this extra piece of history, some of which I had already obtained with the help of a friend of mine, Christine. I am indebted to both for helping us understand a bit more about Emma.

The accounts that follow in this book have been put together as a historical account for my family in Gibraltar and any distant relations I have in UK and elsewhere.

Since I am a writer at heart, I have nearly completed a historical novel based on these accounts, but having returned to secondary school teaching I am, as of yet, to finish it. The truth is that I lack the courage to write a sad and unhappy ending. I hope one day to finish the novel, but either way, it has been both interesting and challenging to bring to life these distant characters. I believe history is always more accessible when seen through the eyes of characters that have a story to tell. It certainly helped me to visualise the setting for this book.

Nevertheless, I put all my energy over the past few years into completing this project. It has taken many hours to transcribe all the handwritten diaries, but I have learnt a lot about my family in the process. For one, my great grandfather, Charles, loved to swim early morning in Camp Bay and he was definitely a voracious reader with an appreciation for music and the Arts.

To enable you to read the letters easily, I have added some minor changes to the layout of the original letters and corrected any errors. I have also made **bold** certain comments which are interesting in the diaries and memoirs so that they are easier to spot!

If I have misrepresented any information I apologise, but some of the handwriting was at times hard to read. I have painstakingly attempted to copy these original handwritten letters and must admit that I am in awe that they could be read by the recipient on occasions!

Family is something that we sometimes take for granted but being able to publish these accounts is truly a magical thing. No longer will anyone have to find old records after over one hundred years have passed – as exciting as this was.

Today, we can share our history via the ease of a button. I hope you enjoy reading the entries as much as I did. The past can inspire the way we live and seeing the way my own children become adults it is truly amazing how characteristics get passed on from one generation to the next.

This compilation is a record of the past for the future.

The Letters

of

Bolton & Emma E. Beanland

and

Emmett Abram Beanland,

compiled by

John Beanland, Urmston, Lancs.

Printed at Gibraltar, 1916.

BEANLAND, MALIN & CO., Printers & Lithographers

Bolton Beanland (1841-1874)
Emma E. Beanland (1837-1876)
Emmett Abraham Beanland (1843-1899)

Original Publisher: John Beanland
son of
Bolton & Emma Beanland, (1868-1925)

Original printed version edited by
V. J. Beanland to enable an easier read.

The copy printed in 1915 has many typographical errors, which may have
been from either the original letter or from when the letters were typed up.

PART ONE:

LETTERS

OF

BOLTON

BEANLAND

The original edition published by John Beanland in 1916 has been split into two parts. This allows the letters found to be read in chronological order, since we now have more letters written by Emma Saword in the period of 1874-1876.

Alderney
24th January 1861

Dear Father and Mother,

I have great pleasure in answering your letter. I received your letter last Saturday and I was very glad to receive a letter from you. I got a letter from my brother EMET the same time as I got yours and he wants to get to me as soon as he can. The Captain of our battery is on leave to Guernsey this week and when he comes back on Saturday I shall put in a claim for him as you want me to send you a few shillings. I send you £1 in this letter and I hope you will answer this letter as soon as you can and let me know whether you get it or not.

I will put the order in another envelope for safety. If you need any more money I think I can have another £1 by the time you answer this letter or if you do not need it, I shall give it towards my brother's expenses in coming to me.

Tell James Watson that he has not answered my last letter. Give my kind love to my brother Joseph and sisters Elizabeth and Margaret and Ann and to all inquiring friends.

So, no more at present,
From your son,
Bolton Beanland

Direct to
Gunner Bolton Beanland
No 8 Battery, 15th Brigade, Royal Artillery
Alderney, Channel Island
Or elsewhere

Guernsey
28th June 1861

Dear Father and Mother,

I have great pleasure of writing a few lines to you hoping this letter will find you in good health as I and my brother are at present. You must excuse me for not writing to you before now. I forget now when I got your last letter, but I think it was about Whitsuntide.

I had a letter from Manchester last week and I answered their letter and told them that I would send them our likenesses. They said that they expected being at Burnley at the fair, so I told them that I would direct the likeness to you for them so that they would be able to get it when they go to the fair. We have got our likeness took now ready for sending so you must expect it a few days after you get this letter. I shall have it registered so that my father will have to sign his name to it when you get it.

I cannot tell you anything particular in this letter.

Our Emmett seems to like Guernsey very well. He goes bathing almost every day in the sea. There is a fine sandy beach in front of our barracks for bathing. We have plenty of shot and shell firing here, with 32 pounder guns, which just pleases our Emmett. To rights, I like it very well only it always makes my head ache with the noise.

I must conclude my letter, hoping it will find you all in good health. We join in sending our kind love to our sisters and brothers and to Mary Watson and all inquiring friends.

Our Emmett would like to send J. Johnson some tobacco, but he cannot. It is so cheap that he never has no less than one pound on hand.

So no more at present.
From your affectionate sons,
A and B Beanland

Answer this letter when you get the likeness.

Guernsey
10th September 1861

Dear Father and Mother,

I dare say that you will have begun to think that we had forgot you. I hope this letter will find you all in good health as we are both at present.

I received your likeness last month and I am very glad of it. The reason that I did not write to you sooner is because I did intend to send you some money, but with my brother coming to me and having so many new things to get I have not been able to send any. But, if all is well, I will send some next week. I have received one or two letters from our Ann since I wrote to you before. I got a letter from Manchester last week and I am glad to hear that they are all in good health.

I should think that our Edward is about big enough to begin to write letter and I would like to get a letter of his writing. I am very glad to tell you that our Emett is well and seems to like the artillery almost better than I do myself. I don't know what reason he has for not writing to you, he never writes to no one but Billy Burrows.

Dear Father, I am very glad to tell you that I have been teetotal now near 9 months, thank God for that. I can tell you this cheap drink here makes sad havoc with some of the men. There has been one man flogged and a great many done 2, 3, 4 and 6 months in prison for nothing but getting drunk.

Give my respects to my brother Joseph and his wife and all my brothers and sisters and to Mary and Richard Watson and to all inquiring friends so no more at present.

From your son,
Bolton Beanland

P.s. Please answer this letter when you get the money.

Guernsey
19th December 1861

Dear Father and Mother,

I received a letter from Burnley today and I think it is from you. It is addressed to "Dear Brother", but it has my name at the end of it. But, no matter about that. I should have written to you now if I had got no letter at all.

I am sorry to tell you that my brother put in for a furlough yesterday and it was signed today. He had got everything packed ready for starting tomorrow morning, and then an order come today for no. 7 & 8 Batteries to proceed to Woolwich on Monday morning to go through a few weeks course of drill and then embark for America. So, his furlough was torn up when that order came, and I scarcely think that either of us will be able to get a furlough. But, I will get our Emmett a furlough from Woolwich if possible.

I am sorry to disappoint you in this way, but I hope you will rest content for I can assure you that we are both glad at having the chance of going to America.

There is a great morning for the **death of Prince Albert** in Guernsey. All the shops in town are half-closed and all the flags are at half-mast.

I will write to you again when we get to Woolwich. Please tell J. Watson where I am going to.

We both send our kind love to all friends at home, especially to Sarah & to Grandmother, and sisters & brothers. I must tell you that I have got some presents in Emmett's knapsack for little Tommy, Edward & Joshua Watson, which I am sorry to take out again and make away with as he cannot get a furlough.

So no more at present from your affectionate sons,
Good night
A & B Beanland
Gunners R. A.

Publisher Note:
Albert, Prince Consort of England (1819-1861), died aged 42 of typhoid fever on the 14 December 1861 at Windsor Castle, then buried at Frogmore Castle.

Woolwich
13th January 1862

Dear Father and Mother,

I have great pleasure in writing to you hoping it will find you all in good health as we are both at present. Thank God for it.

I think I am writing to you before my turn, but it doesn't matter very much about that. The reason that I write to you now is because there is a man of our battery gone on 7 days to Burnley. The same man that the young woman was inquiring for when I was on furlough last year, his name is William Barnes.

I am sorry to tell you that neither of us is able to come and see you this winter, but we are likely to remain here a long time, now that the America affair has turned out for the best. If we remain here till summer, we will try to get to see you and it will be better than going now.

Dear father, it is not because we are not entitled to 7 days pass, but it is because we have no money. Enough, I am glad to tell you that my brother has only been in trouble once since he came to me. That was at the Guernsey races last August. He has got **7 days extra drill for stopping absent at the races**.
I have not been in any trouble myself since I listed. I shall be getting a penny a day extra in about 6 months more as good conduct pay.
I like soldiering better every day and I am sure Emmett does the same.

I am glad to tell you that both of us went to London yesterday to hear Spurgeon preach. I have been to London 2 or 3 times to hear him, since we came here.

We both send our kind love to brothers and sisters and Sarah and Grandmother, and Richard and Mary Watson and to all inquiring friends.

So no more at present from your sons,
Abraham & Bolton Beanland

Answer this letter. Tell me how the trade is. Good night.

Woolwich
13th February 1862

Dear Father and Mother,

We received your kind and welcome letter today and I am glad to receive a letter from you. Also, to hear that you are all in good health as we are both at present. I don't hear very often from home now. I don't know what the reason of it is, but I suppose that they have not much to spare for letter writing. I am sorry to hear that the times are so bad.

I am surprised at you sending so many stamps, but as it happens they come in very useful for I have got a book that I intend to send you as a present and I know you will like it. I have read it through myself. You must look out for it in a few days after you get this letter and I wish you to lend it to my father after you read it.

I have not been up to London lately, but if all is well, I shall be there on Sunday 23rd instead.

Emmett and I is going to Greenwich Hospital and through the park.

Dear Brother, there is some talk about us going to London in May to do duty at the Great Exhibition. I should like some of you to come to London. When the exhibition opens, I think there will be plenty of cheap trips. You see what it is to be a soldier. To see all the fine things of this world.

Give my kind love to my grandmother, and to Mary Ann and Susanna and to all inquiring friends.

P.s. I cannot find out Thomas Johnson. If you can get his direction and send it to me, for I would like to find him out. Tell me whether he is a gunner or driver & what battery and which Brigade. Answer this letter by return of post.

So, no more at present from your affectionate brothers,
A & B Beanland
Direct as usual.

Publisher Note:
The Second Great Exhibition was opened by HRH The Duke of Cambridge on the 29 March 1862. The Duke of Cambridge's daughter married the Duke of Teck. Their daughter, Princess Mary married Queen Victoria's grandson, The Duke of York who later ascended the throne as King George V in 1911, on the death of his father, King Edward VII. The Exhibition was rated as a World Fair and was held at South Kensington, London, on the site that now houses the South Kensington Museums including the Science Museum.

Woolwich
12th March 1862

Dear Father and Mother,

I received your kind letter today, and I am happy to hear that you are all in good health as we are both at present. I will take care that you don't write two letters for my one this time as you say I did last time.

I am sorry to hear that Sarah is not well and I hope she is better by the time you receive this letter. I am happy to hear that Margaret is getting on well. I think I shall soon have the pleasure of coming to see you, but I would rather some of you come down to London to see us as there will be plenty of cheap trips to come to the exhibition and I am sure it will be worth coming to see.

I am very happy to tell you that my brother, Emmett, expects to draw £1-10-0 this week. It has been due to him from government ever since he came to me. It is money that is allowed from government to pay the expenses of the difference between an Artillery man's kit and an Infantry man's kit. The way Emmett wants to do, is to wait till we get our new clothing in April then both of us get 7 days pass.

I am glad to hear that Thomas Johnson has landed home. I would like to see him before he went, but I could not find him.

I saw a Burnley lad today, my sister, Margaret, will know him. I dare say **he was the piece hooker at the Mackintosh shed when I was a tenter** for her. His name is John Whittaker. I had a good chat with him about old Cowil and many more.

I must write a few lines to my brother Joe.

So no more at present from your affectionate brothers,
A and B Beanland
Royal Artillery

Woolwich
12th March 1862

Dear Brother,

I am happy to hear that you are well. You must excuse me for telling you when you write a letter. Take more care in spelling your words. The writing is good enough, but nothing looks so bad as a letter with bad spelling.

I saw a Burnley lad today. He knows you very well & I think you know him. His name is John Hargreaves. If you hear any one inquiring about him. He is a gunner in no. 10 Battery.
Depot Brigade,
R. A.
Dear Brother,
I must tell you that I like soldiering better every day, especially now that I am promoted. Although I am at present (while I am writing now) getting my tea without butter. That's what you would not like. But, you know that I can go to London for a few days when I like and get my pay all the same and, if you think of me on Monday 17th when you are at your looms, I shall be at a wedding. A friend of mine in our battery is going to be married. The fact of the matter is I would rather be a soldier than not, although I know I am to blame for leaving home.

Give my kind love to Elizabeth and to all enquiring friends. Tell Jim Watson, when you see him, that I am waiting for a letter from him.

Dear Brother, I cannot promise to send you a book yet, as they are rather expensive, 3 shillings and six pence each, but I will try to send you one after a while.

Give my kind respects to all inquiring friends. Be sure to answer this letter soon.
So no more at present from your affectionate brother,

B Beanland
Direct thus
Bomber B Beanland
No. 8 Battery, 15th Brigade, R. A. Woolwich

Woolwich
5th April 1862

Dear Father and Mother,

I have great pleasure in answering your kind letter that I received from you a few days since. I am glad to see that my brother has improved a little in spelling and I hope he will take it as no offence by me sending back the letter so that he can see the mistakes that he made.

My brother, Emmett, don't practice writing so much as he used to do. He don't care much about it, especially since I was made a bombardier.

I am truly sorry to hear of what has happened to my Brother John's wife. I hope she will soon recover. I can scarcely tell how to answer the question that Henry Watson asks in the letter about what country girl I have got, but she is neither black nor Irish. But, she is a Londoner, so I will leave him to guess what country she belongs!

I hope you will have a good "Good Friday" as I expect to have a good one myself, as I shall be in London if all is well. There is another wedding coming up at Easter Monday.

I am getting quite used to London now. I shall be off to the exhibition as soon as we come from Shoeburyness. That will be about the latter end of June.

There is a great talk about us going out to Canada about July. I don't care how soon we go for I am getting very near tired of Woolwich. If it was not for going to London now and then I should not care to stop here any longer.

It is now nearly a month since I heard from my sister, Harriett. I don't know what the reason of it. Tell my sister, Margaret, that I should like to get a letter from them.

Give my kind love to all brothers and sisters and to Sarah and to Richard and Mary Watson and to all inquiring friends.

So no more at present.
From your affectionate son,
B. Beanland
Sent to Church St, Burnley, Lancashire

Diary entries from 31st October – 29th November 1862

Friday 31st October 1862

We paraded at Woolwich at 7:30 a.m. headed by the Royal Artillery Band amidst the shouts of a great crowd of civilians. We embarked in a steam tug at T PIER Royal Arsenal and steamed down to Gravesend and embarked on board H.M. Ship Adventure. There we lay at anchor till 10 a.m. the following day.

Saturday 1st November 1862

Weighed anchor at 10 a.m. and sailed smoothly down the river on our way to the West Indies. At 11 a.m. we all mustered on the poop to be divided into three watches.

We afterwards got our sea-kits, which consisted of 1 white slops, 1 white shirt neckerchief, 1 red cap, 1 box of blacking, 1 boll pipe clay, 1 lb of sea soap, 1 lb of tobacco.

We passed the Goodwin Sands at 12:30 p.m. Dover Castle at 3:30 p.m.

Sunday 2nd November 1862

We paraded for Divine Service at 10 a.m. The prayers were read by the captain of the ship. The weather was fine all day. Passed the Eddystone light house at 7 o'clock in the evening.

Monday 3rd November 1862

We are now out of sight of land. The wind rose a little this morning, which caused the ship to roll a little and the men to lie about the deck sea-sick! Divine service held the same as yesterday. Weather fine all day.

Tuesday 4th November 1862

The wind rose this morning, which made the ship roll very much all day.

Wednesday 5th November 1862

The wind settles during the night. It rained till about 10 o'clock and then turned out to be a beautiful afternoon.

Thursday 6th November 1862

It has been very fine all day. We begin to feel the weather a little warmer. Also, the days get longer, the sun just rising at 6 o'clock. This morning the sickness is nearly over now amongst the men. I have myself escaped sickness altogether so far.

Friday 7th November 1862
A fine day and favourable wind.

Saturday 8th November 1862
Sighted land at 11 a.m. and arrived at Madeira at 3 p.m. and sailed about off the island all night.

Sunday 9th November 1862
Cast anchor just in front of town at 8 a.m. Madeira belongs to Portugal. Several of the natives came on board with fruit and the ship was surrounded with bum boats all day.

Monday 10th November 1862
Commenced taking in coal at 6 a.m. which continued all day.

Tuesday 11th November 1862
Weighted anchor at 8 a.m. and sailed at 8:30. The day was very fine and warm.

Sunday 16th November 1862
Nothing of importance since we left Madeira. The weather has been very fine with a favourable wind. We are now that we are in the tropics and the sun so hot that we are not allowed on deck bare-headed. We are now about 2½ hours behind the English time.

Tuesday 18th November 1862
We are now more than 1000 miles from land and the ship is sailing away almost as steady as if she was in the Thames.

Wednesday 19th November 1862
A very dark and cloudy morning till about 8 o'clock when it commenced to rain in torrents. The soldiers work on board ship taking in sails. A cry was heard, "A man overboard!" The sailors rushed to the life boat, which was manned and lowered immediately. One of the sailors, as soon as he heard the cry, jumped overboard and swam after him. He fell off the foreyard arm.

Another man fell off the place at the same time and dropped on board and broke one leg. Shortly after the accident, a very large shark was seen round the ship which followed us during the day.

The rain cleared off about noon and it turned out to be a fine afternoon.

Thursday 20th November 1862

The man that jumped overboard yesterday was rewarded with £12 from our officers. It was the third life he had saved in the same way. He is to be recommended for a medal from human society. There is scarcely any wind all day, which makes it very hot between decks. One or two sharks were seen during the day. A great many flying fish are seen. Every day, one or two have been caught.

Publisher note:
Following internet research, Malcolm Beanland established that an award was recommended when the ship arrived at Port Royal, Jamaica. Given by The Royal Humane Society. The Bronze Medal was awarded "To Able Seaman, J. Widgeney for his valour in assisting a man overboard from HMS Adventure, 19th November 1862, en route to Jamaica."

Friday 21st November 1862

The wind rose a little this morning. It is so warm now that most of the men prefer lying on deck all night rather than go between decks into hammocks.

Saturday 22nd November 1862

Some very heavy rain fell during last night, but the day has been very fine.

Sunday 23rd November 1862

This the fourth Sunday on board all the sailors and marines commenced wearing white clothing and sun caps. We had nearly 13 hours of sun today.

Monday 24th November 1862

Sighted the Islands of Antigua at 6 a.m., the first of the West Indies Islands. We also passed the Island of Monserrat, Nevis and St Christopher during the day. We were 800 miles from Jamaica at 9 o'clock this morning.

Friday 28th November 1862

Nothing of any importance has passed since Monday. The weather was fine and the sea very calm all week. Sighted Jamaica at 6 a.m. and received the pilot on board about 9 o'clock and reached Port Royal about 3 p.m. We lay in the river all night.

Saturday 29th November 1862

We disembarked at 8 a.m. this morning and marched about 300 yards to Port Royal Barracks.

THREE YEARS LATER...

Port Royal, JAMAICA,

7th December 1865

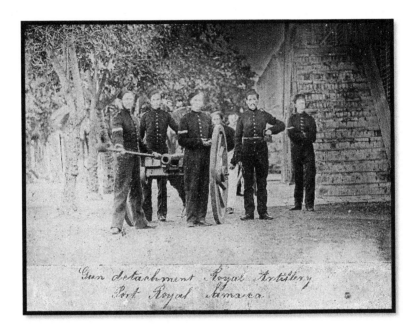

Port Royal, Jamaica,
7th December 1865

My Dear Parents,

I think it very strange that I have not heard from you for so long. I really think that I am entirely cut off from your remembrance, since I have done so well for myself. For I am sure I have got the best wife in the world and I thought you would have been so pleased to hear of it.

I wrote to you early in September, and I enclosed a letter, for London, which I asked you to post for me. I got an answer from you, but you did not say whether you had or had not, or would or would not post it.

I have since heard from London that the letter never was received from you. Now, I do not like it. For I do not think I am deserving such indifference from you if you thought it too much trouble to post it. I must ask you to be kind enough to return it and I will not trouble you with anymore.

I am sorry to write in such a strain as you will get this about New Year's Day. I wish you all a happy one, and hope you will all have had a Merry Christmas.

We are not going to America now, we are under orders to proceed to **Gibraltar** early in spring. I am very pleased at the prospect of going away from Jamaica for we are now over 3 years. But, I am happy to say that Jamaica is once more at peace. The **Rebellion** is entirely crushed out, though has been a great number of men killed, and not a few women even. It caused a great many troops to be brought here from different places, the 17th Regiment came from America but have since returned.

I was very sorry to hear of the sad bereavement that happened to James Watson. I'm sure he must miss her very much.

I hope this will find you all enjoying good health as I am thankful to say we are both at present. My dear wife wishes to be kindly remembered to you.

With fondest regard I remain your affectionate son,
Bolton

Publisher note:

Interestingly, Bolton does not mention his new wife's name. Perhaps, he got married and then informed his parents after the event. Obviously, it would have been practically impossible for the family to have attended their wedding.

The "Rebellion" refers to the Morant Bay Rebellion in October 1865. The rebellion and the resultant deaths of Bogle and Gordon precipitated the beginning of a new era in the development of Jamaica. The British Government became compelled to make changes including outstanding reforms in education, health, local government banking and infrastructure.

In 1865, Jamaica became a Crown Colony. Bogle and Gordon are regarded as two of Jamaica's National heroes.

It was on the 5th September 1865 that Bolton Beanland, Corporal in Her Majesty's Seventh Battery, 15th Royal Artillery married Emma Elizabeth Saword of St Catherine, Gentlewoman, at the Cathedral Church, Spanish Town, Jamaica by licence signed H Rees Webbe DCL Cantab Curate & Chaplain.

150 years later, Chester Castle in 2016

Chester Castle,
6th August 1866

My Dear Parents,

I am very sorry to disappoint you so, in not being to Burnley today, but it is equally disappointing to me. But, through unavoidable causes, I shall not be able to go this week, as only one sergeant is allowed to be away at once, and there is one away on leave already. But, if all is well, we shall go on Tuesday the 14th.

Emmett could go this week, but I would much rather we all went together. It is rumoured that we are to remain here until October, then embark for **Gibraltar** and I think I shall be glad to get back again for it is miserably cold in Chester. I don't know if it is bad in Burnley.

At any rate, I hope we shall not remain in England all winter for I don't at all like the colds, and **Gibraltar is a beautiful climate. Neither too hot nor too cold and everything is very cheap there**.

No doubt you will get a letter from Emma's father this week, as we told him to write there as we expected to be with you this week. If you get one addressed to Mrs. Beanland, from London, send it here as soon as you can.

I hope this will find you all quite well as I am thankful to say we are at present.

Let Jim Watson know when I am coming to Burnley. Say that I am very sorry he should be so disappointed, for I know he is looking out for me know.

With kind regards to all inquiries,
I remain your affectionate son,
Bolton, Sergeant Beanland,
7th Battery, 15th Brigade, Royal Artillery

Burnley, Lancashire, 1866

Bolton & Emma Beanland

Chester Castle,
8th January 1867

My Dear Parents,

I just write to tell you that we are going to Gibraltar. I believe we are to sail about the 15th in a Merchant Steam ship called the St Lawrence, but we are going to leave Chester on Wednesday next from Portsmouth and stay there a few days before we embark. We are not going in a man of war as was expected.

It is a bad time of the year to sail in as it is so very cold, and it is generally very rough in the English Channel in January, but I hope and trust that we shall have a safe passage though. It is but a short one as we shall go in 6 or 7 days.

I am glad for one thing that we are going to a little warmer country. I will write to you again when we arrive in Gib.

We join in kind regards to all hoping this will find you all quite well.

I remain your affectionate son,

Bolton

Publisher note:

I managed to go to Chester to visit the Cheshire Military Museum, which was were the Garrison was situated. Harriett must have been born in this building. I highly recommend a visit to this beautiful city.

Chester Military Museum, 2016

Bolton Beanland's first son, John, must have paid many a visit to The Garrison Library as he researched and found an extract from the Gibraltar Chronicle dated 23rd January 1867.

The first Beanland family to live on the Rock, arrived in Gibraltar on the 23 January 1867.

Extract from Gibraltar Chronicle Jan 23rd, 1867

"The steamship "St. Lawrence" arrived during the night from Portsmouth with the 7th and 8th Batteries of the 15th Brigade R.A. under the command of Col. Dixon VC and drafts for the different Regiments in Garrison. We hear that the steamer experienced heavy weather in the Bay of Biscay. On Friday the 25th inst., the "St. Lawrence" will take on board for conveyance to Bermuda the 2nd and 3rd Batteries, 1st Brigade R.A under command of Col. Thompson C.B."

Extract from the Shipping Intelligence on the 23rd

"British steamer "St. Lawrence" J James, 9 days from London and 7 from Portsmouth with mails and stores for Bermuda cons. To Messrs J Peacock & Co (cl)."

Gibraltar
27th May 1867

Dear Parents,

I dare say that you think I am very neglectful in writing to you, but you must know that I have not near so much time to spare as I used to have. As we have plenty of hard duty here, besides our charming little daughter takes up a great deal of my time. She is getting on beautifully, as lively as a monkey all day.

Publisher note:
Bolton & Emma's first child, Harriett Mary Beanland, was born at Chester Castle on the 5th November 1866.

I saw the letter you sent to Abraham. He got it yesterday. We are very happy to hear that you are all well, but you will think it strange that I did not know that he had commenced to be teetotal until I saw your letter yesterday. So you see, we don't have much to say to each other. He had been to see us, I think, about twice since we last came here. He came and had tea with us last Sunday and nursed baby a while. But, he never told us anything about himself or having written home, but I am very happy to see that he intends keeping the pledge.

There was a grand Review here yesterday, celebrating the anniversary of Her Majesty's Birth day. It was very pretty to see the guns firing from the Rock. At one end of the Rock, there is a passage made right into the Rock and guns placed tier above tier to the top, and holes made in the face of the Rock to fire through, so that, looking from the bottom, they resemble port holes of a ship several hundred feet high. Nothing can be seen but the flash of the gun from what seems to be a small hole in the Rock. It is almost incredible the number of guns mounted in Gibraltar. I think it would defy any nation in the world to take it. Although, it is a very small place, only about 2½ miles long and almost perpendicular to the height of 1,400 feet.

I have never been to the top yet, but Emma has and says it is very pleasant and a nice view from the top. Where we are living is about 300 feet from the bottom and the battery stops close to the water side. So it is very tiring. So much up and down hill.

It is very wonderful the different customs there is in different countries.

This morning, as I was going to the Battery, I saw a Jewish funeral. Two men were carrying the coffin which was without lid covered over with a large cloth. There were about 20 men following (but no women). They were not walking two and two, as at other funerals, but all in a drove as if they were going to market, and every few yards, they changed carriers so that everyone should assist, and when they arrived at the grave they turned the corpse and bury it downwards. The copse is wrapped round with a great deal of linen cloth and the coffin is taken back home to wait for the next member of the family.

The Jews are much hated by the Spaniards. It is quite surprising to see how the poor Jew is persecuted about Good Friday and during Easter week. They burn them in effigy from the yards of their ships or do anything to insult them, but a great many of them go away at that time. But, where, I do not know.

It is quite amusing to go through their market any time to see all the different sorts of things they have for sale. I saw the other day some old black clay pipes for sale on one of the stalls.

There was a sad thing occurred here a few weeks ago. A woman apparently died in giving birth to a child and was buried (according to the laws of Gibraltar) within 24 hours after, and in a few days after the child died and was buried with its mother. They discovered that the woman had been buried alive. She had broken the coffin lid and even torn the flesh from her face in her agony after waking up. She was quite a young woman and was only 12 months married.

I have not had any extra employment here yet. It is not near so good a place as Jamaica for getting money, but, however, we enjoy very good health here, which is a blessing to be thankful for. The yellow fever is very bad in Jamaica now.

We join in kind regards to all at home. Let us know how John is getting on with the twins. Hoping this will find you all quite well.

I remain your affectionate son,
Bolton
Write soon
Sgt Beanland,
7th Battery, 15th Brigade,
Royal Artillery, Gibraltar

Publisher note:
They must have lived near the Moorish Castle quarters, near the Prison.
The Duke of Edinburgh, Duke Alfred of Saxe-Coburg, sailed from Portsmouth aboard HMS Galatea on a round the world trip. He stayed in Gibraltar until the 7th June 1867. On the 26th May 1867, he reviewed the Fleet on the Rock. The Duke returned to Spithead, England, on the 26th June 1868.

By Pickering, Charles Percy
(New South Wales. Government Printing Office)
[Public domain or Public domain], via Wikimedia Commons

Gibraltar
2nd August 1867

My Dear Father and Mother,

I got your letter on the 31st July. We are very sorry to hear that Father has been so ill, but I hope he will soon recover. I am sure Mother will be pleased to see that her youngest son is not so bad as soon at home might think he is, for he is sending £1-0-0 for Father. I gave him the letter you sent and he at once gave me the money to send you. I hope you will get it quite safe and let us know soon as you can.

We are happy to hear that brother Joe has got an addition to his family. I hope they are doing well. I have no news to tell you about this place. Our little Harriett is getting on very nicely. Abraham has been doing very well since we came here.

I suppose you have heard about the increase of pay that has been given to all soldiers. It is 2d. per day more now for all ranks from the 1st of April last, but there was none of it paid until 22nd July, when each man got £1-0-0 (4 months extra pay at 2d.). Of course, it caused a great deal of drunkenness among the men for a few days, but it is all over again now.

An Infantry Private Soldier's pay at home now is 1/3. An Artillery Man Gunner's pay is 1/6¼ per day, and Infantry Sergeant is 2/3 per day. Artillery Sergeant is 3/1 a day (£1-1-7 a week).

So I think that is quite as good as being in a factory.

I am happy to say that my mind is still the same about keeping teetotal. It will be one year on the 29th of this month since I took the last beer, and that was in Burnley.

Abraham got his portrait taken. I think he intends sending you one with this letter. We have been to 2 or 3 places to have ours taken, but could not get good ones. I think I shall get mine taken in my summer clothing. Our summer dress is Blue serge trousers, white jacket, and straw cap with a turban on. The turban is over 2½ yards long and twisted round the cap with a cape down the back to keep the sun from the neck.

I must conclude now hoping this will find you all quite well. Emma desires to be kindly remembered to you all and would like to know how John's twins are getting on.

So no more at present.
From your affectionate son, Bolton

Gibraltar
18th April 1868

Dear Father and Mother,

I received a letter from our Joe, and we are all very sorry to hear that Father is so ill, but hope he will soon recover.

Emmett is stopping some distance from where we are, so I sent him the letter as soon as I could, and he came to see us last night, and he gave me 10/- to send you, to which I put 10/- myself. I hope you will get it quite safe. As Father is ill, I am sending the money to Mother, so that Mother will have to go to the post office for it.

I have nothing particular to tell you. We are all getting on very well. Little Harriett is getting on very well.

Very sorry to hear that Grandmother had such a fall. I hope she will some get over it. Answer this letter as soon as you can, for we shall all be anxious to hear how Father is getting on.

With kind regards to all. I remain your affectionate son, Bolton

Address: -
Sergt. Beanland,
3 Battery, 15th Brigade,
Royal Artillery, Gibraltar

Publisher note:
Records show that his father, Bolton Beanland, died in March 1868 – aged 64

Bolton Beanland

Gibraltar
20th August 1868

My Dear Brother
(suspect this is to Joseph, his eldest brother)

Whatever is the matter? Surely something most extraordinary has happened at Burnley, for after receiving letters from home this last ten years, I have at last actually got one from you. Anyhow, it is better late than never, so I am quite glad of it and we are happy to hear that you are quite well.

Rather strange about you being at No 34. You have not given me much idea of how things are at home. I wish you would, for though it might never be a home to me again, I feel deeply interested in the welfare of my mother.

I wish you would write more freely. I do get such dull, unintelligible letters from home in general. I'll tell you a very good maxim for letter-writing, which I practice myself, and I have often to write letters on business to the war office and horse guards, and to officers of all ranks. When you are writing, fancy the person you are writing to, to be actually before you, and put down in the letter the exact words you would say to him if he was within hearing.

I am glad to hear that you have put such a fine stone over our father's grave. I hope I shall some day before very long be able to see it. Glad to hear that little Bolton has got to be such a fine boy. Our little Harriett has been getting on beautifully, except this week she has had the diarrhoea rather bad, which has brought her rather low, but I hope she will soon be all right again.

I have got a fine double perambulator for her. I got it at a gentlemen's sale for 5 dollars, and now that I have got up well in my business I have not that much to do, so she gets plenty of fresh air.

I have nothing particular to tell you about Gib, only that there was two shocks of earthquake on the 18th. The like of which has not been felt here since 1825, but I knew what it was in a moment, for I have often felt the same in the West Indies.

I saw the son of the late King Theodore, he came ashore here as he was on his way from Abyssinia to England. No difference in him from many hundreds of little black boys I have seen, but of course he is a prince, and I see he has been presented to the Queen.

By all accounts it has been a very hot summer in England, even more so than it has been here.

I don't like this place at all. There seems to be something in the air that

42

makes one so languid and sleepy, especially in summer. But, I think about 3 more summers will be enough for us here.

There is a great deal of very heavy work sometimes for the Artillery here, but pay sergeants are privileged men. We have very seldom anything harder to do than writing.

Now, I think I have said enough in my first letter to you. If you will send me as long a one in return I shall be glad.

I am sending for a 5 guinea watch by this mail for Abraham. He is paying me 5/- a month for it. He has already paid £2-0-0 so you may guess how he is getting on. He is very reserved. He very seldom comes to see us. He is living about a mile away from us, at a place called Windmill Hill. He is just the facsimile of what yourself was at his age. Hoping this will find you all quite well.

I remain ever your devoted brother, Bolton
Address: -
Sergt. B. Beanland,
Royal Artillery, Gibraltar
P.s. Many thanks to Mother to little Harriett's presents. She has got 2 little pinafores with them, and has been highly delighted with them, this evening, kissing and making dolls of them.

Publisher note: The Gibraltar Chronicle dated 19th August 1868, reported on the Earthquakes in its third page as follows:
"For the first time for many years past, Gibraltar has been visited by an earthquake. Yesterday afternoon, (18th), two most unmistakable shocks were felt at many different parts in the town and south. Some people assert that they saw the walls of houses shaking, others had their glasses and crockery thrown down from shelves while by many the strange rumbling noise was mistaken for the explosives of some distant magazine. The first shock was distinct and is reported to have lasted some five or six seconds. This occurred at about 5 o'clock in the afternoon. It was succeeded by a second shock very much slighter in every way at about 6 o'clock pm. The movement appears to have been East to West, but it is impossible to assert this with any certainty as only the most accurate observations could in so small a place indicates the line of motion. It was felt at the North Front and also at Spanish Lines and at San Roque. No atmospheric or other prognostications appear to have preceded the shock".
King Theodore of Abyssinia (1818 - 1868) committed suicide on the 13th April 1868. He had previously imprisoned the British Consul, Charles Duncan Cameron in 1864. After prolonged diplomacy, in 1868 British forces under Napier invaded Abyssinia leading to the King's suicide.

Gibraltar
28th August 1869

My Dear Mother,

According to my promise, I again write a few lines with a hope that you are much better when you get this. I am happy to say that we are all quite well at present, though I am rather busy just now, as we are exchanging Barracks tomorrow. So we are packing up, which makes everything in disorder. We only remain in one barracks 12 months at a time. I suppose you would not like to change houses every year.

Of course, that is one of the discomforts of the service, for on every move we get some of our things broken.

There is plenty of sailors knocking about the streets now, as the Channel Fleet is in harbour, consisting of several very large ships. A man of war at the present day is something wonderful. I was on board the ship Northumberland some time since and it was wonderful to see how easy some large guns (22 tons weight) could be worked by two men. We have some very large guns on the Rock, but nothing to compare what they carry on these iron-clad ships.

"HMS Northumberland early configuration USNHC NH 71227" by photographer not identified. Via Wikipedia

We heard from Emma's father since I wrote to you before. He has arrived in India quite safe after an absence of only 83 days, so that in that 83 days he travelled by sea and land about 36,000 miles, and he expects in 2 years to be making £1,000 a year.

I have not heard from my brother Joe for a long time. Will you be good enough to tell him I would like to hear from him? I wonder if you have any difficulty in reading my letter, for I write them very quick sometimes. If you have, say so, and I will take more pains with them in the future.

With best wishes to all.
I remain your affectionate son, Bolton

Publisher note:
The Gibraltar Chronicle reported the imminent arrival of the Channel Fleet to Gibraltar in their issue dated 28th August 1869.

It reported that the Channel Fleet comprising: HMS Agincourt; Minotaur; Northumberland; Warrior; Hercules; Bellerophon; Monarch; and Inconstant, would arrive at Gibraltar. Their first port of call since sailing from Plymouth. It was expected around the 1st September 1869.

From Gibraltar, the Channel and Mediterranean Fleets would sail to Madeira, and then Lisbon. Following a stay of three days in the Portuguese capital, the Channel Fleet would sail for Cork in Ireland, and the Mediterranean Fleet would return to its base at Gibraltar.

Aboard HMS Agincourt were the First Lord of The Admiralty, Mr. Childs, and senior naval staff who met with HE Governor, Sir Richard Airey, and toured the Upper Galleries and other sites on the Rock. HMS Agincourt joined the Channel Fleet as a 2nd Flagship in 1869 and in 1871 was nearly lost when she was grounded at Pearl Rock, in the Bay of Gibraltar.

On the 3rd September 1869, the Chronicle reported that the Presbyterian soldiers of the Garrison, presumably including my great grandfather, through the Minister Mr. Coventry, welcomed the sailors to the Church of Scotland Church at Gunners Parade, today's Governor's Parade

Gibraltar
9th September 1869

My Dear Mother,

I have not much time to write this time, as it is now late at night, and I have been very busy all day. I am to be the guard tomorrow, so I must get to bed as soon as possible, but I intend to write to you twice a month if it is only to say that we are all well, which I am happy to say we are at present.

Emma has a slight cold, but will, I hope, be well in a day or two.

The children are quite well. Harriett is learning to talk finely.

Abraham comes to see us nearly every evening. He is preparing for examination for promotion. I think he is inclined to do well for himself now, and he expressed himself very sorry for being so foolish in Jamaica, as he might now have been Sergeant-Major, if he had only been steady.

I have nothing of importance to tell you.

This is the third letter since I heard from you. I hope you will have a letter written soon. Surely, Edward ought to be able to write now?

What a difference in him and two brothers of Emma's, one is 16 and the other is 14 years old. They have been getting £50 a year each for two or three years now, and last Christmas they got £10 as a Christmas gift from their employers.

I hope this will find you all enjoying good health. Remember us to all enquirers.

From your,
Bolton

P.s. – I dreamed last night that Harry Watson had enlisted and was a sergeant in Gibraltar, and that I made a prisoner of him for disobedience of orders.

Good night. B. B.

Gibraltar
24th September 1869

My Dear Mother,

I hope this will find you better. I had a letter from my brother Joseph yesterday, and he tells me that, which I am sorry to hear, you are worse.

I think this is 4 letters I have written since I heard from you, so I had begun to think you were getting well again, but I suppose it is difficult for you to get a letter written.

If Edward cannot write, will you ask my sister Margaret to do so. And let me know a little of how things are going at home.

I am glad to say that Abraham is quite well. So is Emma and the children. John is getting a fine little boy.

I have nothing particular to tell you of. The weather still keeps very hot and oppressive.

With kind regards to all at home, and I hope for a speedy recovery.

I remain your obedient son, Bolton

Gibraltar

14th October 1869

My Dear Mother

I am very sorry to hear by a scribble of a letter I received this morning (which I think was written by Edward) that you are still so ill. I had begun to think you were getting well again, as it is now some time since I heard from you, but I trust (and think from a letter you sent some time ago) that you have long before now found peace with God. I pray that you may, through your long illness, always find Jesus precious to your soul. I hope you will recover, for I should like to see you again, and I should like very much for you to see our dear children, which I am happy to say are getting on very well, playing around so lively all day long.

I am happy to say we are all quite well in health.

I have not seen Abraham lately, as he is living about two miles from us, but I here that he is attending hospital with a gathering on his thumb.

Edward does not give us much news in his letters. I wish he would tell us a little more.

How is it you are living at no. 30? Who is in no. 36? How is my brother John getting on? What business is he in?

Is it quite settled about the money my father left? I am very sorry to think that his hard earnings should have caused any disagreeableness in the family, but I hope that what there is left is in your possession, and that you will have the full benefit of it while you live.

It is very kind of Aunt Betty to stop so long with you. I daresay they are anxious at Leeds to have her back at home. I should like to know how Bolton Ingram is getting on, and his family.

I must now conclude with kind regards to all relations and friends at home, with a desire for your speedy recovery.

I remain your affectionate son,
Bolton

Glad to tell you that brother Abraham has lately been promoted. He is now in no. 6 Battery.

Gibraltar
21st January 1870

My Dear Mother

It is some time now since I heard from any of you, which gives me some hopes that you are recovering, but I dare say this winter will have tired you much. I hope this will find you all at home quite well, as I am happy to say we are at present.

Little Harriett and John are shouting and playing about the room as happy as can be.

We had Abraham here a few nights since. He promised to write this week. I have nothing particular to tell you of.

There is a rumour that we are going home in summer, but it is not known for certain when we shall go. I shall be glad when we do go, for I am getting rather tired of this place.

I see, by the papers, that there is a great deal of yellow fever in Jamaica since we left. We were extremely fortunate the 4 years we were there, for there has not been so healthy a time since we left.

I should like to hear how my sister Harriett and family are getting on. I cannot tell the time I last heard from them. I hope you will answer this soon, and let us know how you are.

With kind regards to all at home.
I remain your affectionate son,
Bolton

Gibraltar
22nd July 1870

My Dear Mother,

I promised to write you by last mail, but I kept putting it off until it was too late, and now I have commenced I have scarcely anything to tell you.

Of course, you will have heard from Watson that I have got another step in promotion, which I have no doubt you are glad to hear. And I am glad to say I am getting on very well with it. I have not near so much to do as I had being pay sergeant, but there is more responsibility with it.

Great excitement is caused here by the war between France and Prussia, but I dare say you hear as much about it in Burnley as we do here. The French fleet came in here last night, but went out again directly. They had everything prepared in fighting order. It is to be hoped that it will soon be settled for they are two powerful nations and the destruction will be dreadful.

I am happy to say that we are all quite well. Abraham was with us awhile this evening. I hope this will find you a great deal better in health. I should like to hear from you soon, if Edward will be good enough to write.

Remember us kindly to brothers and sisters and all friends at home.
So no more at present.

From your affectionate son,
Bolton
Address:
Sergeant Major Bolton Beanland
No 1 Battery, 15th Brigade
Royal Artillery

Gibraltar
8th July 1872

Dear Brother,

You all seem to be very silent at home. I have not heard from any of you for some time.

I want you to be good enough to send Abe's money with mine to Mr. Benson, Watch Makers, 23 Bond Street, London. I expect soon to be leaving the service and start business here.

I am happy to say we are all quite well.

Hoping this will find you all enjoying good health.

I remain your affectionate brother,
Bolton

Address:
Sergeant Beanland,
3rd Battery, 15th Brigade,
Royal Artillery

Publisher note:
Records show that his mother, Mary Beanland, died in 1870 – aged 70

Mary Beanland

Gibraltar
21st April 1873

Dear Brother and Sister,

Many thanks to Miss Mary Jane, for her nice letter. Also, for the pretty valentine to Harriett, the whole of the children were delighted with it. Many thanks also for your photo. **You will see by the enclosed card that I have at last made a start in my long anticipated business.** So this will be my last letter to you as a soldier as I shall get my discharge at the end of the month. I have got **a nice little shop on the Main Street**, rent £60 per annum.

Mary Jane asks if coal is dear here. Well, they are 2/6 per Cwt, which I think is rather more than you pay, but thanks to this being such a warm climate, we don't require them as much as you.

She also asks what sort of place is Gibraltar. Well, I can say it is a very different place from Nelson (in Lancashire). The principal people who live here are soldiers. I think there are not less than 6,000 soldiers here. The Rock is about a mile and a half long, but the breadth I cannot say for it rises very steep from the water side to a height of 1,400 feet.

The houses in the Town are built like steps, the roof of one in line with the roof of another and nearly all with flat roofs which makes nice play grounds for children or drying ground for the washing women.

At sunset every day, all the gates are carefully locked that lead out of the garrison, so that people in the strongest prison in England are no more secure that we are on this Rock during the night.

No civilian is allowed to be out after 12 o'clock at night without a written permit from the Governor. Then they have to show it to all the sentries they come at.

It is not so good a place as England for nice fruit, though grapes are very cheap, 1d per lb, but they are only in season about 4 months in the year. There are no such things as gooseberries, pears, black or white currants and many other nice fruits.

The principal market day here is Sunday morning till 10 o'clock. It is then as throng as Burnley Market is at 10 o'clock on a Saturday night.

Harriett is getting on nicely with her reading and writing. She will soon be able to write to you.

I enclose for you our photographs, but they are not well taken. I also send two for our brother Joe.

With kind regards and love to the children.
Yours affectionately,
Bolton and Emma Beanland

Publisher note:
This is the only letter found to have been signed by both Bolton and Emma Beanland.

Bolton Beanland's shop in Gibraltar was at 34 Church Street. This was later renamed 219 Main Street. Today, it is the location of "The Book Centre".]

My debut novel, Hybrid, was on display on the shop front window at The Book Centre, in 2013, shortly after publication – 140 years after the initial shop was opened!

LETTERS

OF

ABRAHAM EMMETT

BEANLAND

Woolwich
4th July 1862

Dear Father and Mother,

I take great pleasure in writing these few lines to you hoping to find you in good health. I received a letter from you and were very glad to hear from you.

We land here on the 23rd of June. We was back in Shoeburyness 7 weeks and was glad to get back to Woolwich again.

I like this place very well. I do not think I can get home this summer, but if we stop at home this year I shall come home in December if all is well.

I have heard some strange news here about Mary Ann Johnson getting married, which I am very glad to hear of it. But, you might have told us something about it before now and we could have kept up the spree! I should like to know who she has got married to.

Can tell you that I expect to get married myself and go out to the East Indies shortly.

So no more at present from your affectionate son,
Abraham Beanland

Please give this note to William Burrows.
Direct to
Gunner A. Beanland
No. 8 Battery, 15th Brigade
Royal Artillery

Please do write back as soon as possible for I am expecting to go out every day.

Publisher note:
This letter is riddled with errors in the 1915 printed version. Again, since I do not have the original, it is hard to know where the errors arose, but I suspect Abraham's spelling was not very good since he himself admits he is not good at writing in his letters. Saying this, he was going to get married and go to the East Indies, but we know this never happened.

Chester Castle
24th September 1866

Dear Father and Mother,

I now sit down to address these few lines to you, hoping to find you enjoying the very best of health as it leaves me at presents.

I sent you a letter about 3 days after I came back and never had an answer from you since I was very thankful to you for the tobacco that you sent me.

I am very happy to inform you that there is no word about his going away yet, so I hope I shall have the pleasure of coming down again before I go away. But the next time I come it will be for 7 or 14 days so that I shall have time to see a little more about the place.

I hope you will excuse this short letter as you know that I am a very bad letter writer.

Remember me to all my brothers and sisters and to all inquiring friends.

No more at present from your dear son,
E. A. Beanland

P.s. Please write by return of post
Address to:
Gunner A. Beanland
No. 7 Battery, 15th Brigade
Royal Artillery

Gibraltar
17th April 1867

My Dear Father and Mother,

I now sit down to write these few lines to you hoping they will find you in the very best of health as they leave me at present. Thank God for it.

I was very sorry to hear of my brother John's child being ill, but I hope it will soon get better again. You can tell my Father and Henry Watson that I have taken their example to be a teetotaller since the 1st of April and intend to keep it until I leave the army.

I am very sorry to say it, Father, but I am not very well off at present. But, I hope I shall be able to recompense you for all the trouble I have given you before long. For, I intend to be a little more saving here than I was in Jamaica.

I like Gibraltar very much so far.

I hope by the time you get this that my sister, Margaret, and her child is in good health again, and tell her that I shall make it a present of something and some before long, for I think it is the first of that name in the generation of the Beanlands beside myself.

I was very happy to hear that Grandmother is in such good health and I hope that God will continue to grant it to her.

I must now conclude with my kind love to you all.

Remember me kindly to my brothers and sisters, uncles and aunts, and to Grandmother and to all inquiring friends.

So Good Night and God bless you all.

From your dear son,
A Beanland
Address to:
Gunner A. Beanland
No. 7 Battery, 15th Brigade
Royal Artillery

Gibraltar
5th August 1867

Dear Father and Mother,

I am very sorry to see by my brother's letter that Father has been ill, but I hope he will soon get better. I am sending you £1 with this letter. I hope you will get it quite safe. It is not often I have so much money on hand at once, but thanks to Her Majesty, who has increased our pay by 2d. per day, and dated it from the 1st of April last. They only commenced paying on the 22nd, so we had each £1 back pay to draw.

I have been doing very little since we came here.

There is plenty of cheap wine, but I don't drink any of it.

I don't go to our Bolton's very often, as he lives in a place called the **Moorish Castle, a good distance up the Rock**. Our Battery is stopping at a place called **Prince Albert's Front, down at the seaside**.

I don't go out much at all, for we have a good Reading Room, and plenty of books. So long as I have a pipe full of tobacco and a nice book I am quite contented.

I had my portrait taken the other day. I will send you one with this letter. I think it was very well taken.

I like this place very much, only the duty rather hard sometimes.

I have the chance of becoming a bombardier, but I would rather remain as I am.

We have not heard from Mary Ann in Liverpool since we came here. I wonder how they are getting on.

Remember me to Billy Burrows if he asks about me. I am glad to hear that Grandmother is quite well.

With best wishes to all friends and relations at home.

I remain your affectionate son,
A Beanland, Gr R.A.
Address to:
Gunner A. Beanland
No. 7 Battery, 15th Brigade
Royal Artillery

Gibraltar
6th December 1867

Dear Father and Mother,

I now take the greatest pleasure in addressing these few lines to you in answer to your kind and welcome letter that I received in October last. I am very happy to hear that father is getting better and that little Margaret also is quite well. Tell her that I will not forget my namesake some of these days, when I get a little richer than I am at present, and I hope that will not be long before.

I am very happy to inform you that I am teetotal still and intend to keep so.

I was very sorry to hear of my nephew Edward's deafness, but I am sorry to say that I cannot recommend you to anything, for I never troubled with it. But, I hope he is alright by this time.

I am very happy to hear that Grandmother is quite well and I hope it will please God to keep her and all of you in the best of health.

I must now conclude with wishing you a Merry Christmas and a Happy New Year.

Remember me to my sisters and brothers and to Grandmother and to all inquiring friends.

So no more from your beloved son,
A. B. Beanland

Good night and God bless to all.

***

"Speak Gently"

Speak gently to the wayward heart
That once has gone astray
And lead him to that lowly path
From which he went away
Let Wisdom's words entice him back
From sorrow, grief and care,
And never chide him for his fault,
But of such faults beware.

A. B.

Gibraltar
29th May 1868

Dear Mother,

I have the pleasure of answering your last letter which announced the death of my dear and beloved father, which I was very sorry to hear. I am very happy to hear from you that he died in the fear of the Lord, and that his soul is at peace with our Saviour. It is a great loss to us all, but we must put our trust in the Lord, and be prepared for the worst.

I went down to Brother Bolton's last Sunday. He is looking much better than I have seen him for a long time, and Emma and the child is in very good health, thank God for it.

I am very happy to hear that all the remainder of our family is enjoying the blessing of good health.

My brother was very much pleased with the verses on the card, and so was I, for I thought they was very nice.

I should have answered your letter by last mail, only I was on duty and could not.

I must now conclude with kind love to all sisters, brothers, uncles, aunts, and to Grandmother and to all inquiring friends.

So good night and God bless you all,

Address to:
Gunner A. Beanland
No. 7 Battery, 15th Brigade
Royal Artillery

Gibraltar
5th December 1868

My Dear Mother,

I now take up my pen with the greatest of pleasure to address these few lines to you hoping it will find you enjoying the very best of health as it leaves me at present. Thank God for it.

I am very happy to inform you that Brother and wife and family are quite well. I went down to Bolton's last Sunday and he told me about Grandmother being quite ill, but I hope she will be quite well again by this time.

I sent you a letter about two months ago, but never got any answer from you since. So I hope you will answer this by return of post.

I was happy to hear of William and MaryAnn Riley coming back to Burnley again and I hope they are enjoying the very best of health. There is nothing to let you know of in Gibraltar. It is such a small place.

I must now conclude with kind love to all brothers, sisters, uncles, and aunts and to all inquiring friends.

So no more at present from you dear son, A. Beanland

Address to:
Gunner A. Beanland
No. 7 Battery, 15th Brigade
Royal Artillery

P.s. Remember me kindly to Mr. and Mrs. Riley and family.

Gibraltar
9th August 1874

Dear Brother and Sister,

I am very sorry to inform you of the **death of our dear and beloved brother, Bolton**. He died on the night of the sixth of this month at twelve o'clock. I am sure that **if anyone went to heaven he has gone there**. He has left a wife and five children to mourn his loss. I can assure you that it is a **very great one** for his wife.

We are still going to keep on with the shop, which is doing very well at present. We intend to get some cards printed next week. We shall send you one each as soon as we get them done.

Bolton appeared to be much better last Sunday and all the week up to Thursday morning. On that morning, he took a turn for the worst and died at 12 o'clock that night.

I have no more to say at present.

Hoping that you and your family are enjoying the best of health. Remember me to Brother Joseph and wife, John and wife, and all the rest of our family.

Emma wishes to be kindly remembered to all of you.

Hoping you are all well.
I am yours truly, A Beanland

Publisher note:
Every time I read this letter I feel a lump in my throat. Especially, when you bear in mind that the previous letters, written a few years earlier, comment on how good his health was!

I have to mention that the loss of my cousin, Alastair Beanland, aged just 27 years old, also fills me with sadness. I have included a picture of him as a child in the section of Gibraltar pictures at the end. Truly, a great loss for Gibraltar since I know he would be an excellent teacher today.

LETTER

OF

EMMA ELIZABETH

BEANLAND

Gibraltar
21st December 1875

My Dear Harriett,

I am much obliged to you for so kindly sending me the photographs of Father and Mother and Elizabeth. My little John is sending you a letter this mail and a card for his Aunt Margaret.

Abraham has not time to write this mail, but both of us unite in hoping that you are all quite well.

We all send our love to John and Margaret, Joe and all your children and theirs, and hoping you have a happy Xmas and will have a Happy New Year.

And remain, yours truly,
Emma E. Beanland

Publisher note:
This in the only letter written by Emma included in the 1915 publication, written to Bolton's sister in Lancashire.

LETTERS

Of

EMMA ELIZABETH

BEANLAND

Publisher Note:
The following letters were found in an envelope by
Peter Beanland, grandson of Charles Bolton Beanland,
around 1998, when he was helping to clear out the
Beanland residence at 74 Main Street, Gibraltar. The
death of the last surviving child of Charles Bolton
Beanland, Leonia, my great Aunt, resulted in the
property being lost to the Beanland name forever.

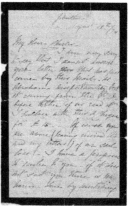

It is his and my belief that no-one had read them in a
very long time…

On the envelope, someone had listed the names:

Harriett Riley – [Older sister, born in 1830]
Margaret Watson – [Older sister, born in 1832]
Joseph Beanland – [Older brother, born in 1838]
John Beanland – [Older brother, born in 1834]
Bolton Beanland – [As told earlier, born in 1841]
Abram (Emmett) Beanland – [Younger brother, born in 1843]

It is my belief that these are the children of Bolton Beanland Senior, born
in 1804. Interestingly, Mary Emmott married Bolton Beanland in 1820.
Emmett was seemingly named after his mother's maiden name.
The only letters within the envelope, however, were those written by Emma
Beanland (wife of Bolton Beanland).

Scrawled in the corner of the envelope was a calculation 1911 – 1841 = 70
years old. Whoever wrote this was, in my opinion, trying to find out how old
Bolton would have been in 1911.

9th August 1874

My Dear Charles,

I know you will be **shocked and grieved to hear that poor dear Bolton has gone so unexpectedly**. I can scarcely as yet believe it, though he has been ill and suffering so long yet he was so patient and so confident that he should recover – that I shared in the same hope though at last I began to fear that he would not live through another winter.

I did think as long as warm weather lasted he was not in immediate danger – he was better than usual the last few days – he was out on Wednesday evening last, but Thursday morning he was taken very ill and **shortly after twelve the same night he died** and was buried on Friday at 5 in the afternoon.

It was sad to lose sight so soon of poor Bolton but it is necessary in this climate – **my good kind husband is gone**. I grieve to think that the doctor never warned us that there was no hope – my issue I think.

His complaint ended in consumption. He spit blood ever since his return from Tangier but he was not reduced in flesh like persons are quickly in that disease – the only consolation to any grief is the hope that he is safe in Heaven and done with suffering – **I don't know what we should have done without Abraham in our distress** – if it was not for him I should indeed be desolate in a strange canal as somehow, I never did or never shall feel at home here –

Give my love to Fanny – I can't write to her this mail. Of course you will now write about business matters to Abraham.

I hope Emma and children are well. I will send you a card as soon as they are printed.

Yours truly, E. E. Beanland

***

18th August 1874

My Dear Charles,

I am very sorry to say that I cannot answer your letter that has just come by this mail as Abraham misfortunately lost it coming from the P.O. before either of us read it.

I enclose with this a cheque for £15. Of course, you are aware (having received A's and any letters) of our sad loss.

I have a proposal to make to you – if it does not suit you there is no harm done by mentioning it.

We find it necessary to have some assistance as Abraham can't manage the shop entirely alone any more than poor dear Bolton. It's too much for one and yet at all times not quite enough for two persons and it's very difficult to find a suitable boy – **how would you like to send Fred, your eldest boy**. He would be at home here. I should treat him as my own – if he only came a year even it would be a change for him. I suppose you will soon think of putting him to something – you were in an office at his age. Think it over my dear Charles.

I cannot write more now – we could not get a cheque in time enough for the Malta Mail – so send this overland.

With love and best wishes

I am your truly, E. E. Beanland

***

[Written in corner of letter]

I enclose a cheque for £10

23rd August 1874

My Dear Charles,

I got your kind and welcome letter last night. It only increases my grief & think how happy he was in the prospect of seeing you. I am afraid it was the excitement that hastened his death – on the Wednesday he said to me:

"I feel no pain only a weakness in my knees. I must brush up a bit and exercise my legs a little or I do not know how I shall get to England"

… and asked me for a clean fronted shirt saying he would dress properly that day – lately he had been too ill and the weather too hot to allow of his wearing any tight clothes. He also ((the day before he died) this all was) wrote letters and went out in the evening. He was taken very ill next morning and day – fixed very much – but in the evening, he started to get better – he literally seemed to only fall asleep.

Alas! What a sorrow it is to lose **such a good husband** as he always was to me – such peace & happiness I had the whole nine years we were married. I shall never be happy again in this world. I never thought of his dying – always thought it more likely I should go first!

Publisher Note:

Does this indicate that she had not been well herself? Several times, she indicated she struggled to cope, the weather not helping?

He is buried in the Presbyterian part of the cemetery at the 'North Front'. I enclose a card – there is a slight mistake about his age. It ought to have been 34th year of his age. He was born on the 25th January 1841.

I had a very kind letter from the "Ford Templar Lodge" here – I wish I could send it you – it shows how much they respected him – Mr. Coventry, the Presbyterian minister here, said:

"Your husband must have been very much respected as many attending his funeral."

Mr. Coventry was very kind & came twice to pray with him the day he died. Bolton and he often used to have a friendly talk together when he was in comparative health.

All his illness commenced with a little cough and cold – even the Doctor Book Practice – it at first – and he was not predisposed to our imptick - none of his family care. But both Gib and Malta are **very bad places for consumption worse than England**. Any man in the service with a delicate chest is always sent home from here as soon as possible.

About Fred – I must warn you that he will find us (if he comes) very rough and ready compared to your house as in Gib they have no idea of comfort in building a house and though we pay such enormous rent – its but a poor place compared to an English house. Still I would make him as comfortable as I can.

I shall be glad to hear from Fanny & will write to her when I have got any sewing done. Am busy making for the children and the baby is rather cross.

Fine. My love to Emma and accept the same yourself

From yours truly, E. E. Beanland

***

31st August 1874

My Dear Charles,

As the Malta Mail is expected tomorrow morning I am writing this afternoon intending to keep this open till then.

I should like to see how we stand with you – as there are a few things we shall require as all our chance of success lies in keeping what the other stationer here do not keep – viz regimental necessities – this Brigade of Artillery going to England about the middle of September and the new ones coming out will require a good many caps – we have only two sergeant's caps left. We have a good many common ones left (gunners) but no fine cloth for do – I do not know how many you sent us last year this time, or rather I have forgotten – but you will have some idea – the sooner we have them the better – there are a few more things wanting.

Abraham will make out the list at the end of this.

I have a very pretty table cloth – poor dear Bolton was anxious you should have it and was going to take it with him to England for you – he had already folded it up – I will send it you the first opportunity I have – poor Bolton not expecting or thinking he was dying had no time to express any wishes in regard to business or anything else.

When he was so ill on his return from Tangier he asked me what I had said in my note to you – he then said:
'I wonder if Charles has any idea I am as ill as I am, but it does not matter the business belongs more to him than to me.'
But, after that he got apparently better and up to the last he expressed his firm commitment that he would recover, and I kept hoping the same.

(Written by Abraham)
Articles Wanted:
Whist Markers
Albums large and small
Foolscap Brols Buled hamt – crumook white cruers.
Marking Mile 1/1 and ced
Elastic Bands (no. 3)
Fountain & Magic Tool stands
Spanish lesson books
Regatta Fame
Book Marlsons
Collins 1 & 2 Drawing books
Plain drawing books
Whiting caps from Hobsons
J pens (Mitchels)

Also, some books plain and buled – we do not know their names so enclose a sheet as a sample.

1st Sept
The Malta Mail is signalled so must close this without delay.
My best love to Emma & children & accept some yourself
from yours truly
E. E. Beanland

***

14th September 1874
My Dear Charles,

As the Malta Mail is still before the English one I will send this overland as it is answerable writing on Cowies account when the mail come in that way – and I have two of your letters 2-answer.

First, as to Freddy, I was in hopes when I proposed it that it might in the end prove a mutual benefit – it would be to mind the shop at times and during his leisure he would be a nice companion for John – take nice walks to frontier and might take Spanish lessons together – which might in future years be a benefit to Fred of course. If he came out it would be my place to pay his passage which would not be much especially as he would only be half price – he is I think not quite twelve? However, I will leave it to you as no doubt you will decide for the best and I should be sorry for him to leave his present situation if it is likely to prove a good one.

The receipts from end March last I will give you chopping add shillings. April - £95; May £91; June £85; July £80; August £62.

Of course in the summer a great many people leave Gib – indeed all also can do so – which makes it slack and poor Bolton being so long ill made a difference. I hope we shall be able to send you more now that the Winter is coming on – the new shop is determined to cut us out if he can – he has started with newspapers this mail for the first time! We shall be glad of any suggestions you can give us about taking stand – and if not too much trouble should be glad of the card you mentioned.

The table cloth I hope to send by a friend in a fortnight or so – many thanks for your offer of a Brooch – a small one I would be glad of.

We want three times the number of chin strips from Hobsons (that was sent last year) and Sergeants Caps we want badly – they are wanted by men now.

1. Sketching Books
2. Best white f-cap plain
3. Dicks cheap classics
4. Penholder containing ink
5. Meciters
6. Metallic books f-edge
7. Wally Ink and pencil scrapers
8. Wax tapers in coil
9. Jackets with alphabet to Index
10. Roman Catholic Prayer Ruler
11. Cayure f-cap
12. Letter Clips
13. Fancy Bone Parker dees

And also send a nicely bound edition of "Esquire William" Cowie Sad. Some cheap ones about 1/6-knot this is wanted with a nice binding about

4/- or 5/- say also a small cheap edition of "Pilgrims Proper's".

I am afraid I shall not be able to obtain a cheque this week though I have money enough for a small due – and it is rather a loss getting a money order.

Hoping you are quite well and all the family.
I am my dear Charles
Yours Truly, E. E. Beanland

We shall want some more Christmas cards – we have some left – I will look over the many articles and tell you what we have another week.
***

2nd September 1874

My Dear Charles,

I received yours of the all right – I was afraid you would be disappointed at the small remit – I could have sent more but was anxious to pay the **Court for the letter of administration which cost altogether £15**. It is not quite settled as I have great difficulty in getting securities indeed considering expense and annoyance. I am almost sorry I had anything to do with it.

As to taking stock that will take some time as I have 3 young children the eldest only 4 years old at home all day. No one to relieve me of the duty – as Harriett and John the two eldest are obliged to go to school every day **the rules are too strict to allow of my keeping them at home** – and Abraham is anxious to do his best but he has not been accustomed to keeping accounts like poor Bolton was – we have a boy or rather young man in the shop now. He is smart and active. We pay him 8/- week which is the cheapest we can get – he seems respectable and may be as honest as the day – but if he is not, **we are at his mercy**.

I have tried already minding the shop – children – and house till I was **too ill to do anything**, and it all came upon poor Bolton with what result we see. It is quite impossible to do without a third person in this place. I must either have a perfectly honest boy in the shop, or mind it myself and get a respectable woman in the house to do the work and look after the children, which will be more expensive – and running great service beside as if I happened to get a bad character in (and they are seldom to be trusted as you do not get characters here with servants like in England). I should be required by the new law here to send her off the border and pay a fine of a hundred dollars besides paying doctors' bills or any expense she might make.

Abraham is obliged to carry bread – groceries – vegetables and butchers meat every morning – many times he is too tired to eat his breakfast as nothing is sent here – and many other times he has to move out in the day after bills and printing and papers – perhaps Emma has a nephew who would be glad to come – it is as much for your benefit as ours – that we get someone honest as **the better we succeed the sooner we can pay you – we owe nothing as poor Bolton hated running in debt** – except the Doctors bill which will not come in till Christmas – and will not be much.

We have several Bills due to us. I could not get a cheque this mail either – so send an order for £20. I could have sent £35 but for this law affair. About xmas cards half the quantity you sent last time will do.

Also we want –
1."Pickwick" Pens
2.Tissue Paper
With best love I am, Yours truly, E. E. Beanland
***

30th September 1874

My Dear Charles,

I enclose an order for £10 – as I am not able to get a cheque this mail. I sent £20 overland last week, hope you got it all right. Shall not send any more cheques overland as I have been told it's not very safe at present. I enclose a short note to Fanny – please forward it to her.

As I shall endeavour to send regularly either on order or cheque every mail now. I should like you to make a rule of taking something towards paying off the dreadful fare – as **I owe you all that account owes and whole of the capital you advanced first**? Or does it include it? I must confess I hardly understand it myself, this of course I am sure you have put it all right at any rate I shall be glad when I am a little more square with you and Cowie as well – I forgot whether I mentioned Almanacs and diaries for the New Year?
Captain Gilbard is not going to publish his Gibraltar Almanac any more as it does not pay – not enough sold.
Hoping you are all quite well
I am Charles, Yours truly, E. E. Beanland
***

20th October 1874

My Dear Charles,

I enclose in this a cheque for £19 – no letter from you this mail. I hope you have got the cheque for £10. I sent the mail before last (overland) there being no Malta Mail – and also the table cloth you ought to have by this. Please let the brooch be as you suggested for hair and photo.

Mr. Cowie wrote me last mail expressing sympathy and support at my loss – but also expecting a hope that (as the quarterly a/c shows a Balance of nearly £80) this "being a large account on the terms, we do business with you we trust, you will endeavour to cover it by food remittances before the end of the year" – so I should like!

Publisher note:
The brooch was found and photographed, but unfortunately is now missing so I was unable to check the colour of his hair!

To raise his spirits if possible by sparing as much as we can so as to lower it a little. I think £30 would in future be a good thing to keep it at. We got the Boresale right.

Please send the following as soon as you can per Cowie as we are much in want of them –

1.Mitchell J pens and others
2.filletts – 292 – 293
3.small pass books ½ d 1 d 2 d
4.White J cap plain
5.Blue E cap plain
6.Highly Burnished Envelopes no. 4
7.Faund letter Clips

I shall persist in sending things we do not – for mistake. "Delight and

Increase" – he had already plenty, and "Minion Note Paper". We also have album dance – it is not very good either. Could buy cheaper here – The Ledgers also very had damaged corners – nothing to compare to what Mr. Nassie sells here. Also drawing blades dearer and not so good a quality as Ewins.

Abraham is getting on very well at the shop – he is compiling a ledger for taking stock which will prove very good (I think) on the same plan as they had in the Canteen. They used to take stock once a month there.

Do not trouble about getting "Inquire Within" bound on purpose – a plain ordinary one will do – also send a full Masterful "Pilgrims Papers" only plain bound.

Please send me a common pair of Patterns for going out in the yard – this wet weather 6 d or 9 d a pair they are I think – cannot get such things here.

Thanks for your offer of sending wearing apparel, we are not in ward of any just at present.

One white you might get me at your leisure – enough "Junk Misso" (Blade) to make me a best dress and mantle – it is no use going in for very cheap things in Blade here as the cheapest are the dearest in the end as they get shoddily so soon on account of the dust here.

Abraham has been busy sending cards to all the Affairs of the new Management lately come here – also the new Brigade of Artillery – I note your remarks about last but with other business eventually no doubt if a person had the means they might do almost anything in the way of business – Abraham has learnt a very good trade in England Brush making but I do not think it would answer so well here as all the Spaniards buy 1d Browns to do their work with, and the English people here Officers and soldiers got the best of Browns and Brushes out of store for nothing. But it is strange what things sailors come in here asking for – "Bladering – Hair Oil" "Thread – Needles – Cigars" it would be possible to sell almost anything here.

I am sure a good English Shoemaker would get enough work to make his future as it's a most difficult thing to get a pair of shoes or boots mended – they all think themselves shoon misending shoon.

In England you can get boots mended as good almost as new. A serious expense as far as children are concerned not being able to get them well mended.

Yours truly, E. E. Beanland

27th November 1874

My Dear Charles,

The mail is late this week. **Fred has got over his homesickness**. I think he is quite at home now I may say – he is very sharp in the shop. Will you send me some old pieces of flannel like his shirts for the purpose of mending them? I enclose the sum of £15 – namely one bank note for £5 and an order for £10. I always take the no.'s. I also send by this mail a sample of lacky kind of paper – also the insides of Sir Frat Balls for you to take to Howard's as it is impossible to sell them as they are so it is better to send them back, than keep them as they would be a dead loss in that case.

Send Fred's top coat please, it will be **useful in wet weather**.

Fanny sent me her photograph – please give her my thanks when you see her.

The answer to your remarks about this house – reply there is no help for it – strange as it appears to a person accustomed to the low rents in England – it is exceedingly cheap – so everyone who knows the rent says – formal pay £6 – per month for just his shop alone and partition half off for a dwelling place – how they exist I know not – as they have five or six children – and a servant. Surely, they will have fever in the hot weather.

To have a really good house and shop would be almost £150 – a year.

We have no water local on as yet which is very expensive and also inconvenient.

Abraham and I, seeing that we content, are not liked to better ourselves have been thinking of proposing to the landlord – rather he proposed to us sometime after to lay it on – he hearing one half – and we the other of the expense – and as it is a common practice here for a landlord after a tenant has imposed the place – to **either raise the rent or evict them** (which is done at a very short notice sometimes – and I do not know where we should go if we were turned out).

We have been thinking of taking the house for 12 months at a time instead of monthly as it is at present him either raising the rent or turning us out at too short a notice.

The reason we got this house in the first instance so cheap was it had been rather what might be called as milady shop – ever so many tenants taking it and each one failing of it two or three months trial of it – so he was rather glad of a good tenant.

Yours my truly, E. E. Beanland

2nd February 1875

My Dear Charles,

I kept from writing until the last minute, thinking that perhaps you had enclosed a note in one of the parcels per Cowie, is. I have not much time for writing and the **baby is crying for me to take him as well**. We have the enclosures, but have not had time to look over them yet. I am not able to send you much this mail as Business has been immensely slack the last two weeks. I enclose £7 past Co Order.

Hoping you are quite well (I must finish at once as the Baby won't let me write more)
Yours truly, E.E. Beanland

***

16th February 1875

My Dear Charles,

Both mails are just in sight, so I must write without waiting for yours - I wrote last mail enclosing a cheque for £12 and an order for £10 in all £22. I now send an order £8 - if he had - had the papers and other things. I might have sent £20 - being the monthly parcel - it is to be helped it will not occur again - as customs are very high and mighty sometimes - the Light Mess of the 4th Regiment have taken their Custom from us, on a/c of the misfortune last week although it certainly was no fault of ours. However, we are much the same as before as a fresh Battery of Artillery gave us the supplying of their reading Room - the end of last week.

The "Taper Stand", you sent is not a stand at all - it is a proper candlestick. The gentleman wants and he is waiting very patiently a Patent Stand for one of the Curfee Tapers - do you recollect the stand that Grandma used to have? Well something like that would do - these must be stands for the curled up Tapers - Abr tells me the mail closes at once so must finish writing.
Yours Truly, E.E. Beanland

***

26th February 1875

My Dear Charles,

The Malta Mail is rather late this week. I trust it will bring the Bon of which, as yet we have heard nothing. I wrote last week enclosing £8 – this mail I send £18 – we got the things of the Lisbon on Wednesday – when you can spare the money a couple of dozen (men) best Bats and the same amount of second quality will be required as the Cricketing season in commencing – but Abraham is writing to you this mail so I need not mention re as he will give you a list of anything that is wanting.

Fred is writing as well – we are all quite well thank you – and hoping you are the same.
I am yours truly, E. E. Beanland

P.S. We have a person as customer a 'Bart' an Honourable and the last arrival is a Viscount! When Fred took a paper to his house he was rather astonished to see what a small home he lived in. A respectable chimney sweep, a bricklayer would have it better in England.

[On the next page, written by Abram (Emmett)]

Dear Charles,

We got the case last Wednesday last quite safe. The goods were just what we wanted. We were just run out of large envelopes.
The second-hand books were very good with a few exceptions. I looked them over yesterday to find that when they are sold they will have fetched about £1, 16 or £1, 18.
I could not put a very large price on many of them. The large one that cost 1/6 I am very sorry to say is no good at present. I had a Roman Catholic Priest in the shop and I showed it to him. He tells there are four rolls of it in all, so this one is no good without the other three, what do you think would be the best to do with it?
I received the pamphlet last mail. I think it would be of great use in some of the large offices. I should like very much to try it but I think the price is rather too much for us at present. I hope in time we shall be able to get such things.
We are in want of a few more things:

Morning note paper & envelopes & Bd Birad, Med & Marrow.
Envelopes roughly Burnished no.4
Fools cap Blew Plain & white Riled
White blotting paper
About 18 match Bats & 18 Practice

We are quite out of all these things.
I think Fred has written a longer letter this week than usual, he is quite well in health. I was noticing him this morning how fast he is growing out

77

of his clothes. His working suit is getting too small already.

Hoping you are all quite well
I remain yours truly,
A. Beanland

***

Beginning of Letter missing...

Do just as well, we shall be glad of a little foolscap as soon as possible - as to the poems. I mean well boned ones suitable for presents, to sell at almost 3/6 or 4/- each. It seems useless to give you any further list of requirements - but I may just mention that we shall soon be out of "Cement of Pompen" also. White blotting paper, and we are also quite out of the ...

United Service Pencils
Long Wood Penholders
White Ivory or Bone Penholders

And when you are able, some violet Tuls would be suitable. Excuse haste and scrawling as I have been writing the greater part of this standing.

And with love to yourself and all the rest.
I am Yours Truly, E.E. Beanland

I am well myself, only not strong as in the Summer the bad smells do not improve my appetite - and I cannot carry him and take a good walk, as the baby is so heavy. **I cannot carry him far and he does not walk yet**, but when he is able to walk I hope to be able to get a little more fresh air. **It is quite impossible to keep one's health here, without a good walk every day.**
I am glad of any news you may have to tell me, though I sometimes wonder how you manage to get through so much business as you do.

***

5th May 1875

My Dear Charles,

I wrote last week but quite forgot to tell you how much I was sending either last week or the previous one - but I see by yours received yesterday that you had the mail I sent of £9 - and this week I sent £20 - we having received the compensation for the missing case. They however only gave the actual cost of the things. No compensation for loss of time or profit -

Ab tried hard to get the selling price of them but they would not do it - they however gave me the case and contents do they will sell for waste paper - so I got not quite £12. However, I think they acted as fairly as could have been expected. I think as Mr. Cowie's recount is so heavy that it would be as well to fine him the whole of the £20 - this Mail as I hope to be able to send you at least £20 - again next mail, as the fleet is in.

Fred's hat comes to £5 and boots half solving 3/6-

You mentioned Emily Turner in your letter lately – is Mrs. Turner still living? I think father has done right in going to his own House. Both common sense and duty would dictate his being there.

Hoping you are quite well.
Yours Truly, E.E. Beanland

P.S. when you are sending another case you might send a few shirts - also 3 pairs of Cricketing Leg Guards - 3 Pairs of Batting gloves - also 3 pairs of Cricketing gloves.

***

6th July 1875

My Dear Charles,

I have yours of the 30th June to hand this morning and hasten to answer it as the Mail closes in a couple of hours. The goods per Lisbon are very good and an useful assortment but one thing we wanted very badly you omitted, viz - fibolscap plain blue, please send

Sir Beaness as soon as possible. Also five thousand Blle - bordered envelopes Barack, and five thousand Blle bordered extra Borad - also two thousand Official envelopes, plain, not Off - but I find more things are especially required so I will supply a list at end of this letter. I have not been able to look over the Fan's yet so hope to report in them next time - please do not send any more of the "cotton" on beds that you sent with the small wares. It is not a good quality. I have tried it myself. "Chadwicks" is the best and the only maker that I ever use - a great deal is sold here.

I have been thinking of sending my sewing machine along with Fred and asking you to take it to Wiles and Fibbs (the makers) and asking them either to take it back and allow for it and send me a new one, or clean and repair the old one. They do take old ones back in exchange. If I had a new one I should prefer one with a Bar to cover the top, they cost a little more but it is necessary in this damp climate to keep them covered as everything turns so soon rusty with the sea air (I suppose)

Mine has paid for itself but is very much in want of repair. I have had or more than four years. Wilcox & Fibbs is best for Household use. I think if mine is repaired or exchanged for a new one, I can - especially when Harriet is a little older - **make a good many articles of baby linen and children's underclothing, which would sell very well in this place**. Especially if you could get me Calico, Linen, and Shaper and Holland at wholesale price.

Harriet and Emily could, when grown up, keep the shop supplied with their own creations. So I should be glad if you would go to the Makers and make enquiries. I will try to explain it to Fred. It is very simple - indeed they will give you books of directions.

I send you £15 - last mail. This mail I enclose £20-17-4

Hoping you are quite well.
I am Yours Truly, E.E. Beanland

Please send these things as soon as possible.
1.6 Beans Ficap Plain Blue
2.5000 Broad Blle B- Envelopes
3.5000 ether Barad Blle B- Envelopes
4.2000 official Plain/ no half/ do
5.5000 no.4 Highly burnished do
6.1000 Fouzien White do
7.2 doz FCap Matts Books ruled faint
8.2 doz do Plain
9.2 doz Past lunato do ruled faint
10.2 doz do plain

***

7th October 1875

My Dear Charles,

I am obliged to write overland this week as there is no Malta Mail at all. It has broken down so a telegram reports - have a cheque for £10 so (although I have been warned not to do so) still I am risking it overland for fear you should be short. You will receive the tablecloth next week. I hope it is on board H.M. Ship "Simoon".

I shall be glad when the things come as we are getting rather short of some articles.

With love to all
I am dear Charles
Yours Truly, E.E. Beanland

***

17th Nov 1875

My Dear Charles,

The English Mail is not in yet, so I cannot send of this without waiting to hear from you. I enclose a Post. O. O. For £6 and a cheque for £10. We had the Duke of Connaught in again yesterday morning, he came in for an exercise book. He chats quite freely and pleasantly with Abraham, he told A that a new game is coming out - played with Draughtsmen and that we shall have plenty of call for them, so whatever other games you omit sending **do not forget to send some more Draughtsmen**, as we have only one set left - we have plenty of Draught Boards and therefore do not want any of them. **The Prince is very pleasant, no pride about him.**

Please send the game of Beqique ordered last mail as soon as possible per Cowie as they are for General Soused's children - and they want them soon. Our name is getting known pretty well. We send papers to Cadiz, Malaga, Tangiers, Casablanca, and we had a circular from a house in Venice the other day, a large glass bead Tiering.

Hoping you are all well, and with love to all.
I am Yours Truly, E.E. Beanland

P.S. The diaries are a very good selection - what a waste De La Bere's were for 175. We have not sold more than two or three of them. I feel quite vexed when I look at such a heap of fine fill Diaries left in hand - however it could not be helped.

***

28th Dec 1875

My Dear Charles,

I wrote last mail enclosing £20. I now send the same amount - the week before I sent £21-11-10. Many thanks for the kind present you sent of sweets, the children were delighted. I hope you are better of your rheumatic. **It is very damp and chilly here**. I have never seen such wet weather before here - people cannot complain of not having rain enough this winter, it does nothing else day after day.

I want you to get a Church Service with Hymns - ancient and modern. The person who requires it said he would not mind paying £1 - for a nice one - a good dark binding not too fancy (it must also not be either too large or too small, a medium size). Black B - note paper to mark square envelopes - also Black B envelopes (square and plain). Sent about the things I mentioned last mail as soon as you can please - we did not have any too many cards as they nearly all went off. I think the demand increases - we were the first to introduce these here, and now Coulox Shops, drapers in fact everybody seems to keep them. I noticed that Fiemed in his Oclat copied us - in (all foods sold at fixed prices).

Mrs. Mc Carter made an effort to take to periodicals again. At least she admits so.

We should have been perfect if we had a little more tissue paper. There was much greater call for it this year than last.

Hoping you are quite well. I am.
Yours very Truly, E.E. Beanland
P.S. I have got another cheque so that I am sending you £25.
***

18th Jan 1876

My Dear Charles,

I have just received yours of the 5th Jan. How is it that your letters are always a Mail behind mine now? We got the fire screen last mail and your two last letters have been the same. I am glad you have the remits safe, as I am genuinely anxious until I hear of their safe arrival. I enclose £15 this mail. I sent £27 last mail and £20 - the preceding one. I think I answered your questions in my last or last letter but one.

The Duke continues a custom, he sent his steward down yesterday for a good many things, some of which we had not got - such as Whitley-Brown paper of a good quality for kitchen use. Also Mossello's Tule. He says it is very much used in England.

Please send the two staff sergeants' caps, they are a fresh order.

Abraham has been thinking lately that if he can manage to do a **little business on his own account** - with what he can save out of his pay (of course keep it separate) in such things for instance as freemasons Regalia

82

- if it would not be putting you in too much trouble to make a few inquiries at your leisure, but he must tell you frankly **he would not able to pay you any commission** - as his means are small and he will only get 20 per cent on them himself.

Please excuse this badly written letter as I am **suffering from face ache** and I have the two youngest children troubling me.

With love, I am Yours Truly,
E.E. Beanland

***

April 20th, 1876

My Dear Charles,

I send this overland as the Malta Mail was in here on Sunday and it was quite impossible to get an order. I now enclose one for £15. I should not have had any to send, but for some bills that were paid, as last week first of all the mail breaking down occurred there Good Friday, then Saturday.

I have shut all day, and the same on Monday besides **going to the expense of Flags and Candles over the Prince**. I hope he will not come here again in a hurry. The Wine Book that Isaacs did was very nicely done for, better than one I have done here, and cheaper.

I must say though that I should like to have a better quality of note paper and FC as their present strode does not suit everyone. I should like to get some very superfine to suit the most particular of them. I thought that sending the money direct to Cowie would not only save you some trouble but also make Cowie more attentive - by his getting the order quicker, as if you recalled the first year we started at least a few months after, he proposed the same thing mainly when written to about his irregularity - knowing he is decidedly after this month. So if you do not mind the trouble, it is all the same to me only I should like to keep him always under £50 - of course I know there are slack months in Summer when I only send about £40 - in that case you must give Cowie say £33 - and take £7 yourself that leaves nothing for stationery - but of course other months leave avoid margin, at least £10.

Thanks for your offer of getting wearing apparel - **the silk cloaks you sent out for Harriet two years ago still looks nice, it was a very good silk**. We do not want anything at present, but if we do I will let you know.

Hoping you are all quite well.
I am Yours Truly, E.E. Beanland

Publishers note:
Emma Elizabeth Beanland nee Saword passed away on the 31st July 1876.

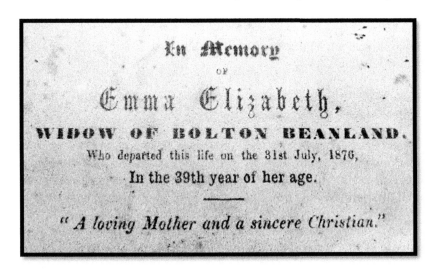

MEMOIRS

of

HARRIETT BEANLAND

By Malcolm Beanland

Publishers note:

Malcolm Beanland wrote this article for the Gibraltar Heritage Journal. The entire memoirs he referred to can be found in the subsequent section. I am in awe of Harriett for being able to write these memoirs in such an engaging manner.

In addition, Malcolm added some interesting aspects of her writing, whilst noting historical facts that add to the account.

I came across this Diary, handwritten by Harriett, Bolton's eldest daughter, for the years August 1874 – May 1876 and that contains many interesting anecdotes and captures life in Gibraltar as seen through the eyes of a small child.

In those days, keeping a diary was an important record kept within the family and I recall that my grandfather Charles Bolton Beanland and my father did keep yearly records that unfortunately with the passage of time have not survived.

Publishers note:
Since this was written two diaries for Charles Bolton Beanland have come to light, which are also included in this book.

The period of heavy mourning so fashionable in Victorian days following the tragic early death of her father in August 1874, is captured vividly in a Diary that her daughter Harriett kept when she wrote:
"We did not go back to school till our black clothes were ready. Mourning in those days was a serious matter. Fashion dictated that for widows and orphans, one whole year of deepest mourning without any alleviation of black crepe cloth. For the following six months, the darkness might be relieved by a thin line of white or purple round the neck, wrists on bonnets. During the second half of the second year black lace alpaca could be worn instead of crepe. This was followed by half mourning for the third year. After the third year the bereaved were considered to have done their duty and the embargo on colours, jewels and gold ornaments was lifted."

The period of deep mourning even extended to attending public functions.
"Of course all public amusements were barred the first year entirely and only mild functions allowed the second, the third year one could attend the opera or an informal dance but not a ball!"

She then recalls returning to school a few days after her father's funeral recalling how some of her friends at school had English fathers married to Spanish mothers.
"When I returned to school in my black dress, I was treated by my school mates with a sort of shy deference. Caroline Chalmers also commiserated, for she too was fatherless, but her father had died more than three years ago and so she was wearing colours. She was a nice girl but had the misfortune to be lame. Her mother was Spanish, so she was half Spanish and half English.

Bessie Robinson and several others in the School were the same half castes"

She then recalled going to see her father's grave at North Front.

"The first Sunday after we were duly robed in our mourning clothes, mother took us all, including Uncle Emmett, in a cab to the North Front. As we walked through the Cemetery to the Presbyterian ground, I was reminded of the day of the funeral. I thought we all looked so strange in black. Mother defied convention and dressed the younger ones in white frock and capes with a ruche of black ribbon around the edges. I had been deputed to carry a bunch of flowers to place on the grave but mother said it might wither away so John and I hunted about and found a rusty tin can. We found a well half full of water and ran back to see if we could have a drink from it, but mother very earnestly told us on no account to drink water from any well in the cemetery as it was poisonous, and we would surely die! I suddenly asked why there were wells if people hadn't to drink. Mother explained that they were there for the purpose of watering the flowers on the graves and that we would have to get a nice jar for father's grave and bring flowers every week to put it in. We liked the idea and it cheered us up."

And going to Church.

"That same Sunday afternoon, mother took us to Church, not the King's Chapel, but a strange church we had never gone to before. It was a large square building with a huge gallery on each side. There was a black pulpit very high up and a smaller one or reading desk underneath. The minister was the same one that had read the service at Father's funeral. There were no stained windows as in King's Chapel and no organ. I took a dislike to the ugly church and its old minister and hoped we should never go there anymore. But mother told us severely that it was father's wish that we should attend that Church and little girls had to do what their elders wished. The Sunday after that we went to the Presbyterian Sunday School and left King's Chapel for ever."

She then recorded her baby brother Charles, my grandfather, being christened.

"When Charlie was three or months old, an interesting event took place. He was christened at the Presbyterian Church one Sunday evening after the service. The congregation had dispersed, and the only ones present at the ceremony to my recollection were Mother, Uncle Emmett and us children. It was the first christening we had ever been present at and we gazed with much interest as the venerable old minister Mr. Coventry took Charlie in his arms and held him to his breast as he sprinkled a few drops

of water from a white basin on the reading desk on baby's face! Whether Charlie was scared at the nearness of Mr. Coventry's long white beard or the strangeness of the scene in which he was the principal actor, he gave vent to some loud yells and a tradition lingered long in our family that he actually kicked Mr. Coventry in the face! Mr. Coventry paid us pastoral visits after this at certain intervals."

An extract from the "History of St Andrew's Church of Scotland" records that John Coventry was the Minister of the Church in August 1874. He was an Edinburgh man, and for 16 years between 1868 - 1884 was the Minister. At the age of 60, he died in Scotland whilst on recuperative leave from Gibraltar. John Coventry was a kindly man who took a keen interest in the welfare of Scottish soldiers stationed in the Colony. His period of office is notable for the efforts he made to consolidate the plans and work of his predecessors. His memory is perpetuated by a marble tablet in the Church.

Later on in the Diary, she records of the family assembled on Sunday mornings after breakfast and what was thought of Catholics.

"We were all assembled, including Uncle Emmett, in the sitting room while Mother read a chapter in the bible and afterwards we all knelt while she read several prayers from the Book of Common Prayer. Mrs. McKendry, the family maid, did not join us but I assumed it was on account of the washing up of the breakfast things. Later I discovered that she was a Catholic and I was informed by Anne Park, my school friend, that Catholics worshipped idols! And could never go to heaven. Some of the missionary tracts we had been given at Sunday School were garnished with pictures showing black people prostrate before ugly images so I took for granted that they were "Catholics!" only I wondered why they turned black. I asked mother if all Catholics turned black and she said, "Nonsense what makes you think such a thing."

She then records the end of 1874.

"The end of 1874 drew near. The year that brought us our darling baby brother and our first great bereavement in the death of our father. Among the events in the year might be mentioned the end of the first Gladstone ministry when Lord Beaconsfield, became Premier. The capture of Coomasi and the end of the Ashanti War and the annexation by Britain of the Fiji Islands."

Benjamin Disraeli, Lord Beaconsfield, became Prime Minister of Great Britain, for the second time (1874-1880).]

Harriett then looks back during her school days in 1875, when aged 11.

"I have no recollections of how we spent Xmas Day that year, but I remember going back after the holidays to school and writing the date 1874 as usual at the top of my copy book when to my surprise the teacher came round and told me to alter it to 1875. I realised that we had begun another year. I also learnt the meaning of the initials B.C and A.D. I was at that time in the fourth class, (the lowest) in the Masters School where I must have entered the previous year but have no recollection of when John entered. The hours of School were from 9 to 12 and 2 to 4 in the winter and from 8 to 1 pm in summer. There was no heating apparatus whatever in the Masters School (as it was called) and I remember feeling very cold in winter. The room seemed very grand and large to me after the small yellow washed Infants School next door. It was whitewashed had a row of large windows each side and long coloured maps were hung on the walls between each window. There was plenty of fresh air at any rate! Rows of desks and seats filled one side of the room to the centre in front of which were arranged blackboards and easels for each class. In the centre of the room was the master's desk to which delinquents were sent for punishment by the teachers who were forbidden to use the cane themselves. The teachers were all soldiers in uniform, but the Master was a civilian. I do not remember who was Master when I graduated from the Infant School that grand personage seldom troubled himself about the small fry at the far end of the room.

The School opened with prayers the children standing but no hymns that I can remember. The curriculum seemed to consist of reading from well-thumbed dirty and exceedingly dry little books, writing on slates and copy books and sums on slates simple addition and subtraction.

We went out to play for a few minutes at 11am in the road that was our only playground. The narrow strip of yard round the School led to the Masters quarters which adjoined the school and was therefore taboo to the children.

I think I have mentioned before that there was a class for illiterate soldiers and very funny it was to us children to see big men learning the A B & C cards. The soldiers came out to play the same time as we did only they just stood about smoking short clay pipes. In wet weather we crowded into the ante-room where our hats and coats were hung and it was very disagreeable."

Meet Mr. Bacon, our School teacher.

"This year I think saw the advent of our new School master, Mr. Bacon. He brought a wife and large family with him. In spite of her numerous olive branches, Mrs. Bacon became the mistress of the Infants School replacing Mrs. Robson who had retired. Mr. Bacon was a tall stout man with immense side-whiskers. His wife was a gentle rosy-cheeked woman

with faded hair a resigned expression. She was never seen without a baby in her arms and a new one seemed to arrive every year! The irruption of all these large plump rosy golden-haired children into the R.A School (Royal Artillery School) caused quite a sensation."

Arrival of Abdul, our Moroccan servant.

"One day we had a visit from an old friend of the family whom we had nearly forgotten our faithful Moorish servant Abdul who had come to Gibraltar to escape being made a soldier against his will. Mother was much pleased to see him and brought him to the house to see us. Abdul refused mother's invitation to stay for breakfast but promised to call again. We were very sorry to see him go and urgently begged mother to take him on again as our servant instead of Mrs. McKendry!"

Down to the Races at North Front and the tragic death of her teacher.

"I was very fond of making dolls clothes at home and often when Uncle Emmett took John and Arthur to the Races on the North Front I would elect to stay at home and amuse myself with my pillow case full of scraps and making garments for my family of dolls... The Infants School too seemed different to how it was when I was a pupil there. There were some of my old teachers, Lizzie Hume and her sister Mary Ann. Lizzie Hume seemed very delicate. She was a gentle faced young woman of 21 who seemed older than her years. She stooped very much and coughed a good deal. At last there came a time when she was too ill to teach anymore and soon after came the startling news that she was dead! The authorities arranged that the school should be closed and the children she had taught should attend the funeral considering that she had been a teacher for some years and was greatly liked and respected by everyone.

As the procession with its school children walking down two and two and carrying flowers passed down the Main Street the shops were all closed and sympathetic crowds lined the pavements, the men were all bareheaded. How keenly the solemn procession brought back to me another procession little more than a year ago! It required all my resolution to keep back the tears as I walked along and on arrival at the grave my grief felt overwhelming for it was quite close to Father's grave. Mr. Coventry conducted the service too and at the close the children had to sing "There is a Green hill far away" which they had practiced at school in the morning and lay their flowers in the grave as the coffin was lowered. But we were too full of emotion to sing more than a few lines of the first verse when we all broke down sobbing and weeping unrestrainedly around the grave of our beloved teacher, the adults alone continued the hymn and the last verse was not sung. The painful scene soon ended and Uncle and Mr. Hume and other gentlemen hurried the poor children into the waiting cabs at the Cemetery gates and got home without delay."

Father's grave and School picnic at Campamento.

"Before the end of 1875 a handsome tombstone had been erected over Father's grave consisting of a wide stone platform with two steps and a square pedestal supporting an upright marble cross. That emblem was decidedly rare in the Presbyterian portion of the cemetery so ours was very easy to find. A wreath of everlasting flowers hung on the cross. At that time the hideous artificial wreaths under glass domes had not been invented!"

An interest in birthdays.

"That year was the first that we took an interest in birthdays. We were given pocket money every week and got quite enthusiastically about buying presents for each other. I teased mother into telling me her age but she would only tell us her birthday which was on the 31 October.

I couldn't decide what to buy her but then decided on a black brooch with a floral design which I had seen in a jeweller's shop. Mother was busy ironing and when I returned I presented it with "Many happy returns of the Day" She was greatly surprised and pleased with her present, kissing me very affectionately in return.

How little I thought that that was Mothers last birthday on earth. It was a great comfort to me in after years to think that I had remembered to give her that little present which she wore constantly. I wish that I had treasured the little brooch for her sake but with a child's carelessness I left it lying about years after and finally lost it.

Buying Christmas presents with 10/- shillings

For some reason (presumably because she was too busy) mother was not able to make the annual journey to "London House" to buy our presents for Christmas and was wondering who she could send for that purpose, when, John and I, volunteered to go, stoutly declaring, that we were old enough to go shopping for mother. After some hesitation and many injunctions to mind the cab and carts and always to look before crossing a road to take hands and not run or lose the money.

Dear mother saw us off on Christmas Eve, John (being the more trustworthy) being deputed to carry the money, ten whole shillings wrapped in paper and a list of the presents for everyone including Uncle and Mrs. McKendry. We arrived at "London House" in Scud Hill and were smilingly greeted by Mrs. Batchelor to whom mother had sent a note informing her of our errand. She blandly exhibited dolls, rocking horses and other toys in glorious profusion all over the shop, but John (tightly clutching his precious money) cautiously proceeded to inquire the prices of almost everything in the shop till Mrs. Batchelor lost patience and flounced off making some remark to her husband, "those tiresome children". I blushed scarlet and nervously nudged John with a whisper to make haste and buy something. But John was determined to make the most of his money then Mrs. Batchelor wanted John to give her the list of presents and she would choose presents for all, but he stuck to it like glue and then after much hesitation and changing of mind, he selected (with no help from me) what he thought was suitable for everyone. I was the hardest to please. At last laden with parcels and no more money left (John did some hard bargaining to make the 10/- last out) we triumphantly left the shop (I thought Mrs. Batchelor wouldn't want to see us there again!).

We were rather tired by the time we reached the Saluting Battery (Rosia Road) and sat down one of the benches counting the parcels when he said, "Oh I have forgotten Uncle" When we told mother, she gave John two shillings and sixpence to buy Uncle a meerschaum pipe!"

Harriett recounts the excitement of the visit to Gibraltar of The Prince of Wales, later King Edward VII to Gibraltar, in January 1876.

"Early in the New Year, Gibraltar was ablaze with excitement and illuminations in honour of the visit of the Prince of Wales on his way from India. The ship he came on, (the "Serapis") a great white vessel lying along the New Mole carried a regular zoological garden of animals of all kinds from Elephants to performing fleas on board, all presents from the various Rajahs and Kings in India. The public was allowed on board the three days or so the Prince was in Gibraltar.

The city was en fete! The houses all along the Main Street were decorated with flags and wreaths. The public buildings were lavishly decorated. The Officers Mess opposite us was simply covered with evergreen foliage and bunting. I think a Welsh Regiment occupied it for over the main entrance was a niche and in it was the figure of a Druid with a long beard and playing a harp, as the procession went by. At intervals there were triumphal arches. Every road and street in Gibraltar was outlined with fairy lamps so that at night the illumination must have looked splendid to the lookers on at Algeciras and Campamento.

Mother made two big flags of red, white and blue bunting to hang out of our front windows with big rose tags tied at the ends of the poles.

On the eventful day that the Royal procession was to take place there was the greatest excitement in our home. All places of business had to be closed by 10 am, crowds of people passed up and down the streets staring at the decorations. Our two big flags were out soon after breakfast. Uncle nailed the poles to the window ledges to keep them firm. How pleased I was that we had windows in the Main Street and could see the procession without any trouble. Mounted police cantered up and down the street keeping the crowd behind the barriers and shouting directions to unfortunate cabmen who couldn't or wouldn't understand that they were to go along the Line Wall instead of the Main Street.

Our shop was closed in good time though people would keep coming and wanting to buy more tissue paper for making flowers. We children and Mrs. McKendry were at the windows when a fierce mounted official shouted something at us and hammered at the door below! Uncle came upstairs in a hurry and told mother that the police wouldn't allow the bunches of flowers on our poles as they were hanging down and might fall into the Royal carriage and perhaps hit the Prince! So the poles were unfastened the rose tags pulled off (to my regret) and the poles replaced in a great hurry. Soon after that another official riding by commanded us to raise our flags higher. They were so big that they hung quite low. This means that some more work of un-nailing the poles and Uncle got quite cross about it. At last our banners were tilted to the right angle and I kept wondering what would happen if one of the poles gave way at a critical moment!

At last our patience (strained to the uttermost) was rewarded, we heard the joyful sound of the regimental brass bands approaching. People burst into loud cheering and the procession moved in sight. We frantically cheered and waved our hands (though we were nearly squashed with Uncle and Mrs. McKendry leaning on top of us. Mother and some friends were at the other window and the windows were very narrow! Especially when an open brougham passed below containing ladies and gentlemen, the Governor, his wife and other notables. Most people thought the Prince was in that, but I saw him quite plainly riding a horse behind the carriage. He was just like his portrait above our chest of drawers and wore a scarlet uniform covered with sashes and medals. He was a stout heavy faced young man and he gravely saluted the people each side of the road. I had a hot argument with Mrs. McKendry afterwards, she insisting that the Prince was driving in the carriage and not on horseback.

His Royal Highness did one piece of useful work that day. He laid the foundation stone of the New Market. Up till then, Gibraltar Market consisted of a number of dirty squalid booths where meat, fruit and vegetables were sold of indifferent quality.

Uncle took us on board the 'Serapis' one afternoon to see the presents and the animals. We were greatly taken with the big white (!) elephant though disappointed with the colour, we thought it would be as white as a clean tablecloth. The monkeys were a source of great amusement! There were Bengal tigers in cages and many other creatures too numerous to mention or remember. We saw cases containing blazing jewels and wonderful carved sandalwood things but it was the animals we were interested in.

When relating to mother all the wonders we had seen while she was bathing us that evening (we always got a bath before bed-time) I couldn't help inventing the story that I had given the elephant a bun and he had taken it with his trunk. John, not to be outdone, said that he had shaken hands with the biggest monkey! Mother laughed heartily at our innocent fabrications.

When the Prince departed in his big white ship, down came all the decorations and I deeply regretted the taking down of our flags, I was under the impression that they were to remain up for good. I asked if I could have the bunting for doll clothes but was refused!"

The Gibraltar Heritage Journal, Issue No 7 dated 2000 records an article on the visit of HRH, The Prince of Wales to Gibraltar, Visual Artefacts of 19th Century Gibraltar by Larry Sawchuk & Jane Padiak pages 99 to 112.

Visitors from the Moorish Castle and the lady who had a shop in Scud Hill.

"Sometimes on getting home after school we found mother had a lady visitor or two. We were trained to politely say "Good afternoon" and leave the room till the visitors had gone. Mrs. Oates The wife of the Governor of the Castle Prison was a frequent visitor besides Mrs. Wigley and Mrs. Batchelor was another. She was a very sharp strict old lady and she had a large shop on Scud Hill called "London House" where mother used to buy us toys. We liked the shop but not the lady!

In winter we often suffered from colds and mother made treacle toffee with pecan in it for a remedy. Needless to say the colds were very lingering."

A strict but loving mother.

"One afternoon, I was returning from School with Bessie Robinson down the road from Gunner's Parade when I saw mother in the Main Street just passing Howard's Shop with Charlie by the hand (he was able to walk by then) and Emily holding on to her skirt the other side thought how nice she looked in her black dress and bonnet with white edging round the forehead and the two children in white with black ruche round thin capes. I told Bessie that was my mother. She looked surprised and said, "Why! Your mother looks like a lady!" (And she looked every much one with her quiet refined dignified manner) I said shortly "Well she is one!" Bessie stared and said, "Why don't you run to her, are you afraid?" I told her that mother strictly forbade us running up to her in the street or shouting to attract attention if we met her!" "My, your mother is strict!" said Bessie."

OUR LIVES

AS CHILDREN

By

Harriett Beanland

August 1874 ~ May 1876

Publishers note:

This diary was found in 1997 by, Marie-Carmen Beanland, wife of Malcolm Beanland, great grandson of Bolton and Emma, at 74 Main Street, Gibraltar.

It is obvious from the tense of the text that these entries were made several years later, but there is nowhere on the memoirs that tells us when Harriett wrote them. I have edited Harriett's writing into paragraphs for an easier read.

Interestingly, the first entry page was annotated as page 89, which means other entries are missing – this is a real shame.

Chapter XII

Mourning Clothes. Pennipers. The Grave. The Presbyterian Church. Sunday School.

We did not go back to school till our black clothes were ready. Mourning in those days was a serious matter. Fashion dictated that for widows and orphans, one whole year of deepest mourning without any alleviation of crepe cloth, no jewellery allowed except dull jet. For the following six months, the darkness might be relieved by a thin line of white or purple round the neck, wrists or bonnets, and bright jet ornaments, earrings allowed instead of dull jet.

During the 2nd half of the second year, black lace alpaca or silk could be worn instead of crepe, and white lace collars and grey gloves with silver ornaments. This was followed by half mourning for the 3rd year, that is grey or lilac coloured clothing, but no bright colours such as blue, red, yellow, or white, and gold ornaments instead of silver or jet allowed.

After the 3rd year the bereaved ones were considered to have done their duty and the embargo on colours, jewels and amusements was lifted.

Of course, all public amusements were barred the first year entirely, and only mild functions allowed the second, the 3rd year one could attend the opera, or an informal dance but not a ball!

The day after Father's funeral, Mother overhauled all our outdoor clothing to decide what had to be sent to the dyers and reached down her band boxes from the shelf over the landing at the top of the stairs from which she extracted her bonnets. I thought they were beautiful, ones I admired greatly was the black lace trimmed with red geranium in velvet, and the strings were of lace. Mother gave them to Mrs. Wigley who demurred saying that Mother would be able to wear them herself when she was out of mourning!

To which Mother replied, **"Take them. I shall never go out of mourning!"**

I listened awestruck and thought how much she must have loved Father if she was purposing never to go out of mourning for him!

Dear kind-hearted Mrs. Wigley, what would Mother have done without your help and affection during those dark days!

When I returned to school in my black dress and wispy hair tied in black ribbon, I was treated by my school mates with a sort of shy deference for a day or two. Even teacher Lacey spoke to me in a kinder tone.

Annie Park was back at school, she had been away for some time, her mother had been sick. She said a few kind words to me with the concluding

96

remark in a mournful tone, "You are like me Harriett now, you have no father!" She was a very sensible, womanly little girl for her age which was the same as mine but for three months.

Caroline Chalmers also commiserated, for she too was fatherless, but her father had died more than three years ago and was now in colours. She was a nice girl with a beautiful face, but had the misfortune to be lame. Her mother was Spanish so she was half Spanish and half English. Bessie Robinson and several others in the school were the same, half castes.

If any girls in the class wore black dresses the others used to ask if they could wipe their pens on them! Our pens were always needing wiping, the ink was so poor that great clots used to be always at the bottom of the inkwells, and got on to our notes when we dug our pens in. My fingers used to get pretty inky too & need wiping so I found a black frock a great convenience and didn't in the least mind my companions using it for their pens & fingers either. Annie Park was not so complacent. She absolutely refused to allow her black frock (we were the only girls in black) to be utilised as an ink rag. She always dipped the point of her pen daintily in the ink, as she never got any clots on it, and never got any ink on her fingers. She tried to harden me into refusing to lend my dress but I was too easy-going and feared to lose popularity by not being willing to oblige, besides I needed my frock to wipe my own pen & fingers on, so could scarcely refuse it to others. Annie tried to instruct me in the art of dipping only the point of the pen in the well, but without success.

The first Sunday after we were duly robed in our mourning clothes, Mother took us all (including Uncle Emmett) in a cab to the **North Front** to visit Father's grave. As we walked through the Cemetery to the Presbyterian ground, I was reminded of the day of the funeral. I thought we all looked so strange in black! I hardly knew Mother with a deep wide crape veil over her black bonnet. Emily and Baby didn't look so bad. Mother defied convention and dressed them in white frock and capes with a ruche of black ribbon around the edges and they looked very nice. Mother had to carry Becidge of course, I thought he looked like a big white flower edged with black. Little Ems looked very sweet in her white pique cape, the black ruche on it made her little plump face and golden hair look fairer still!

Arthur and John were in black Knickerbocker suits with white ties and white stockings. I have a black merino frock with one frill for school. I had a black hair ribbon and white cotton stockings, black patent leather boots with bead tassels in front and black cotton gloves.

When we arrived at the grave, I saw a long narrow mound of earth with a black metal plate & number on it at one end. Mother couldn't remember the number right, so Uncle went back to the Cemetery gates to find out… but it was Father's grave after all. Mother stood by it and wept. Uncle stood a little way off with his hat brim on his mouth and his handkerchief in his hand.

John and I stood near the grave, and shed a few tears because we saw Mother crying. Arthur and Emily being too young to understand were chasing each other round the tombstones and laughing with glee. I was scandalised at their turning the cemetery into a playground, and with John's assistance tried to capture and quieten them, but we might as well have tried to catch butterflies!

Baby Charlie started crying dismally when he saw Mother full of grief, and Mother had to go & sit on a tombstone to nurse him. Uncle put a shawl on the stone for Mother to sit on, it was one she brought to wrap round Baby in the cot for the wind was always fresh and cold on the North Front.

I had been deputed to carry a bunch of flowers to put on the grave, and I stuck it in the earth on the grave, but Mother said it might wither, so John and I hunted about and found a rusty tin can in the grass.

There was a big glass jar with flowers and full of water on another grave, so Uncle poured some water out of it into our tin and we put our flowers in and stood the tin at the head of the grave. John and I then wondered about and read the names on the tombstones. We also found a well half full of water, and ran back to see if we could have a drink from it, but mother very earnestly told us on no account to drink water from any well in the cemetery as it was poisonous and we would surely die! I sullenly asked why there were wells if people hadn't to drink. Mother explained that they were there for the purpose of watering the flowers on the graves, and that we would have to get a nice jar for father's grave and bring flowers every week to put it in. We liked the idea and it cheered us up.

Every Sunday after that we used to drive to the cemetery and carry flowers to put on Father's grave. John & I took turns in carrying the flowers.

That same Sunday evening Mother took us to Church, not the King's Chapel, but a strange church we had never gone to before. It was a large square building with a huge gallery on each side. There was a black pulpit very high up and a smaller one or reading desk underneath. The minister was the same one that had read the service at Father's funeral. He read the big Bible at the reading desk and prayed with his hands lifted up, and went up into the big round pulpit to preach. He wore a black gown, not a white surplice such as Mr. Magee had. There were no stained windows as in King's Chapel and no organ. The people sat down to sing and stood up when the Minister prayed. The singing was slow and spiritless I thought without any organ to accompany it.

John and I thought it was very funny and giggled most of the time. We sat in one of the side aisles under a gallery. On the front of the gallery opposite was a large clock. It ticked very loudly when the Minister was praying or preaching. The pew we were in was a very long one with no cushions. There were not many people in church. Artie stood up on the seat and stared at the people behind us. Mother pulled his frock and made him sit down. Ems went to sleep on her lap. Baby was at home in bed. John & I whispered and bittered so much that Mother looked quite annoyed, at last she signed to John to come & sit the other side of her. Then I tickled Artie and made him squeal out, mother sternly whispered to me to go & sit at the end of the pew by myself! Even there I contrived to catch John's eye & we would both splutter with suppressed laughter. Poor Mother! She must have been quite ashamed of our bad behaviour! I took a dislike to the ugly church and its old minister and hoped we should never go there anymore!

After the service the Minister came up to Mother and shook hands. He looked at us & I thought that Mother was apologising for our bad conduct in church.

When we came out she told me very sternly that she wouldn't tolerate such misconduct in Church in the future and if I couldn't make up my mind to behave better I should be locked up in the coal cupboard instead of going to church!

I said, 'I don't like that horrid old church!'

Mother replied severely that it was father's wish that we should attend that Church, and little girls had to do what their elders wished and not please themselves!

The Sunday after that we went to the Presbyterian Sunday School, and left King's Chapel for ever

The school began at 10 o'clock and lasted 50 minutes so as to close in time for the children to attend church with their elders. The classes were held in the vestry - a long wedge-shaped room adjoining the church. It was a very dark place with only one window covered with close woven wire netting looking on the parade ground, and there were a number of long benches for us to sit on. There were some dingy cardboard texts on the walls. One was: - "Jesus said, those who seek me early shall find me."

The second one used to puzzle me a good deal.

John & I were separated, he was put into a boy's class and I sat with two or three other little girls, Bella Hume was one of them. John looked rather wistfully at me as he went away. At King's chapel nobody had taken the trouble of classifying us so he always used to sit beside me, patiently nursing his straw hat on his knees.

I felt very strange and shy. A lady with rosy cheeks and bright black eyes came to teach us. Her method was asking questions. It came to my turn. She asked who created me. I was going to answer "God", but the question was such an obvious one that I suspected a trap for the unwary, and after some hesitation answered "Jesus" instead. Miss Campbell (that was the lady's name) looked annoyed and said "no" & turned to Bella who gave the right answer, to my mortification. Then Miss Campbell asked me who redeemed one, but I gave it up, my theology was too limited for the Presbyterian catechism! I couldn't answer any of the other question that Miss Campbell asked from a little book that she had, so she ignored me and talked to the other girls. I stared at the walls and furniture, and was heartily glad when the time came for closing.

That evening we went again with Mother to the Presbyterian Church, but this time we sat in one of the cushioned pews in the middle of the church, and not in the side aisle as formerly.

Chapter XIII

Mrs. McKendry. Charlie Christened. Pastoral Visits.

Life seemed to go on pretty much as before. I do not think we missed Father quite as much as we would have done if Uncle Emmett had not been living with us. He was rather like Father, but not as tall and a little broader. In face he was fresh coloured and had a big moustache and no whiskers, whereas Father had been very pale and had worn short whiskers and a moustache not as large as Uncle's. Uncle Emmett's voice was very much like Father's but louder and more imperative. The only time I heard Father speak in Uncle Emmett's tone of voice was when he said, 'Emma, have you given this girl permission to cut her hair?'

John's voice when a man was (and is) like Father's while Emily has inherited Mother's voice which is rather a contrast.

I have often heard Mother comment that she couldn't get reliable servants and having heard Mrs. Wigley say that she would do her best to get one, I wasn't surprised one morning to see a strange woman sweeping the veranda. She was tall and strut and seemed middle-aged to me. She looked very dignified and entirely different to the skimpy, Spanish servant girls we formerly had.

I stared at her pretty hard, and at last asked her if she was Spanish. She told me to mind my own business, in very good English. I stared harder than ever, and asked if she had come to be our servant. At this, she swept away vigorously and gave me a scornful glance. We took a mutual dislike to each other on the spot. I went off in search of Mother hoping she would satisfy my curiosity as to the stranger, but she was busy downstairs, it was mail day, and Uncle impatiently ordered me off.

At dinner time, mother told us that the woman was Mrs. McKendry, who had come to help with the work and that we were to be good children and treat her with respect. For spite of the fact that our new domestic was tall and stout and had a somewhat grim and severe expression due to a heavy chin and thin lips. I did not feel in the least in awe of her, and am sorry to say took a childish delight in teasing and annoying the lady, and so many were the complaints in consequence that Mother firmly forbade me to go near her.

Mrs. McKendry, we found was exceedingly touchy and quick tempered. The only one of the family she took to was baby Charlie, and in time she simply idolised him! **Mother was unable to nurse Baby after Father's death, and Mrs. McKendry who had recently lost a baby of her own was able and only too willing to take entire charge of the little fellow**, who throve exceedingly well after this, to mother's satisfaction no doubt, for I once heard her say she didn't believe in giving babies the bottle.

When Charlie was three or four months old, an interesting event took place. He was christened at the Presbyterian Church one Sunday evening after the service. The congregation had dispersed and the only ones present at the ceremony to my recollection were Mother, Uncle Emmett and us children. It was the first christening we had ever been present at and we gazed with much interest as the venerable old minister Mr. Coventry took Charlie in his arms and held him to his breast as he sprinkled a few drops of water from a white basin on the reading desk on baby's face!

Whether Charlie was scared at the nearness of Mr. Coventry's long grey beard or the strangeness of the scene in which he was the principal actor, he gave vent to some loud yells and a tradition lingered long in our family that he actually kicked Mr. Coventry in the face!

Whether that was so or not I can't remember, but I know that he kicked one of his little woollen booties off in the struggle he had in the Minister's arms, and we children had to hunt on the floor for it afterwards, while Mother sat down with Baby and soothed his ruffled clothes and feelings! The simple ceremony was soon over and we returned home to go to bed.

Mr. Coventry paid us pastoral visits after this at certain intervals. These were very solemn affairs not at all like the modern parson's casual call as to the parishioner's health and a hasty 'Good Day! & off!' Oh no! When our minister called (if we happened to be at home) we were sent to have our hands & faces washed and then were ushered into the sitting room where Mr. Coventry sat with his big Bible in his hand. Mother gave us our little Bibles and we all sat round on chairs in solemn silence while the minister read a chapter, which we followed by pointing along the text with our fingers for fear we should lose the peace, Mother reverently looking at the page in her Bible, while Ems sat on her lap and tried to turn over the leaves with her little hands!

When the chapter was finished, it was followed by a long extempore prayer in which Mr. Coventry asked for a blessing upon the widow and orphans in their affliction. At the close we all said 'Amen', got up from our knees, shook hands with Mr. Coventry and went out, Mother usually remaining behind for a few words with him before he took his leave.

These pastoral visits made a great impression upon me, though I took very little interest in the chapter reading, and could understand very little of the prayer. I felt instinctively that the "Widow & Orphans" mentioned in it, referred to ourselves & that it was that that caused Mother to hold her handkerchief to her eyes!

Chapter XIV

Family Prayer. Uncle Emmett. Xmas Tea-Party. End of 1874

It was about this time too that we had Family Prayers on Sunday mornings. We were all assembled (including Uncle Emmett) in the sitting room after breakfast, while Mother read a chapter in the Bible and afterwards we all knelt while she read several prayers from the Book of Common Prayer. Mrs. McKendry did not join us but I assumed it was on account of the washing up of the breakfast things. Later on we discovered that she was a Catholic, and I was informed by Annie Park that Catholics worshipped idols (!) and could never go to heaven! Some of the little missionary tracts we had been given us at Sunday school were garnished with pictures showing black people prostrate before ugly images. So I took for granted that they were "Catholics" only I wondered why they turned black! I asked mother if all Catholics turned black and whether Mrs. McKendry would?

Mother seemed surprised at such a question and said, 'Nonsense! What makes you think such a thing?'

I had the vaguest idea about "Heaven" except that it was a nice place somewhere in the sky where Father had gone! I was very curious to know where Mrs. McKendry slept at night! Mother wouldn't tell me, and I got too hostile a reception if I went bothering Mrs. Mc. K. herself with questions (especially personal ones!)

We children did not seem to get any better acquainted with Uncle Emmett as time went on. He took little or no notice of us, was mostly in the shop & except on Sundays got his meals at different times (in order to mind the shop while Mother got her dinner). I think he was mostly away on Sundays too! He slept in the sitting room, and I concluded that Mrs. McKendry slept there too, as there was no evidence of her sleeping in Mother's room or ours!

We missed the R. A. School picnics this year through **being away at Tangiers**, to our great disappointment, but we were told when Christmas drew near that we could go to the Sunday School Soiree! I was greatly mystified as to the meaning of the word "soiree".

Well, on the eventful afternoon John & I were dressed in our best & sent off to St Andrews for the Tea Party was held in the vestry where we always had Sunday school. A little crowd of excited children were round the vestry door as we came up and at the ringing of a bell they all rushed in took their places on forms each side of the two long tables covered with white cloths, cups & sauces.

In the melee, John & I were separated & to my regret I found he was far away down the second table. I felt dreadfully shy & forlorn amid my gay companions who were all laughing & talking. Suddenly, the bell rang again & there was a hush as Mr. Coventry stood at the head of the table & said a long "Grace". As he raised his hand we all stood and as the forms were high there was a good deal of pushing & scraping & I dropped my handkerchief.

Grace over, we scrambled up on the forms again, and several ladies came around pouring tea into our cups from big jugs and handing round bread

& butter & bread & jam. This was the signal for a perfect hubbub of talk and laughter.

I was rather discontented that a large piece of bread & butter had fallen to my share. I thought I could get enough of that at home & expected something better at a tea party! But, I was elated at the thought of drinking real tea which we never got at home and was just raising my cup to my mouth when a boy who sat opposite said, 'Stop! You mustn't drink that!'

I put it down in surprise & alarm; and the boy made an ugly face at me. I suppose he was only in fun, but I wasn't used to being teased & didn't know how to take it! He was a fair, freckled boy about 10 or 11 with white eyelashes & a very turned up nose. He teased on, interfered with the children each side of him & cheeked the teachers who were serving us.

Once he got a box in the ears from a young lady who was his aunt, but I don't think it hurt much. This lady also had a very top tilted nose & a huge chignon with curls! I was very thirsty & again tried to drink when my tormentor scared me again!

It was the same when cakes & buns were being passed, he shouted at me every time my timid hand tried to reach the plate. I sat miserable.

A lady stopped & said, 'Little girl, you are not eating anything?'

I tried to tell her why, but my throat was too full for words, it was all I could do to kept from crying outright!

My cheeky tormentor called out, 'She doesn't want any!'

The lady said, 'Nonsense!' & walked on.

I was astounded at his audacious untruth, but could say nothing, and he added insult to injury by proceeding to fire crumbs of bread at me. One hit me on the nose, I turned my face and another hit me in the ear. I looked wildly around for help but no one was taking any notice & the ladies with cake & buns had ceased to come around.

Everyone was supposed to have had enough.

My tea was cold, and I had had nothing to eat. I spied Johnny at the end of the other table munching contentedly away at a big piece of cake & longed to rush to him for protection & comfort!

The children were becoming quite rowdy, pieces of bread were flying about, cups were upset, some little ones were crying & amidst all the din the bell rang followed by silence and another long "Grace" from Mr. Coventry, which made me realise with anguish that the tea party was over and I had had no tea!!

In the rush from seats that followed, John & I came together as we were swept by a throng of boisterous youngsters through the door leading to the church. I thought the soiree was all over & clutching John's hand I said passionately, 'Come home! Johnnie! I hate soirees!' But the children were crowding into the front pews and in front of the pulpit as hung a big white sheet while a big shapely thing shrouded in white was standing in the minister's big square family pew to the left of the reading desk.

Johnnie stared at these mysteries & said, "Let's stop! There's something to see!"

I sullenly followed into a pew & we followed the example of those in front of us by standing on the seat. Behind us there were numbers of grown up people, I looked eagerly to see if Mother was among them but she was not. A gentleman in the reading desk said something but there was too much noise to hear what he said and the din rose the crescendo when the lights went out & nothing could be seen but the big white sheet in front of us.

Soon there was silence & subdued "OH's!" of admiration as the wonders of the magic lantern were unfolded to our delighted eyes! This was a complete surprise to us & I quite forgot about my tea-less condition! At last, after an hour of rapture, the lights were turned up to my regret, but another delightful surprise was in store for us! The object that we had regarded with much curiosity was unveiled and proved to be a Christmas tree of noble proportions loaded with toys & tinsel & little coloured candles which were lit one by one to our breathless admiration. At the very top of the tree was a beautiful doll which I secretly hoped would fall to my share (but did not). One by one the children's names were called out & they went up to receive a toy from the tree. I heard mine called & shyly made my way to the front to receive a jet bead necklace on a card! Full of disappointment I went back to my seat. John had got a trumpet & was quite proud of it!

If the noise had been loud before, it was absolutely deafening now! Trumpets & drums squeaked & banged, rattled were whizzed. I caught sight of my tormentor whirling a big one round his head & snatching at a little girl's doll! I cowered in terror for fear he might see me & was edging out of the pew when I found Uncle was beside me. We eagerly showed him our toys & he said he had come to take us home.

When we got there we found the shop was shut, it was nine o'clock! Mother fondly welcomed us & asked if we had enjoyed ourselves. At once the recollection of the tea-party came over me & I burst into tears. Mother was greatly concerned when I informed her that I'd had nothing to eat or drink & said she would find out who the boy was who had given me such a bad time. I was regaled with some hot milk & bread & soon after forgot my troubles in bed!

The end of 1874 drew near. **The year that brought us our darling baby brother, and our first great bereavement in the death of our father!**

Among the other events in the year might be mentioned the end of the first Gladstone ministry, when Lord Beaconsfield became Premier, capture of Coomassie & the end of the Ashanti War; & the annexation by Britain of the Fiji Islands.

Chapter XV

Visitors. "Becidge". Toffee for colds. "Lizzie destruction". Photographs. Cousin Fred.

I have no recollections of how we spent Xmas Day that year, but I remember going back after the holidays to school and writing the date 1874 as usual at the top of my copy book when to my surprise the teacher came around and told me to alter it to 1875. I realised that we had begun another year. I also learnt the meaning of the initials B.C and A.D. I was at that time in the fourth class, (the lowest) in the Masters School, which I must have entered the previous year, but have no recollection of when John entered. The hours of School were from 9 to 12 and 2 to 4 in winter, and from 8 a.m. to 1 p.m. in summer.

There was no heating apparatus whatever in the Masters School (as it was called) and I remember feeling very cold in winter. The room seemed very grand and large to me after the small yellow-washed Infants School next door. It was whitewashed had a row of large windows each side and large coloured maps were hung on the walls between each window. There was plenty of fresh air at any rate! Rows of desks and seats filled one side of the room to the centre in front of which were arranged blackboards and easels for each class. In the centre of the room was the master's desk to which delinquents were sent for punishment by the teachers who were forbidden to use the cane themselves. The teachers were all soldiers in uniform, but the Master was a civilian.

I do not remember who was Master when I graduated from the Infant School, as that grand personage seldom troubled himself about the small fry at the far end of the room.

The School opened with prayers, the children standing, but no hymns that I can remember. The curriculum seemed to consist of reading from well-thumbed dirty and exceedingly dry little books, writing on slates and copy books and sums on slates simple addition and subtraction.

We went out to play for a few minutes at 11am in the road for that was our only playground. The narrow strip of yard round the School led to the Master's quarters which adjoined the school and were therefore taboo to the children.

I think I have mentioned before that there was a class for illiterate soldiers and very funny it was to us children to see big men carrying the A.B.C. card! The soldiers came out to play the same time as we did only they just stood about smoking short clay pipes. In wet weather we crowded into the ante-room where our hats and coats were hung and it was very disagreeable.

Sometimes on getting home after school we found Mother had a lady visitor or two. We were trained to politely say "Good Afternoon" and leave the room until the visitor or visitors were gone. Mrs. Valis, the wife of the Governor of the Castle Prison as a frequent visitor besides Mrs. Wigley, and Mrs. Batchelor was another. She was a very sharp strict old lady and she had a large shop on Scud Hill called "London House" where Mother used to buy us tops. We liked the shop but not the lady.

In winter, we often suffered from colds, and Mother used to make treacle toffee with ipecac in it for a remedy. Needless to say the colds were very lingering!

Baby Charlie or "Becidge" as we were fond of calling him, throve exceedingly well under Mrs. McKendry's care. On May 10th he celebrated his first birthday. He was very fond of crawling on the floor, and Kems used to crawl beside him for company!

Once we were plagued with swarms of cockroaches. Mother got some trap for them which were placed under the beds to be under the way. As time went on the pests did not seem to be getting any less, and the traps were declared to be useless until we found that Baby **used to crawl under the beds and considerately set the imprisoned insects free by turning the traps upside down!**

After that we were deported to watch him, & after his baby feelings were ruffled by his favourite amusement being interfered with & himself dragged by the legs from under the valance!

He was a sweet, good-natured little fellow with silky golden hair and a face as delicate as a flower. He was never fat but plump enough to be pretty. Mrs. McKendry adored him and couldn't bear him out of her sight.

When ironing she used to have him beside her in his high chair where he was quite happy & contented with a few play things, till John & I used to rush in from school when so much hugging, kissing & pulling about went on that we often made him cry whereupon Mrs. McKendry would fiercely drive us out of the room scolding us loudly!

Arthur and Emily were still in the nursery stage, and used to play happily together on the verandah. Arthur was a quiet child, but Emily was a plump busy little person always trotting about holding on to Mother's gown wherever she went. Arty would patiently put one block on another until he had quite a high tower and would chuckle with glee; Kems would trot up to him, scatter the blocks in all directions & run as fast as her little fat tootsies would let her! Arty would give a wail and again proceed patiently to build up his castle, till another onslaught took place.

Mother always took Charlie & Emily out for an airing every fine afternoon, I think we had no pram. Then she always carried Baby in her arms. One afternoon I was returning from school with Bessie Robinson down the road from Governor's Parade when I saw Mother in the Main St. just passing Howard's shop with Charlie by the hand (he was able to walk then) and Kems holding on to her skirt the other side. I thought how nice she looked in her black dress & bonnet with white edging round the forehead and the two children in white with black ruching round thin capes. I told Bessie that was my mother.

She looked surprised and said, **"Why! Your mother looks like a lady!"** (And she looked every inch one with her quite refined dignified manner) I said shortly, **"Well, she is one!"**

Bessie stared & said, "Why don't you run to her, are you afraid?"

I told her that mother strictly forbade us running up to her in the street or shouting to attract her attention if we met her!

"My! Your mother is strict!" said Bessie.

On Friday, the children at the R. & Master's school were marched down to the different church's they belonged to for one hour's religious instruction from 11 to 12 a.m.; we of course being out with a few others of St Andrews. Mother was greatly amused when I told her we went to the "Liggie Destruction" on Fridays!

Mother had her photograph taken with Charlie & Emily that year. Baby is seated on her lap with one dear little fool just peeping from under his frock & Kems is nestling up against Mother with my jet necklace (which she soon commandeered after the soiree!) round her little neck & holding a Moorish basket in her hand. We had vainly tried to induce her to leave go of it before going to the photographers but she stuck to it like glue!

I forget what month in 1875 our cousin **Fred Saword** arrived from London, but Mother one day told us that a cousin was coming to see us soon. We were greatly excited.

We knew we had an Uncle Charles, Aunt Emma and lots of cousins in London, and we had two photos on the sitting room mantel piece showing a thin gentleman with whiskers, and a thin child with long thin legs on his knee; and the other showing a stout lady holding a baby on her lap; these we knew were **Uncle Charles and Aunt Emma**.

I pictured cousin Fred as a tall, rosy-cheeked boy and was greatly disappointed to find when he arrived that he was dark & pale and very little bigger than myself!

I remember we were called into the shop very early one morning (or else very late one night) for the door was closed and there was Mother welcoming our cousin, a pale solemn looking boy with a scotch cap, and black suit. It seemed so odd to hear him address Mother as "Aunt". We shyly shook hands with him, he did not kiss us (as I thought he would) but was very quiet & civil, though his big dark eyes stared at us with some curiousity.

I unfortunately do not remember much about his stay with us except that he was a great tease & plagued us most of the time, though he was very quiet & civil to Mother and Uncle Emmett.

The person he most enjoyed teasing however was poor Mrs. McKendry! They were hostile to each other from the first, and his pranks used to drive her to frenzy! Many were the complaints Mother had to listen to from one & all!

I forget whether he went to school, but I think he used to help in the shop. He used to chase Bessie Robinson and me if he saw us while on an errand. Once he chased us all over the castle ramps. If he happened to catch us, he pulled our hair unmercifully, tossed our hats into the road, and made himself agreeable in many other ways.

I don't think anyone was sorry when he left, but in justice to the lad **I think he was lonely and home-sick**, he had no companion of his own age to associate with & no doubt hated the shop and mean dark little house we lived in, and at the same time was **too young to appreciate the beauty and romantic history and associations of Gibraltar**.

One night I was wakened out of sleep by Fred rushing in to say "Goodbye", he was going back to England.

I heard Mother (who was with him) say, "Don't waken the other children," as he scampered through the room gathering up his belongings.

As he was going down-stairs I heard him exclaim, "Aunt! I haven't got my nightshirt!" and rush upstairs again.

Mother called out, "Make haste Fred, the cab is at the door!"

He rummaged about the bedroom, grumbling loudly, and at last called out, "I'm coming!"

I fell asleep & in the morning we were told that Fred had gone, he had gone on board the mail the night before.

I don't think we shed any tears!

Chapter XVI

Mr. Bacon. Arthur goes to school. Abdul. Lizzie Hume.

This year I think saw the advent of our new school master, Mr. Bacon. He brought a wife and large family with him. In spite of her numerous olive branches, Mrs. Bacon became the mistress of the Infants School replacing Mrs. Robson who had retired.

Mr. Bacon was a tall stout man with immense side-whiskers. His wife was a gentle rosy-cheeked woman with faded hair a resigned expression. She was never seen without a baby in her arms and a new one seemed to arrive every year!

There were two big boys, Herbert and Frank, rosy & chubby, a girl Agnes with golden hair, rosy cheeks & blue eyes (whom I immediately fell in love with, dethroning Annie Park from the first place in my affections!), a smaller girl, Flowey, and a small white-haired boy, Arthur, beside the baby whose name we did not know. The irruption of all these large plump rosy golden-haired children into the R.A School (Royal Artillery School) caused quite a sensation! Agnes was in our class (the 3rd then I think!) and she was quite a self-possessed little queen! The boys vie with each other in paying her attentions which she regarded with supreme indifference. Annie Park was jealous of her from the first!

Arthur Beanland

Arty attained his fifth birthday on the 30th of August and started going to school! John & I were very proud to escort him (each taking a hand) to the Infants school, where kind motherly Mrs. Bacon welcomed him and no doubt made him feel quite happy in our absence. I suppose John & I felt very big and important as we went to the Master's school! After school we went to take Arthur home, Mrs. Bacon telling us he had been very good! He was a calm, philosophical little fellow, nothing seemed to trouble him much (except getting his bricks knocked down!). At home, he played a good deal by himself, being the middle child, he did not seem to have a companion.

John and I were too old for him, and Emily and Charlie seemed too young! He was too old to trot round after Mother, yet too young to go with John & me! Mrs. McKendry had no time for him, & Mother and Uncle were always too busy, besides the youngest children took up Mother's time mostly. He must often have been lonely, but he did not complain or worry any of us!

One day we had a visit from an old friend of the family whom we had nearly forgotten, our faithful Moorish servant Abdul who had come to Gibraltar to escape being made a soldier against his will. Mother was much pleased to see him and brought him to the house to see us. John & I came rushing down the stairs (it was before breakfast) leaving the landing gate open at the top to greet him when screams & bumps were heard and down the stairs came rolling Kems and Baby!

Finding the gate open and hearing unusual voices below they thought, I suppose, that their presence was also required hence the debacle!

It was some time before they were soothed and quieted and butter rubbed on the bumps (our stairs were not padded). Fortunately, no bones were broken!

Abdul refused mother's pressing invitation to stay for breakfast but promised to call again. We were very sorry he had to go so soon, and urgently begged Mother to take him on again as our servant instead of Mrs. McKendry!

When I was promoted to the Third Class (standards were not known then) I found to my dismay that I should have to spend an hour every afternoon (from 3 to 4) in the Infant's school doing sewing, which I abominated! Even the pleasure of being near Arty & being able to see him in school scarcely compensated me for being forced to that doleful drudgery.

I was very fond of making doll's clothes at home and often when Uncle took John & Arthur to the Races on the North Front I would elect to stay at home and amuse myself with my pillow case full of scraps, cutting out and making garments for my family of dolls, but that was very different to sitting on a form in a stuffy schoolroom hemming endless strips of calico for no object whatsoever!

Mary Ann Hume & Lizzie Hume

The Infants School too seemed different to how it was when I was a pupil there. There were some of the old teachers, **Lizzie Hume and her sister Mary Ann**. Another teacher was a bright red-faced girl named Emma Winter. She had brothers and sisters in the Master's school.

Lizzie Hume seemed very delicate. She was a gentle faced young woman of 21 who seemed older than her years. She stooped very much and coughed a good deal. At last there came a time when she was too ill to teach anymore and soon after came the startling news that **she was dead**!

The authorities arranged that the school should be closed and the children she had taught should attend the funeral considering that she had been a teacher for some years and was greatly liked and respected by everyone.

As the procession with its school children walking down two and two and carrying flowers passed down the Main Street the shops were all closed and sympathetic crowds lined the pavements, the men were all bareheaded. How keenly the solemn procession brought back to me another procession little more than a year ago! It required all my resolution to keep back the tears as I walked along, and on arrival at the grave my **grief felt overwhelming for it was quite close to Father's grave**.

Mr. Coventry conducted the service too and at the close the children had to sing *"There is a Green hill far away"* which they had practiced at school in the morning and lay their flowers in the grave as the coffin was lowered.

But we were too full of emotion to sing more than a few lines of the first verse when we all broke down sobbing and weeping unrestrainedly round the grave of our beloved teacher, the adults alone continued the hymn though they too were greatly over-come, and the last verse was not sung.

The painful scene soon ended and Uncle and Mr. Hume and other gentlemen hurried the poor sobbing children into the waiting cabs at the cemetery gates and got us home without delay.

Publisher note:
In 2004, distant relatives of Lizzie and Mary Ann Hume (Eileen & Cecil) visited Gibraltar and confirmed that both had died of T.B. (Phthisis Pulmonalis) within two years of each other. The same illness that took Bolton, and probably Emma too.

However, the date of Lizzie Hume's death was 1977, not 1975, as Harriett has led us to believe if this event was to take place a year after her father's death. Because I believe this account was written retrospectively, perhaps, Harriett might have got confused and is describing how she felt a year after the death of her mother.

Either way, this quote from Eileen is relevant:

"The army brought the first Hume teachers to Gibraltar and the Army took the last Hume teachers away from Gibraltar".

Chapter XVII

Father's Grave. School Picnic. The broken Chair. Happy Memories. Family News. Birthday Presents.

Before the end of 1875, a handsome tombstone had been erected over Father's grave consisting of a wide stone platform with two steps and a square pedestal supporting an upright marble cross. That emblem was decidedly rare in the Presbyterian portion of the cemetery so ours was very easy to find. Mother had placed some pots with choice geraniums growing, at each corner of the platform which covered the vault.

We always went out in the cab every Sunday to visit the grave and attend to the flowers. A wreath of everlasting flowers hung on the cross. At that time the hideous artificial wreaths under glass domes had not been invented, so that graves did not then present the appearance of a pastry-cook's counter!

The **annual school picnic took place at Campamento** during the summer holidays, and this year there were three of us to go in the waggons! I have already described this joyous affair [probably in an earlier diary we no longer have access to], but may add that this time I did not distinguish myself by fainting through the heat, and that more of us were frightened by the familiarity of the Nigger Minstrels (!) this time.

John was so clever with tools that Mother made him a present of some toy carpenter's tools for his birthday. He was always hammering and nailing wood together. He made a little book shelf for Mother which pleased her greatly.

"Why Johnnie! You are a genius!" she exclaimed with delight.

One Saturday afternoon, he actually made a chain, and called me into the yard to look at it. I tested its durability by sitting on it, but whether I was clumsy or sat down too hard, I found myself sprawling on the ground!

John burst out laughing at first, but seeing the ruins of his chain he gave a loud wail, "Oh! What have you broken it for?"

I got up feeling cross at my ridiculous position & retorted, "I didn't break it. It's a silly old chain, that's all!" and I gave a spiteful kick to the unfortunate remains.

Now, one may insult an invention, but one must not insult his handiwork!

This was too much for John to swallow, though he was one of the most placid and sweet natured of boys. He gave a yell & went for me! It didn't take me long to get into a rage, and the next minute we were pummelling & pulling each other's hair like a couple of little wild cats!

Mother hearing the row, rushed out to see what was the matter and separated us with difficulty. We both wept & complained of each other vociferously. By judicious questioning she got to the truth. John was rebuked & told it was very unmanly for boys to strike girls, and very naughty to fly into a passion over an accident! He soon became penitent. I knew it was my turn. I was severely rebuked for being so rough & careless as to break my little brother's chain that had cost him so much trouble to make, and for being so cruel as to fight & thump him afterwards. That, as his elder sister, I ought to help him all I could and take care of things he made!

Mother then made us apologise to each other, kiss and make friends, after which she examined the broken chain and encouraged John to put it together again, showing him how to strengthen the legs so that the seat would not collapse if anyone sat on it. Thus was the little fellow made happy and cheerful once more!

Dear wise mother!

How careful she was not to discourage effort in any of her children!

My pet productions were dolls' clothes and she gave me unstinted praise for my neat sewing though I am afraid her efforts to induce me to go in for more useful work were unsuccessful!

The Saturday after, John proudly exhibited a chain that looked the finished article! He invited Mother to sit on it, but she prudently declined. However, Arty, Kems & Baby were allowed to sit on it, and great was the admiration for John's handiwork.

Even Mrs. McKendry (who usually threw cold water on our ambition designs) condescended to look and admire! John looked at me & said "you can sit if you like, but (anxiously) don't be too heavy." I declined the honour feeling it better to be over-cautious than risk another accident!

After Charlie was weaned Mrs. McKendry used to have Sundays off. We know by then that she used to go to her own home to sleep at night as we hadn't room for her, and Mother insisted on her having Sundays as a holiday when Charlie was able to do without her. No doubt she would have liked to have taken Charlie with her!

Uncle was often away too on Sundays, so with the shop being shut we enjoyed having Mother all to ourselves! I volunteered to help with the work, and after breakfast would seize the palmetto broom & zealously sweep the verandah & stairs, raising plenty of dust in the process. John would dust the legs of the chairs, & enthusiastically propose all kinds of unnecessary work such as cleaning windows, white-washing the yard wall (which sadly needed it!) & bees-waxing the furniture! I clamoured to do the washing up but was only allowed to wipe, till the mortality among the tea-cups became so alarming that Mother gave me a less expensive job!

There was no afternoon Sunday school at St Andrews. On wet afternoons, Mother would tell us Bible stories. How we loved to crowd round her, Charlie in her lap of course. John & I were fond of stroking her silky dark hair so smoothly parted above her dear forehead! Arty liked the story of Goliath best, and during the week would chop off any number of imaginary giants' heads! Kems didn't like this story, she used to bury her face on Mother's lap & scream & stamp her little feet. We all liked her story of Joseph & his wonderful coat which we imagined to possess all the colours of the rainbow!

We went to Sunday school at 10, staying to the service in the church afterwards at 11. Mother always managed the Sunday dinner so as to be able to get to the morning service. I well remember seeing her enter and walk up the aisle with Baby & Kems clinging to her black dress all the way to our pew where John, Arty and I would be already seated.

Ours was the last pew but one at the back of the church next to the wall & facing the pulpit. A Mr. & Mrs. G. Torrie with a tiny fair girl & Mr. & Mrs. R. Torrie with two dark handsome little boys occupied the back pew with sometimes an old lady & gentleman Captain & Mrs. Charlton. Those were the days of family pews! The centre of the church was full of them, the side aisles & gallery being reserved for the troops.

Each side of the pulpit were two great square pews with seats all round

& a little table in the centre. One was for the use of the Minister's family and the other for the officers. Mr. Coventry's family consisted of his wife, a stout motherly lady with a very handsome face, his grown up handsome buxom daughters and a young son named David.

In front of our pew sat the Reid family. In front of them, the Humes. In a line with us, but divided by a partition the height of the pews was the Fromow's pew. Behind them against the wall sat the Dallas's. In front of the Fromow's were the Pattersons. The services were exceedingly dull and in the evenings badly attended. The morning service was the fashionable one. When it was over, the members of the congregation would stand outside in little groups chatting pleasurably with one another before going home.

We did not always attend the evening service. On summer evenings after tea we used to sit on the verandah steps with Mother who would tell us about the stars and the wonderful animals that would inhabit the world in prehistoric times. How we loved those talks & Mother's company.

That year was the first that we took an interest in birthdays. We were given pocket money every week, and got quite enthusiastically about buying presents for each other! I teased mother into telling me her age but she would only tell us her birthday which was on the 31st of October.

I couldn't decide what to buy her but then decided on a black brooch with a floral design which I had seen in a jeweller's shop. Mother was busy ironing and when I returned and presented it to her with "Many Happy Returns of the Day!" and she was greatly surprised and pleased with her present, kissing me very affectionately in return. I think John's present was the book-shelf he made, his finances probably being pretty low after generously donating to Charlie's, Emily's & Arthur's birthdays!

How little I thought then that that was Mothers last birthday on earth. It was a great comfort to me in after years to think that I had remembered to give her that little present which she wore constantly. I wish that I had treasured the little brooch for her sake, but with a child's carelessness I left it lying about years after & finally lost it.

Chapter XVIII

Pet's. Presents. Xmas parties. Pocketing. Paints. Prince of Wales visit. Tall yarns.

We were all very fond of animals, I never remember a time when there was not a cat or a dog or bird in the house. In Fathers' time we had canaries, but one after another they fell victims to our cats, till we found it impossible to keep both. The cats won. They were Mother's favourites. I often saw her sitting with a cat on her knee and another on her shoulder while she sewed or knitted, and encouraged by her sympathy we children brought home every poor stray cat we found, put a ribbon round its neck & gave it a saucer-full of milk, sometimes to Mother's vexation emptying the jug which left us without any tea!

At last, an embargo had to be placed upon the importation of pussies, especially when those who were installed commenced having families of kittens! Uncle had the job of drowning them while we stood round the pail tearfully begging the lives of "that dear little one with the white paws!" or "that one with the striped tail!" till Uncle had to ruthlessly command us to go away in order to let him finish the sacrifice in peace!

Someone gave John a couple of rabbits (or else he bought them – I forget which). He kept them in the old bread oven in the yard & in a short time there were some little bunnies! Mother gave him lettuce leaves to feed them on. The old brick oven was so dark & impossible to keep clean that the rabbits got to be rather a nuisance & eventually found their way into another kind of oven, and then on to our dining table in the form of rabbit pie.

John wept on having to give up his bunnies, but Mother explained that we had no proper place to keep them in, and that it wasn't kind to the poor rabbits to keep them in a brick place. When John got older **we would all go to England where we should have a nice garden for the rabbits** to play in & how nice that would be! John wiped his eyes with his grubby bit of handkerchief, and was comforted.

He spent the rest of the afternoon in asking questions about England and enthusiastically set to work to make a rabbit-hutch (with Arthur's help) to stand in the "garden". I think he imagined the garden **would be the size of the one we had in Tangiers.**'

My idea of England was a place full of flowers and green fields and people with fair hair and rosy cheeks! Fred had somewhat disillusioned me, he was as sallow and dark as any Spaniard!

Christmas drew near, and we began to think about parties. The usual Soiree was to take place at the Presbyterian Church, and there was to be a school treat at the R. A. to which we were going.

Although it must have been a sad Christmas for poor Mother being the 2nd without dear Father. Still, she resolved that we should be happy. For some reason (probably being too busy) she was not able to make the annual journey to "London House" to buy our presents for Christmas, and was wondering who she could send for that purpose when John and I volunteered to go, stoutly declaring, that we were quite old enough to go shopping for mother!

After some hesitation and many injunctions to mind the cab and carts and always to look before crossing a road, to take hands and not run or lose the money!

Dear mother sent us off on Christmas Eve, John (being more trust-worthy) being deputed to carry the money (there may have been more than 10/-, I cannot quite remember), ten whole shillings wrapped in paper and a list of the presents for everyone including Uncle and Mrs. McKendry.

We arrived at "London House" in **Scud Hill** and were smilingly greeted by Mrs. Batchelor to whom mother had sent a note informing her of our errand. She blandly exhibited dolls, rocking horses and other toys in glorious profusion all over the shop, but John (tightly clutching his precious money) cautiously proceeded to inquire the prices of almost everything in the shop till Mrs. Batchelor lost patience and flounced off making some remark to her husband, "those tiresome children".

I blushed scarlet and nervously nudged John with a whisper to "make haste and buy something." But John was determined to make the most of his money! He asked me what I would like. I pointed to a big doll in a gorgeous silk dress. He calmly inquired the price.

"Ten shillings!" snapped the lady.

John looked reproachfully at me. I wildly pointed to a doll's pram.

"How much is that?" he asked.

But Mrs. Batchelor was exasperated by this time, we had been in the shop over an hour & nothing bought yet!

She replied sharply, "How much have you to spend?"

On being told, she scornfully said, "Oh, that pram is five dollars, you couldn't buy that!"

If she had said £5.00 I couldn't have felt more crestfallen.

Then Mrs. Batchelor wanted John to give her the list of presents and she would choose presents for all, but he stuck to it like glue and then after much hesitation and changing of mind, he selected (with no help from me) what he thought was suitable for everyone. I was the hardest to please. At last laden with parcels and no more money left (John did some hard bargaining to make the 10/- last out) we triumphantly left the shop (I thought Mrs. Batchelor wouldn't want to see us there again!).

We were rather tired by the time we reached the **Saluting Battery [Rosia Road]**, as we had been standing all afternoon, so John proposed a rest and we sat on one of the benches and counted our parcels. John went over them with glee and immense satisfaction (I wish I could remember what the presents were, but I cannot unfortunately) feeling sure that everyone would be satisfied

Suddenly, he paused with dismay & said, "Oh! I have forgotten Uncle" Alas! It was true.

We had got something for Mrs. McKendry because Mother had impressed it on us to be sure and buy her a present which would come from us.

We looked at each other in consternation. I believe John proposed going back to "London House" to get something for Uncle on credit to be paid for later out of our pocket money, but I stoutly refused to accompany him!

Our unfortunate discovery rather dampened our pleasure but we got safely home with all the parcels and told Mother of our mistake, which she soon set right by giving John two shillings & telling him to buy Uncle a meerschaum pipe! So he got the best present of the lot!

Of course, the presents were jealously kept till the next morning & then placed on the breakfast table. I was discontented with my tin bath till John suggested that it would do to wash the kitten in, which proceeding Mother promptly vetoed!

I believe Mrs. Batchelor told Mother afterwards that John would make a fine business man when he grew up, the way he laid out those shillings at her shop!

By the way, I can remember one present.

Emily had always been fond of a battered old Dutch doll minus arms or legs, so John bought her a big new one with a very shiny black head! When Emily had it presented to her she screamed and hid her face on Mother's bosom refusing to take or even look at the doll in spite of John's coaxing! At last, Mother had to tell John to take it away, as Emily was really frightened of its big black head. Arthur annexed it however, and we found him later busily engaged in licking the black paint off, and teaching Charlie to do the same! They were promptly hauled off to be washed with dire threatening as to what would happen if the paint got into their little "tummies!" and the unfortunate doll consigned to be chopped up for firewood, till Mother thought of scrubbing off the paint with salt & hot water.

It emerged from the ordeal looking very faded & featureless having nothing but a wooden nose left! Eyes, lips & rosy cheeks had vanished with the "hair". Kems however condescended to accept it, clasped it to her little bosom and took it to bed with her every night.

119

I do not remember anything about the 1875 Soiree, and I don't think any naughty boys kept me from enjoying me tea. The R.A. tea party was a novelty. The tables, I think, were laid in the Infant school which was so decorated with flags & holly that we hardly knew it! Our teachers too were all in their Sunday clothes, & it was a pleasant novelty to have them passing us cake & jam & bread instead of slates and books.

After tea, we all went into the Master's school and there was a huge & very gorgeous Xmas tree in full blooms! How eagerly we stared at the beautiful presents on its boughs! There was the same kind of joyous noisy crowd of children as at the soiree the year before!

To my disappointment I did not get a doll but a book. I looked at it contemptuously. I associated books with lessons in school & thought it too bad to have such an unwelcome present given me. In the crowd, I bumped up against my old chum Bessie Robinson, she was bewailing the fact she had received a game of "Lotto" from the tree. I told her I have a book and didn't want it! She suggested an exchange. I agreed. We swapped!

John was the joyful recipient of a box of paint, and I think Arthur got a drum. I wasn't much more pleased with the box of "Lotto" than I had been with the book. I opened it, there were lots of little discs with numbers on and a paper with full of dry directions. I felt quite an ill-used person!

Mother was waiting to receive us, smiling and ready to listen to our descriptions of the party. She sympathised with my look of appreciation of "Lotto" saying she never cared for games herself. Till John let out that I had been given a book. When she heard of the exchange I had affected, she was quite angry with me, saying that she wished I could get fond of reading; I was so backwards at school.

When I was in bed that night, I laid awake and heard Mother telling Uncle at supper about my little transaction, & expressing her vexation that I should have given a book for a worthless game!

I never played "Lotto" needless to say after that, still it was not wasted – the discs & different parts of the puzzle came in for playing "shops" in the verandah steps.

I do not remember any entertainment besides the Xmas tree at the R.A. treat that Christmas, but I remember how disgusted I was to see all the boys at the tea-table (and many of the girls) busily engaged in pocketing all the cake they could, when they had eaten their fill! I even detected John doing the same thing and lost no time in administering a reproof!

John replied, "I'm taking this home for Mother!"

That completely altered the case!

I blushed to think that I had not thought of taking any home for Mother or anyone else & accordingly stuffed my pocket full. I hope those at home enjoyed our contributions next day!

John's box of paint proved an unending source of enjoyment to us, for Arthur & I loved to dabble with the brushes John generously allowed us the use. Before long everything in the house showed vivid traces of green, vermillion & sky blue! Towels, curtains, furniture & walls as well as fingers, faces, books, & clothing looked as if trying to emulate the hues of Joseph's coat! Mrs. McKendry complained loudly about the damage, declaring that the colours would not wash out of the clothes & towels & c, while it took all her time cleaning furniture &c.

Mother had to interpose and forbid us trying our brushes on anything that came handy. We were given an armful of old fashion books to paint and some rags to wipe our hands & brushes on, and the house gradually resumed its usual air of respectability.

Early in the New Year, Gibraltar was ablaze with excitement and illuminations in honour of the **visit of the Prince of Wales on his way from India**. The ship he came on, (the "Serapis") a great white vessel lying along the New Mole carried a regular zoological garden of animals of all kinds from elephants to performing fleas on board – all presents from the various Rajahs and Kings in India

The public was allowed on board the three days or so the Prince was at Gibraltar.

The city was en fete!

The houses all along the Main Street were decorated with flags and wreaths. The public buildings were lavishly decorated. The Officers Mess opposite us was simply covered with evergreen foliage and bunting. I think a Welsh Regiment occupied it for over the main entrance was a niche and in it was the figure of a Druid with a long beard and playing a harp, as the procession went by.

At intervals there were triumphal arches. **Every road and street in Gibraltar was outlined with fairy lamps so that at night the illumination must have looked splendid to the lookers on at Algeciras and Campamento.**

Mother made two big flags of red, white and blue bunting to hang out of our front windows with big nosegays tied at the ends of the poles.

On the eventful day that the Royal procession was to take place there was the greatest excitement in our home. All places of business had to be closed by 10 am, crowds of people passed up and down the streets staring at the decorations. Our two big flags were out soon after breakfast. Uncle nailed the poles to the window ledges to keep them firm. How pleased I was that we had windows in the Main Street and could see the procession without any trouble. Mounted police cantered up and down the street keeping the crowd behind the barriers and shouting directions to unfortunate cabmen who couldn't or wouldn't understand that they were to go along the Line Wall instead of the Main Street.

Our shop was closed in good time though people would keep coming and wanting to buy more tissue paper for making flowers. We children and Mrs. McKendry were at the windows when a fierce mounted official shouted something at us and hammered at the door below!

Uncle came upstairs in a hurry and told mother that the police wouldn't allow the bunches of flowers on our poles as they were hanging down and might fall into the Royal carriage and perhaps hit the Prince! So the poles were unfastened the nosegays pulled off (to my regret) and the poles replaced in a great hurry.

Soon after that another official riding by commanded us to raise our flags higher. They were so big that they hung quite low. This necessitated some more work of un-nailing the poles and Uncle got quite cross about it.

At last our banners were tilted to the right angle and I kept wondering what would happen if one of the poles gave way at a critical moment!

At last our patience (strained to the uttermost) was rewarded, we heard the joyful sound of the regimental brass bands approaching. People burst into loud cheering and the procession moved in sight. We frantically cheered and waved our hands, (though we were nearly squashed with Uncle and Mrs. McKendry leaning on top of us. Mother and some friends were at the other window and the windows were very narrow!) especially when an open brougham passed below containing ladies and gentlemen – the governor, his wife, and other notables.

Most people thought the Prince was in that, but I saw him quite plainly riding a horse behind the carriage. He was just like his portrait above our chest of drawers and wore a scarlet uniform covered with sashes and medals. He was a stout heavy-faced young man, & he gravely saluted the people each side of the road. I had a hot argument with Mrs. McKendry afterwards, she insisting that the Prince was driving in the carriage and not on horseback.

His Royal Highness did one piece of useful work that day. He laid the foundation stone of the New Market. Up till then, Gibraltar Market consisted of a number of dirty squalid booths where meat, fruit and vegetables were sold of indifferent quality.

Uncle took us on board the 'Serapis' one afternoon to see the presents and the animals. We were greatly taken with the big white (!) elephant though disappointed with the colour, we thought it would be as white as a clean tablecloth! The monkeys were a source of great amusement! There were Bengal tigers in cages and many other creatures too numerous to mention or remember. We saw cases containing blazing jewels and wonderful carved sandalwood things but it was the animals we were interested in.

When relating to mother all the wonders we had seen while she was bathing us that evening (we always got a bath before bed-time) I couldn't help inventing the story that I had given the elephant a bun and he had taken it with his trunk. John, not to be outdone, said that he had shaken hands with the biggest monkey! Mother laughed heartily at our innocent fabrications!

When the Prince departed in his big white ship, down came all the decorations and I deeply regretted the taking down of our flags, I was under the impression that they were to remain up for good. I asked if I could have the bunting for doll clothes but was refused!

Chapter XIX

John's investment. Our 'carriage'. Fairy Tales. Examinations.

We children always had porridge or bread and milk for breakfast. On Sundays we had weak tea (a spoonful of tea to a cupful of milk) bread & butter and a boiled egg each or fried sausage, or bacon & fried egg. Mother often lamented the difficulty she had in procuring really fresh eggs. I remember we often encountered eggs of the vilest odour at breakfast time which had to be hastily removed from the table.

John asked if we couldn't have some fowls to lay eggs for us. Mother said that if he saved up seven shillings he could buy some fowls. He did so in a very short time. How, I don't know. I got just the same pocket money, but could never manage to save a penny! Uncle said he would give him 3d. a week for cleaning his boots every day. Mother said she would pay him 1d. a pair of her boots cleaning. John accepted the work willingly. He used to sit on a little stool (of his own manufacture) at the foot of the yard steps, with his sleeves rolled up and his little white arm nearly buried in Uncle's big boots while he energetically plied the big blacking brush.

John & I used to clean our own shoes every morning before going to school, while Mrs. McKendry cleaned Arthur & Emily's. John's idea of buying livestock seemed such an immense undertaking to me that I was entirely sceptical about it ever coming to anything. But, one fine morning John and Uncle went to market and returned with four beautiful fowls, a cock and three hens, all as white as snow; at least the hens were white, I think the cock was dark.

Wasn't Mother surprised and pleased, and wasn't Johnnie as proud as Punch!

They were beauties certainly, I did not think there could be finer birds anywhere. Uncle said they were the best in the market and we believed him! They strutted about the yard picking up the corn that John threw for them & the splendid rooster opened his wings and crowed! What a crow!

I am sure it could have been heard at the Signal station! Mrs. McKendry was full of admiration for John's beautiful fowls and had even more admiration for his pluck & perseverance in obtaining them!

She turned to me & said playfully, "Ah! When are you going to save up and buy something sensible like John?"

I made a mental resolution that I would save and do something wonderful with my money, for a start pestered Mother to tell me how many dogeys (threepenny bits – our weekly pocket money each) there were in a shilling! She told me I was old enough to know and I was, but too indolent to make the exertion of remembering.

At last, (with John's help), I found that it would take 28 weeks to save 7/- if I never spent anything at all, more than half a year! That made my resolution very tottery indeed. The very thought of going without meringues all that time was enough to damp my ardour! Especially when I had no object in view, no use for going in for fowls, when John's took up all the yard space there was!

Mother had some difficulty in getting us off to school that morning. I think we were all late, something new for John! At dinner time we raced home to feast our eyes on our "farmyard". The cluckies were making themselves quite at home and the yard in something of a mess! Mother made an agreement with John that she would pay him the market price for fresh eggs – 1/- a doz. & he would have to buy the food for them. He declared that the first egg would have to be a present for Mother!

Early next morning, Uncle greeted us with the wonderful news that one of the hens had laid an egg! John proudly presented it to Mother and stipulated that she was to have it for her breakfast! Mother was very much pleased, but wanted to share it with us. She said it was such a big egg for one person, but John was obdurate. Mother must have it and no-one else; so she gave it to Mrs. McKendry to boil with careful instructions not to let it get hard. Mrs. McKendry's methods of egg boiling were scarcely scientific. She would put the eggs in boiling water, put it on the fire & often forget all about them. Sometimes they would be nearly raw, other times hard as bullets; she used to guess the time they were cooking & was not a good guesser!

It wasn't long before we had to face the problem of finding a more suitable place for a fowl-run, as our meagre yard soon became filthy and Mother was afraid that with summer coming on it would be impossible to keep the fowls. Uncle suggested taking them up to the stable. I pricked up my ears & wanted to know what stables! Then it came out that Mother was the proprietor of a cab & horse, & they were housed in a stable somewhere in tow, I think somewhere near the theatre. We were sorry to part with the fowls though we could go & see them every day & John of course had to go & feed them daily & collect the eggs.

So the cab we used to drive to the cemetery in on Sunday afternoons was ours! This gave us a great feeling of importance. We spoke of it as "our carriage!"

When the spring came, Mother allowed me to discard my black dress to my delight, and I had a lilac muslin made for best and a grey frock for school. But **my friend Annie Park was again plunged into deep mourning by the death of her mother.** I was very sorry for her and told Mother.

She said, "Poor Annie is quite an orphan now!"

I felt what a dreadful thing it must be to have no father nor mother, but never dreamed that such might be our unhappy fate.

John had always worn a little grey felt hat for school so long that we derided it, it had become so shabby! Still John stuck to it and resisted all attempts to replace it with a new one. We derisively called it a "dustman's" hat! The "basura" man had an old felt hat something like it when he came into our yard every morning to collect the refuse. But all the ridicule failed to wean John from his beloved grey felt!

In March, the school examinations took place and the pupils in the "Master's" school had to journey for two or three days to the South Barracks school to be examined, all except the 4th class. John & I went up to the South Chapel (as it was called being used for a Garrison chapel on Sundays) for the first time that year. It was a great ordeal to me. I had no idea what horrors we would have to undergo in "examinations".

We had to meet at the R.A. School and were marched, escorted by our teachers, to our destination, via Castle Road, Hargreaves Parade, the

Alameda and Scud Hill. It seemed a very long journey in those days, and when we arrived at the school we found children from all the other Garrison schools assembled in the spacious yard overlooking Rosia Bay.

So many strangers made me feel miserably shy.

Then we were marched into the (to me) huge building and were seated at desks one yard apart from one another to prevent copying. We had to write with pens & ink on sheets of foolscap, no slates. The silence & strange surrounding filled me with awe! Our teachers were standing in a group near the door; they were allowed to bring us anything if we held out our hands, but not allowed to speak to us.

A strange man came around to hear each of us read aloud. I think I made a fearful hash of my reading through nervousness. I was told twice to "speak up", then the examiner shut his book abruptly & passed on to the next victim. I caught a glance of annoyance on my teacher's face which added to my misery and mortification. I felt I had "failed" and wondered what would be done to me! It was a great relief when it was all over and we were free to return to the R.A. once more.

On Good Friday, Uncle took John & Arthur to some sports on the North Front, but I had to stay at home with a sore throat. It wasn't bad enough to interfere with the dolls' dressmaking, I was busy putting them out of mourning & into colours, & had no time to lose.

It was about this time that I discovered the charms of reading, & was brought about in the following way. Mother came upstairs one wet afternoon with a new book from the shop "**Grimms Fairy Tales**". She gathered us round her, and read story after story to our great delight. We were quite fascinated by them and were never satisfied. Every afternoon we would eagerly clamour for "more stories!"

One day, to our great discontent, Mother was too busy in the shop to come and read to us. Paints had lost their fascination since "Grimms" came into our lives. John & Arthur went off to play. Charlie & Emily were having their afternoon nap as usual.

I discontentedly turned over the leaves of the book that we were so absorbed in, wishing that Mother would come & read as usual, when curiosity led me to read a short story with a singular title, I forget what, but, I found that I need never wait for anyone to read to me anymore after that. I devoured tale after tale till I was summoned to tea. Thus a new world was opened to me! **Reading was transformed from a dreary task to the greatest of pleasures.** Mother never had any occasion from that time to chide me for my indifference to books. On the contrary, I used to neglect everything else if I had a book in my hands! The trouble was to get me to stop reading!

I even read the Bible in church during Mr. Coventry's long dreary sermons, though I found that a little too dry and unintelligible at first. Still it helped me to pass the longest hour in the week!

Chapter XX

Mc. Williams. The Sewing Class. R.A. Discipline. Large Hand. Songs in School. Uninteresting Sermons. Magazines. Pen Portraits.

After Easter, we had a new teacher at the R.A. – a corporal Mc Williams who was a handsome young man with a red face and a bad temper. He was engaged to Mary-Ann Hume who was one of the teachers in the Infant school and sister to Lizzie Hume who died. **Rumour had it that he was previously engaged to Lizzie, but on the death had transferred his affections to Mary Ann.**

I think he was a good teacher, but for two defects. He had favourites and easily lost his temper with the dull schoolers of whom I was one. He used to shout & storm at us & often threw books at us or banged us on the head with them!

Discipline at the R.A. was I am afraid at a low ebb in those days. The noise from the different classes was often so great that Mr. Bacon used to have to bang his cane on his desk to enforce silence, or he would come round to each class & thrash some of the most unruly boys, till something like order was obtained, but not for long however! Still it was better than that in the Infant school where order seemed to be utterly unknown.

Poor Mrs. Bacon couldn't attend to her family & home & school at the same time, so the latter had to be neglected. In the afternoons when the girls in the Master's School went for sewing, the teachers sat & gossiped or quarrelled. Mine, Mary Ann Hume had a temper quite as virulent and overbearing as that of her beloved.

If the infants got too noisy and unmanageable she would get up from her chair at the sewing table (where she was not needed) rush between the desks in a passion caning & cuffing every child indiscriminately whether good or bad till she had reduced them to whimpering silence. There was no attempt to teach the unfortunate infants.

They were simply huddled to forms where they had to write (if they felt inclined) pot hooks & hangers on greasy little slates all the afternoon: utterly neglected. Some poor little mites fell asleep from sheer weariness, resting their little heads on the hard desks till they fell off the form with a bump followed by roars & tears. This frequently happened during the afternoon, yet none of the teachers present thought it their duty to look after the poor little things!

The dreary ill ventilated school room with its dirty yellow walls with a few dingy pictures too dirty & high up to tell what they were about; dirty windows & often filthy bare floor would be a strange sight to the modern kindergarten teacher!

All honour to Germany for leading the way and showing the world what infant teaching might to be like! And all Dishonour to careless money-grabbing, child-despising England – the richest country in the world in money, but nearly the poorest in educational facilities!

As for our sewing, it was a perfect farce! We girls dawdled away our time doing nothing. We were given dirty little strips of calico to hem that had been hemmed and unpicked many times before. Sometimes the needles & thimbles were not given out till nearly closing time. But if we were not taught sewing we were certainly & most effectually taught how to waste time! Then when our brothers surpassed us in the Master's school it was put down to our inferior female intellects!

John certainly overtook me at school though nearly two years my junior!

The fatal influence of that infant school "sewing" class undermined my whole character. I became a first-class dawdler! I made no effort to acquire anything, learning was a thing to be shirked. I could see no object to be gained by learning lessons in any way, and nobody ever tried to interest me in anything.

I did as little work as possible to avoid being caned, was always glad when school was over. Our teachers were merely soldiers who had passed an examination to qualify themselves as teachers, they had absolutely no training as such.

One or two took an interest in the work, but the remainder got through it with as little trouble to themselves as possible. For a few weeks before the annual examinations we were coached & whacked & stormed at. We recited our tables or spelt aloud at a deafening rate, wrote interminable copies with pen & ink, my blots earned me many a rap.

To do myself justice, I had developed into a beautiful writer at first, with a fine copper-plate hand that was the admiration of the whole class; it was the only thing I could do well & therefore took an interest in it.

When Mr. Bacon arrived, he was imbued with the latest fashion in writing of the park-paling type! I loathed large hand writing and refused to change mine. At times, I was forced to write large hand in the copy books, but I deliberately took no pains with it.

Unfortunately, bad habits are easily learnt & hard to shake off! Had Mr.

Bacon left me to myself I would have gradually adopted a larger handwriting without being forced, but he bullied and caned me to such a degree that I grew desperate & careless.

One day, after looking at my neat dictation, he roared, "I'll make you stop writing that small hand!" & he crushed my hand with his, twisting my fingers till I could have cried out. Then he set me a large hand copy & dared me to write a hair's breadth less than that! I was boiling over with rage & disgust.

I deliberately wrote that copy with letter not less than an inch high, not caring a rap for the consequences.

Mr. Bacon came & looked over my shoulder when I had finished. He looked at me and I looked back at him. Something in my face must have warned him that he had better not go too far or there would be an explosion, so he went away without a word. But my writing was ruined from that time. I did not care, but I nursed a grudge against Mr. Bacon in my heart that lasted for many years and made me overlook the things I ought to have been grateful to him for.

Mr. Bacon was very musical and introduced singing into the school. We learnt many delightful songs that John & I have remembered all our lives & that have given us untold pleasure, such as, "Come & see the daylight dawning", "Spring! Spring! Merry Spring!", "Among the fields so pearly! "Men of Harlech" "Sweet Spring is returning", "Welcome Christmas, welcome here" "The Schooner Hesperus", "Cold the blast may blow" "Canadian boat song! "Glide along my bonnie boat" (part song), "Ring, ring the bells" "Oh the sports of child-hood" and hymns such as "There is a green hill", "Three in one & one in three" (which attracted me by its solemn time & mystical words), "New every morning is the love", "Abide with me", "Now the day is over" (which always went flat before the last verse was finished!), "Nearer my god to thee", & "Jesus, lover of my soul."

He also introduced a little sermonette after the usual morning prayers, to which I used to listen with great interest, they were far more interesting than Mr. Coventry's long prosy sermons. Mr. Bacon must have been a Tory of the old school for he used to give us the impression that such people as Puritans and Dissenters held very wrong opinions, and it was our duty to be very loyal to the Queen and all that were in authority under her!

The Catholic children were exempt from attending prayers & Bible reading, and I rather envied than their liberty to stay in the porch till 9.30!

The same lack of discipline and general slackness used to permeate the Sunday school also. Mother took us away from King's chapel because we never learnt anything there, but I've no recollection of ever learning anything at St. Andrew's either.

After the opening hymn & prayer, the children were divided up into classes. Our teacher would ask a few desultory questions & read a book to us the rest of the time. I seldom listened being more occupied with noticing the details of the teacher's dress – one young lady used to wear very high-heeled shoes. Sometimes we sat without any teacher at all, and I wearily yawned the time away after puzzling as to the meaning of the grimy texts on the walls!

Down the right-side of the vestry were book shelves with glass doors through which I used to gaze at very dry-looking dusty volumes. "**Humboldt's Travels**" were there in several big volumes. The only thing taught successfully in that Sunday school was the art of wasting time.

The singing in church was very slow & tuneless, the psalms in phrase were usually sung. The Free Church hymnbook wasn't introduced till some years later. Old Mr. Coventry was a very dry & prosy preacher, but he had a habit of tilting himself on his toes that I thought was very funny. He had a decided Scotch accent; the opening prayer in church was always the same, one petition was "Give our senators wisdom" for years I thought it was, "Give whose senators wisdom" & wondered what senators were!

What a relief it was when the last paraphrase was given out, how impatiently I waited till the slow verses where drawled through, & Mr. Coventry's slow closing prayer came to an end with an empathic "Ay-men".

The congregation seemed to come to life then, coats were quickly donned, sleepier children roused & a brisk stir apparent in all the pews. I was usually the first to get out into the fresh air & glorious sunshine pervading Gunner's Parade. I think it was the only time in the week that I moved with alacrity!

Finding that both John & I were fond of reading, Mother ordered two delightful magazines for us every month named "Little Folks" and "Chatterbox". Mother herself took in two magazines, the "Leisure Home" and "Sunday-At-Home". There were serial stories in both, and we waited with eager impatience for the monthly big case containing all the magazines. I wondered what connection there could be between book magazines and powder magazines. There was a huge powder magazine near the castle with a sentry always marching up & down guarding it. We shuddered to think what might happen if a spark fell into the powder!

Mother said it might blow the whole city up as well as the R.A. School! We wouldn't have minded the loss of the school, but we didn't want our shop blowing up or the stable where John kept his fowls!

It wasn't very long before Uncle hired another stable to house our fowls & equipage, it was at the foot of Scud Hill, rather a long way for poor little John to go & attend to the wants of his pets. However, Uncle solved the difficulty by offering to call every night when he took his usual stroll after closing the shop at 9 o'clock, to feed the fowls and collect the eggs.

At first, there was a gratifying number of eggs produced every day when John looked after them himself, but after the removal to the South district there were not quite as many.

Mother suggested in answer to John's enquiries that possibly the shortage was due to the fowls moulting, and that in time there would be more. John (practical laddie!) wanted to know what moulting was & the duration & frequency of the attacks, and lived in hopes of a speedy revival of the egg trade! On Sunday evenings Uncle took us (John, Arthur and me) up to the stable to see the poultry, while Mother had a rest after tea.

We did not attend church in the evenings then. In the afternoons there was always the drive out to the North Front (where there was always a refreshing breeze no matter how hot the day) to visit Father's grave! How carefully Mother picked off any dead leaves on the beautiful plants round the tomb-stone. They had lovely blooms and the pure white marble cross rising from its pedestal in the centre made me think our grave was the handsomest in that cemetery!

It certainly had the best appearance of any in the Presbyterian section. We always paused to read the inscription a good many times. It was…
"To the memory of Bolton Beanland, who died August 6th, 1874, aged 33 years."

Underneath was the text…
"Lord, remember me when Thou comest in Thy Kingdom."

I thought it a wonderful co-incidence that Father had died the same age as Jesus.

Not far off was Lizzie Hume's grave, just a head stone with her name & age & the inevitable text which I think was, *"Just as I am without one plea!"* The letters were not clearly cut & John & I used to have hot arguments as to whether the last word was "plea" or "flea".

I often recalled the tearful scene at the funeral, and wished that Lizzie had not died.

I never remember seeing any of the Humes at the cemetery when we were there, but perhaps they went during the week.

How we enjoyed those drives in "our carriage", especially on the return home, with the comfortable prospect of tea with toast or jam & cake awaiting us on arrival for Mrs. McKendry (or "Chacha" as Charlie called her) preferred to stay at our house with Charlie's company, to having lonely Sundays off in her own lodgings without him!

The moment the cab stopped she was ready with the shop open (we only had that one entrance) and would seize and kiss & hug Baby as if she hadn't seen him for a month! The little fellow was very fond of her too and would trot after his Chacha everywhere.

His second birthday took place on May 10th and a great fuss we made of it. As I remember him then, **he was a fair, delicate looking little fellow with heavy dead gold hair, big grey eyes, soft pink cheeks & lips, and a most winning expression.** Everyone fell in love with him and wanted to kiss him, but he had rather an objection to being kissed by anyone but Mother and Chacha. He was a little king and would only bestow his royal favours on a chosen few.

Arthur and he got on well together, I think John & I pulled him about too much in our desire to show our affection. They would play with blocks for hours on the floor, till a certain little pirate appeared in the offing and there would be a general screech, "Chacha! Look at Emily! She's taking our bricks!" Chacha would suddenly appear on the scene and the enemy would be repulsed with heavy loss.

Charlie was slender in body and rather quiet & sedate in manner, a contrast to Emily who was a plump lively little sprite of nearly four years. She had rather dark hair which curled up prettily on her shoulders & forehead, twinkling eyes, a little nose, plump rosy dimpled cheeks, & the prettiest little mouth possible.

She was a talking, lovable child but very wilful and determined. If she took fancy to anything, there was usually a tug of war, and she was often the victor.

I remember getting a pair of boots with bead tassels in front. She took an immense fancy to them & wouldn't surrender them till Mother got her a similar pair! Then she told everyone, even her Sunday school teacher, about her "tassels" and used to sit in church admiring her little feet with great satisfaction.

Arthur was pale and slender to thinness. His hair was nearly as dark as Emily's but straight. He had large blue eyes with dark lashes, but his other features were large which made him look older than he was.

He was such a quiet, grave little fellow that he attracted little notice from others. He was never aggressive, but wouldn't let himself be imposed upon all the same. He was a useful ally, always ready to play with others. He was very fond of playing being the "dustman", with an old basket over his shoulders he would walk up and down the verandah crying aloud, "Basura! Basura!" He wanted to be a dustman when he grew up.

John was plump like Emily, but very fair with almost white hair & skin, & eyelashes. He had beautifully shaped red lips which were always firmly closed and a very determined little chin. His hair was very thick & always rumpled. It grew so fast that it was always 'in his neck'. His plump little white hands were always busy doing something or other. I don't think I ever saw him idle! He was wonderful, good-tempered too, very rarely was he roused into a temper, but when he was his anger rose to white heat! It was something to remember!

Clothes didn't interest him much, he liked old clothes just as much as new, in fact more! Although he was lively and sociable, he was very sensible and practical for a boy of seven.

Mother was exceedingly proud of him, she spoke of him fondly as **"my little genius" "my clever little man" "my right-hand boy".** Yet, unlike me he was never conceited for being praised.

As for me, I was a **plain, thin girl with a pale face, scraggy hair & turned up nose**. My fingers were always inky and my stockings coming down.

That's all!

***

Publisher's Note: That was not all! It turns out that…

'Harriett Beanland, a tailoress, from Nelson, was a member of the local ILP, a poor law guardian and suffrage supporter. In 1913, Harriett Beanland, suffragist, was secretary of the Nelson branch for a year until it was dissolved.'
For Labour and for Women: The Women's Labour League, 1906-1918, by Christine Collette

She is also mentioned in **The Road to Greenham Common: Feminism and Anti-militarism in Britain Since 1820**, by Jill Liddington, page 88.

Having bought a copy of this book, I can quote that Harriett Beanland wrote a letter in 1914 after the start of the First World War.

'One such rebel voice came from a dressmaker in North-East

Lancashire; a week after war began Harriett Beanland dispatched a furious letter to the local paper, denouncing:

"The erroneous impression that this and other countries are at war with one another. They are not. Their governments, composed of men and responsible to the men of each country, and backed by the majority of men who have caught the war and glory fever, have declared war on one another.

The women of these countries have not been consulted as to whether they would have war or not… If they, [men] deliberately shut out women, the peace-loving sex, from their rightful share in ruling their countries and Churches, then all the appeals and sentiments and prayers will be of no avail in preventing hostilities…

Yours, etc

H M Beanland"'

Therefore, it could be safe to assume that part of the reason for Harriett and Emily's departure to Australia in 1915 might have been in protest to the Great War since they did not support this 'war of men'.

Harriett Beanland (1866-1922)

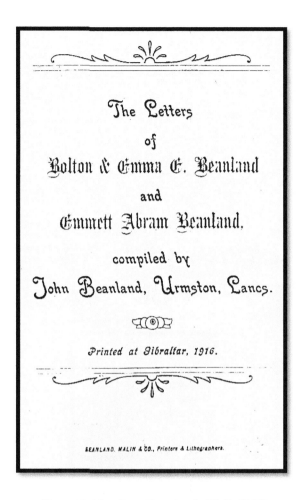

The Letters

of

Bolton & Emma E. Beanland

and

Emmett Abram Beanland.

compiled by

John Beanland, Urmston, Lancs.

Printed at Gibraltar, 1916.

BEANLAND. MALIN & CO., Printers & Lithographers.

Emmett Abraham Beanland (1843-1899)

**Original printed version edited by
V.J. Beanland to enable an easier read.**

**The copy printed in 1915 has many typographical errors, which may have
been from either the original letter or from when the letters were typed up.**

PART TWO:

LETTERS

OF

ABRAHAM EMMETT

BEANLAND

1875 ~ 1883

Gibraltar
6th September 1875

My Dear Brother and Sister,

We have great pleasure in answering your kind and welcome letter you sent, and thank you very much for the photograph you sent. They are very nice, but we should very much like to have one of sister Harriett's. Also, one of my niece, Mary Jane. You see, I have not forgotten her name, although I have been so long away from England. We are sending some photographs of Emma and the two youngest children. One for each. John, Joseph, Elizabeth and Margaret, and one for yourselves.

The next time you write I hope you will send us a good long letter and let us know all the latest news from Burnley and Nelson. I should like to know how our sister Elizabeth is getting on. Also, her son, Edward. You never say anything about our brother John, please let me know how he is getting on. I do not know where he is living or I should write to him. I have never received a letter from Henry Watson, since I have been here. You might be kind enough to give him my address, and then he will know where to write to.

You wanted to know more about our late dear brother, Bolton. He is buried in a family vault in the cemetery for the Garrison. It is outside the Garrison on what is called the North Front. We are getting a very nice tomb put over him.

I have nothing more to say at present. Hoping you are quite well.
We remain your dear brother and sister,
A Beanland

P.s. Tell Joe I shall answer his letter shortly.

Publisher note:
Further sorrow befell the family when Emma Elizabeth Beanland died a year later, aged only 38 years, on the 31 July 1876. She left behind five young children, now all orphans.
Luckily, their Uncle Abraham Emmett Beanland, Bolton's brother, who had shared all Army experiences since they enlisted was at hand and shouldered the heavy responsibility of bringing up his three nephews and two nieces.

Gibraltar
13th July 1877

My Brothers and Sisters,

It is so long since I heard from you that I scarcely remember the date of your last letter. I think I wrote you about 4 months ago, but got no answer to my letter. Did you receive one from me?

How are you all getting on?

I am happy to say that all the children and myself are doing very well. I wrote a letter to my sister Margaret, about three months ago, in answer to one I got from them. Please inquire if they got it, as it may have gone astray.

There is a friend of mine going from here to Accrington, so I am taking the opportunity of sending you a fine present. I am sending a broach made from the Rock of Gibraltar to each of my sisters, also a little broach for one of your girls each, and a set of Moorish shirt studs for my brothers, and I am shipping, by the next mail, some cases of grapes to London to a **Mr. Saword, poor Bolton's wife's brother**.

After he receives them, he will forward a case by rail addressed to you. About 28lbs, so you can divide them amongst all the families, and please let me know how you like them.

Tell my little nephew that I have not forgotten about the letter he wrote to me from Blackpool. I should have answered then, only I had too much trouble on my hands. At the time, with poor Emma being sick and having the shop to look after as well.

How is my niece, Mary Jane? I suppose she is quite a young woman now. Of course, she is the only one I can recollect as a baby.

I am sending a small present to Susanna Johnson. Let me know how John Johnson is getting on, and all my sister Ann's children.

How is trade in Lancashire? I suppose it is like everywhere else. Very dull at present on account of the state of affairs in the East of Europe. I see by the papers that the Turks are getting a little the best of it at present.

Business with me is middling at present, but not so good as in the winter time.

You don't happen to have a photograph of yourselves and the children taken together? I should much like to see them all.

Give my love to all your children. Also, to my brothers and sisters and their children, and tell them **not to forget that they have an Uncle and three little cousins and two nieces, living on the famous Rock of Gibraltar**. I expect some of us will be coming to England in two or three years' time.

Trusting you are all quite well.
I remain yours truly, A Beanland

I can't describe them all to you if I was to try. I should like to see some of you come out to Gibraltar and see this famous old Rock. I could show you some nice sights, when you are grown up a man and business should send you abroad. Don't forget to call and see one of the finest sights in the world.

When you answer this please give me all the particulars, and the best news you can.

Give my love to Father and Mother, also to all your sisters and brothers. Also, to yourself and I hope you are the makings of a good young man.

With kind love to all,
I am your dear Uncle,
A Beanland

Gibraltar
14th November 1878

My Dear Nephew,

I have your kind letter of the 9th October to hand and was very glad to hear from you. I should have written before, only I have had a little trouble about a letter of mine going astray with money in it.

I am glad to hear of your trip to London and Woolwich, and hope you enjoyed it much.

I know the young man Tom English very well. He was in my Battery all the time he was in Gibraltar, and he was a very nice and steady young man.
How would you like the idea of following the life of a soldier? You will see they have to rough it a little sometimes, and what you saw is nothing compared to being on a foreign station, such as the East or West Indies or even in Gibraltar – and this is considered a good station.

I wish I had known you were going to visit London as I have some friends there that would have been glad to see any of my friends or relations. **All of your Aunt Emma's relations live there. One of her brothers, a Mr. Saword, does all my business for me there. I have never seen him myself, but I hear from him every week.** So, the next time you are thinking of going let me know and I will send you his address.

I am sorry to hear that trade has been so bad in Lancashire, but trust it will mend as the times get more settled.

Please tell your mother that I have given up soldiering since I purchased my discharge in 1874, and there is no reserve here. I think I served my Queen and Country long enough (14 years) and then had to pay 10 pounds for my discharge afterwards.

The children are quite well and are getting on at school.

I have sent one of them to a school in England, about two months ago. Little Emily, she is the youngest girl, six years old. The school is so close to London, in **a place called Hampstead**, so she is quite close to her uncle and aunt Saword. She will get three weeks holiday at midsummer, and will spend them with her uncle in London. But, the next time she gets one, that will be the summer of 1880, I shall be glad if you would take her for a few weeks to your home, as she is rather too young to travel by rail yet. But, the next holiday, if God spares us so long, we will arrange to send her down to you.

I am doing very well with the shop and considering last summer was such a bad one I cannot complain at all. The next time you write, give me all the particulars about your uncles and aunts, and what they are doing.

With kind love to all.
I remain yours truly,
A Beanland

Emily Beanland

Gibraltar
10th February 1879

My Dear Brother and Sister,

I have your kind letter of the 27th to hand and was very glad to hear from you, since it is so long since I have heard from you. I am very sorry to hear of your sad loss. Your dear little boy, Abraham. It must have been very sudden – only 24 hours sickness. I hope you both will be consoled with the other dear little ones you have left.

All my children are well, thank God.

I suppose E. Riley told you about my sending dear little Emily to a school in England. The school is in Hampstead, near London. She was doing very well the last time I heard from there, about a week ago.

**Sailors' Orphan Girls' School & Home –
Hampstead: Rosslyn Hill**

I am sorry to hear that trade is so bad in Lancashire. I think it has been bad all over the world really. What are you doing now? Would you kindly tell me, in your next, the amount of wages a man like you can make in a week in Lancashire?

How would you like to come to Gibraltar if you thought you could materially better yourself? For myself, I am doing a very good business and I know that I could do better if I had someone that I could trust and help me a little. I don't mean to say that this business would keep two families, but I can see a way of starting something else besides the stationery line that would pay just as well.

All the children send their kind love to their Uncle and Aunt and to all their little cousins. Please accept the same from me.

With kind love to all, I remain your dear brother,
A. Beanland
34 Church Street

Gibraltar

22nd August 1882

My Dear Brother and Sister,

Just a line to let you know that I am sending you a few lbs of the best grapes by a friend of mine. Captain of the s-ship "General Elliott". He is going to Liverpool, so he will send them on by rail to you. I am sending 20 lbs, so please give Brother Joseph and John a few lbs each.

I shall write them today or tomorrow acquainting them of it. I suppose you got my last letter a week or two ago. Have you shifted your house, as I note it is not the same address as usual?

Please let me know if the grapes arrive in good condition? If they do, I may be able to send you some more some future time.

I remain,
Yours Truly,
A Beanland

Please excuse the short letter as I have no time to write a longer one. You may expect the box about 5 days after this.

Gibraltar
12th September 1883

Dear Father and Mother,

It is now some time since I dropped you a line, to let you know how we are getting on. Well, considering all things, we are getting on well. With regard to myself, I have plenty of work to do and, thank God, good health and strength to do it with.

The children, I am happy to say, are all doing well at school. Harriett is a pupil teacher, and John and Arthur have already passed the 7th Standard – the highest they can get! The school holidays are on just now, so I have sent them all into the country for a month.

I have now fully made up my mind to come to England and see you and the old place once more. I shall start about the 10th or 12th of next month (August) and will be in Liverpool about the 20 or 22, is all is well.

I think the best plan will be to call at **Burnley** first, as that is the nearest, stop a few days there, and then call on brother, John, in Burnley Lane, and stop a time there, and then come on to **Nelson** and stop the remainder of the time with you and brother Joseph.

With kind love to all.
I am your truly, A. Beanland

ABRAHAM BEANLAND

Letter of intent

No. 103, Church Street,
Gibraltar

I herewith take this opportunity of informing you that I am carrying on business in the above-mentioned premises as Stationer, Bookseller and News-agent, and have always on hand, at moderate fixed prices, a large and varied assortment of goods connected with the Stationery trade. All daily and weekly papers as well as monthly periodicals, I supply directly to Reading Rooms, Officers' & Sergeant Messes, jc, and private persons. I also have always in stock all kinds of Army forms.

My long-established name, and the high reputation which my house has enjoyed for upwards of twelve years, will, I trust, be accepted as a sufficient guarantee of the quality of the goods that I supply, therefore, respectfully soliciting the favour of your patronage,

I remain, Sir,
Yours obediently,
A. Beanland.

Publisher note:
In 1883, Emmett formed a partnership with William Malin and added a printing business to the stationers established by Bolton, Emma and Charles Saword.

Emmett married Jinny (surname unknown), as mentioned in Charles diary of 1895-96 (p.210&215). She bore him two sons. Sadly, his second son, George Bolton, died in 1918, close to the end of WW1.

Emmett's widow moved to England, but not much is known of where she went. She sold her share of the business to William Malin, after inheriting it from Emmett, as degreed by his will. Unfortunately, Emmett did not leave any of the business to the children of Bolton & Emma.

Charles arranged to buy this share back from Malin and they developed a successful partnership over the years. At the start of WW2, both Charles and William Malin were evacuated from the Rock. Charles son's, Albert, John and William, stepped up with the help of friends to save the family firm.

Unfortunately, Beanland Malin & Co. closed its doors for business in 1978, after the crushing effect of Spain's decision to shut the frontier. The frontier reopened in 1985, when I was only nine years old. It was a scary prospect to leave the Rock and enter Spain for the first time.

CHARLES BOLTON

BEANLAND

Very Strictly Private

*"Let he or she that cometh across this book
not look therein as it is private."*

C. B. Beanland

1888
Lett's Rough Diary No. 31
Published for Lett's Diaries Company, Limited, by Cassell & Company,
Limited, London, Paris, New York, and Melbourne.
Price 1s. 6d., or with Blotting, 2s. 6d

***

Publisher note:
This diary was found by Peter Beanland, at 74 Main Street, Gibraltar, when they were clearing up the apartment in 1997. There are many sketches within, as well as his notes for learning short-hand writing.

1888

Aug 2 (Friday)

Rose at 6.15 & went for "arrival" after which bathed with G. Hall (water fine, middling high) had breakfast at 8.0 went to work, and this afternoon went round with bills, which I finished today (pretty glad) feel it very hot. Went to shop at 7.0 & saw Fred Moore who says Mrs. McKendry was getting on all right at Dr Charlesworths.

Had very serious thoughts all day (indeed have had for some time past, and determined to turn over a new leaf. Commenced by (draws a doodle). Hope it will keep? I think of learning short hand commencing on 3rd Aug. Harriett says she will too. Hope this will keep too? Commenced this diary, hope this will keep too? Went to bed at 10.15.

Aug 3rd (Saturday)

Rose at 6.15 & went for arrivals, unusual quantity which kept me till 7.30, when I went to printing office & helped to distribute. At 8.0 went to breakfast (I did not bathe this morning intending to this afternoon. At 9.0 went to printing office & at 9.30 went & at 10.30 finished arrivals, at 11.0 went collecting for Uncle but only got 2/6, at 1.0 had a snack, & at 2.30 (having finished collecting) went up in bus (charged 2d) to Frankie's with whom I went to bathe at Camp Bay, after bathing we went to a cave in side of precipice which took us 2 hrs to explore, we went to extreme end and took a string which we went paying out to find our way back, we put our names C Beanland, F. Roderio & G. Lopez on a stone blackened with candles - soon, after exploring cave went and bathed after which came home at 7.0 (as I was late I had to get my tea in 10 minutes & go to shop). Wrote original of letter which I am going to send to Arthur on Monday, saw F. Moore & also Mrs. McKendry who says she gets 8$ a month & is very satisfied. At 9.30 locked up and came home, washed all over & wrote in diary & at 11.30 went to bed.

August 4th (Sunday)

Rose at 7.30 & went with John to bathe at Devils Tongue (high water), we swam as far as the end of the mole head, came back and had breakfast after which went to church at Soldiers Institute at 11.0 came back at 12.15 & read until dinner. Went to Frankie's and after to Camp Bay and went as far as the quarry after which we and forming "fleet" (F. And young Moore were with us) and went about; examined a cave which we mean to explore soon. It is underneath the sentry walking place near the "landing Place". Walked pretty fast home just in time for church (very good sermon this evening) after church went to Frankie's and went with him walking as far as Europa Pass, came back at 9.20 & had supper after which read Boys

Own Paper and went to sleep at 10.30.

Aug 5th (Monday)

Rose at 6.15 and went to printing office after which I went for arrivals (usual Monday quantity after taking a few and bringing them up. I went & bathed with G Hall after which I finished the "arrivals", had breakfast at 8.0, after when wrote Sunday's Diary, and went to printing office at 9.0 finished clearance & shipping gazette by 11.30 when I went in a "shore" boat on board of H.M.S. Colossus with some proofs of some theatricals, stayed on board as I had to wait for a marine until 1.0 when I and the marine came on shore (altogether charged 2f for boat) and went to printing office at 1.30. Went to dinner after which went to printing office to read proofs. At 4.0 went to Police Office to hear the particulars of a drowning case which took place on Sunday last in which two boys were drowned at 5.30. Took "guardians" to the shop and went to tea. Intended writing to Arthur tonight but when I went down Uncle gave me two letters to write. One to Uncle Charles and the other to Cowie & Co. Rather disappointed but as I couldn't help it tackled them didn't finish them until nine as I had to get up every minute to attend to sailors. At nine Uncle came down and I left leaving Uncle to shut up. I went home and then to Frankie's with Virgil's Anead and a Latin Dictionary that I had promised to lend Frankie. I also took last week's Boys Own Paper to lend him. I stayed chatting until 9.45 when I walked slowly down stopping a bit on the Saluting Battery. I stopped at the Rec Room for 1/2 an hour and then went home, had supper and went to bed.

Aug 6th (Tuesday)

Rose at 6.0 and went (as usual) for arrivals, had bathe and came home and had breakfast at 8.0. After breakfast worked at different things until 1.0 when had dinner. After dinner read proofs, etc, went to tea at 5.45 & saw Mrs. McKendry's place also went upstairs and examined the surgeon's rooms which are very nicely laid out with Moorish curios, had tea & went to shop where I did several things and commenced my letter to Arthur. Intend finishing it tomorrow night at 9.0. Closed up and went to Frankie's. We both went out for a walk and stayed on the Saluting Battery until 10.30 when I left him and went home to bed as I was very tired.

Aug 7th (Wednesday)

Rose at 6.0 and went to work and bathe as usual. At 8.0 went to breakfast after which wrote in diary. Returned to work until 1.0 had dinner and went to work, at 4.10 went to P&O Office to collect a package belonging to Uncle from Cowie & Co. At 5.30 went to tea as I had to collect the bill of the A.D.C. of H.M.S. Colossus at the Assembly Rooms. I went down to the shop at 6.30 and read part of "Alain Quartermain" in Longman's Mag (these are the missing ones that I had not read but came in the parcel today). I forgot to mention that in the morning I bought a cap (naval one) at the Jews market which cost me 1/6. At 7.30 I went to collect the bill at the Assembly Rooms but as the chap said he would send the money down tomorrow I went up the South and passed a very enjoyable evening with Frankie walking as far as Rosia & then down to the Saluting Battery where we sat down for half an hour. At 9.30 we separated and I went to the Rec Room to read the Graphic & Illustrated until 10.0 when I went home, had supper, washed my eyes, and went to bed at 10.30.

Aug 8th (Thursday)

Rose at 6.15 and went as usual for arrivals. Missed G. Hall today as I was late & did not go to bathe until 7.0 so had to bathe alone (water middling high) at 8.0 came to breakfast and wrote in diary after which I went to finishing office. At 1.0 came home and had dinner. The goods from Uncle Charles arrived today but no Indian Clubs from Arthur. At 5.45 Uncle came down to printing office & I had to go on board the Temeraire (alongside the New Mole) with a parcel at 7.15. Came back and wrote a bit of Arthur's letter. Down the shop at 8.45. Uncle came down and I had to go and collect the account of H.M.S. Colossus at the Assembly Room & they paid £2.18.0 (if discount) after collecting it. I went on the Saluting Battery and sat down on a seat. During the time the band was playing, I saw Vision walking up & down along with the boy Sords (I think). At 10.45 I came home, had supper, and finished Arthur's letter (thank goodness!!) after which (at 11.30) I went to bed.

Aug 9th (Friday)

Rose at 6.15 and went for arrivals, bathed, and came home to breakfast, wrote in diary and went back to printing office. At 1.0 went to dinner and at 2.0 went back to printing office. Nothing for me today from post. At 5.0 went home & had tea & went down to shop at 7.0. Saw G. Hall and chatted a while with him and at 8.0 commenced original letter to Alf. Scully. By 9.0 when I shut up had written 8 pages. At 9.0 I closed up & went up South, saw Frankie who accompanied me down to the Saluting Battery where we stayed chatting, and planning a submarine dress. At 10.30 we parted and I went home, and supper, washed my eyes, and went to bed at 11.0.

Aug 10th Saturday

Rose at 6.30 and went for arrivals (did not bathe this morning). At 8.0 had breakfast and at 9.0 did some messages for Uncle. At 9.30 this morning had a very curious experience. I was passing the Roman Catholic Church in Church St. when I saw a tall, very dark, being almost for more a mulatto, passing me. He had a short, scrubby beard and was dressed very well. He was going along very fast and as I passed him I thought I recognised his face, and then it struck me that he was that half African half European chap mentioned in that story of the mysterious desertion of the ship "Maria Celeste". He was very like in the face to that man Septimiou Goring in Cornhill magazine pictures. Indeed it so much struck me as being so that I went behind him to see if he had any fingers on his right hand. He had both the hands clenched but I could see that his little finger had been cut off. This so flabbergasted one that I didn't think of following him to see if he had any fingers whole besides but stayed staring after him like a fool.

I told John and Harriett & Emily but they (except John) don't seem to think much of it. At 11.0 went collecting for Uncle and at 1.0 had my usual snack and went up South at 3.0. I should have mentioned that I and Harriett both received short letters from Arthur. He says he has bought the clubs and I suppose will bring them out with him.

I and Frankie saw a bottle floating in the water when we went down Camp Bay. We undressed quickly and got it. It took us a good swim to pick it up as there was a good deal of current. We got it emptied of a knodicum of wine that was in it and after dressing put a paper in it stating when and where it had been thrown in and whoever found it to return it to F. Rodriguez, after this we bathed again and went home and had tea and went to shop. Had to write letter to Uncle Charles tonight so could not do much to Alfie's letter. I finished the original however came home had a wash all over had supper, washed my eyes and went to bed at 11.15.

Aug 11th (Sunday)

Rose at 7.30 and went to bathe with John (low water). Had breakfast and went to post with a letter for Uncle Charles came back and brought 1lb ice for dinner's water. Dressed and went to church (saw vision) and came home had dinner (chicken) at 1.30 and after dinner went up South with F. Moore whom I met on the way. Went down to Camp Bay. The wake was beautiful to look at as it was rather rough with a South Wind. We then went along and climbed to the cave but did not go in. After this we came back and again we have a very long "natta" and got rather exhausted by the time we got back. The diving board has got loose and was in the water, but we pulled it out onto the shore.

At 6.30 we walked home and after resting a bit we had tea and after that washed down and stayed a good bit on the Saluting Battery. Frankie then came with me home and I lent him "**Ivanhoe**" and accompanied him as far as the Saluting Battery, when I came home it was 10.30 and all but Harriett had gone to bed. I got to bed as quick as I could neither reading the Boys Own Paper nor washing my eyes.

Aug 12th (Monday)

Rose at 6.0 and went for arrivals and bathe. Had breakfast and went back to work. At 1.0 came and had dinner and went to work again. At 6.0 came home, had tea & went to shop. Wrote most of Alf Scully's letter. Uncle came down at 8.45 and I went to Rec. Rooms until 9.15 when I went home, had supper, and washed my eyes going to bed at 9.45, as I was rather tired.

Aug 13th (Tuesday)

Rose at 6.0 and went to bathe and took arrivals. At 8.0 came back had breakfast. After this I went up South to see the Black Watch come ashore. At 10.0 I went back to work. At 1.0 had dinner after which I went to work, read proofs, and came back and had tea at 6.0. Went down to shop and finished Alf's letter. After which at 9.0 closed up and went to see Frankie, stayed chatting and came down at 10.0 had supper, washed my eyes, and went to bed (very tired).

Aug 14th (Wednesday)

Rose at 6.20 and went for arrivals, as it was a bad levanty morning. I did not bathe. At 8.0 had breakfast, wrote in diary, washed my eyes and read a bit of "**Little Women**", at 9.0 went to work, I wrote 6 postcards to Messers Winch, Hope, Peckilt, McAuslan, Alvarez, and Lincoln, also one to Frankie asking him for Alfie's address.

At 11.0 I had to go to the Post Office to report a robbery in the Bay, and at 1.0 had dinner, read a bit, and went to work until 6.0. Had tea and went to the shop, I commenced counting the Gib stamps but could not do anything to them as Mr. Everard came in and stayed chatting a bit until 8.0 when Uncle came down!! I went at 8.0 to the Rec. Rooms and stopped there until 8.40 when I went home and read "**Little Women**" until 9.45 when I washed my eyes and went to bed at 10.15.

Aug 15th (Thursday)

Rose at 6.15 and went to work and bathe, at 8.0 had breakfast wrote in diary, washed my eyes, read a bit & went to work at 9.0, at 1.0 had dinner and went to work. Came home to tea at 6.0 had tea and went to shop, at shop I had to make AB a list of books wanted from G. Routledge (I had intended counting out my Gib stamps but could not) saw Mrs. McKendry who told me to go to her place and try on the trousers she is making. F.

Moore came in too and gave me some foreign stamps, he promised to get me some white duck trousers also.

At 9.0 I shut up and went to Mrs. McKendry's where I tried on the trousers, had a bit of supper (1st since about 4 years ago) and after that went home, had supper, read a bit, washed my eyes, and went bed at 10.30.

Aug 16th (Friday)

Rose at 6.30 and went to work, had breakfast and went to work had dinner and went to work had tea and went to shop, didn't do anything important, saw F. Moore, closed up at 9.0 and accompanied F. Moore as far as Southport. Came back, had supper, washed eyes, etc and went to bed at 10.30.

Aug 17th (Saturday)

Rose and went to work at 6.30, didn't bathe today had breakfast and went to work, collected some money for Uncle, went to 21 Bomb House Lane and got the Sunday trousers from Mrs. McKendry, I took them to printings office and pressed them a bit. At 2.40 went home, gave Emily a letter which came by post, packed up my "caving" suit and went up South. Went down Camp Bay and bathed, did not much like to do it but swam out with Frankie as far as to see New Mole, dressed and explored the old cave, found the piece of string, went to end of cave and unloved the string. I had a lantern with me and coming back got separated from the others and my lantern nearly went out, but managed to get back and join the others all right. After coming out of cave bathed again and found the water was not very salted and did not support one as well as usual.

At 6.30 went home, had tea and went down shop at 7.30. I took my Sunday tie with me, but after a lot of changing left it as it was, stayed down shop until 9.30, closed up and went home. Settled my Sunday things, washed all over, washed my eyes and went to bed at 11.0.

Aug 18th (Sunday)

Rose and went to bathe with John at 7.30 (swam pretty far out, high water) came back had breakfast and went to church at 11.0 saw Vision and came back at 12.10.

Read until dinner time, after dinner went up South (2.30) and went with Frankie to Camp Bay, and rubbed ourselves all over with sand (this makes the skin beautifully soft and fresh) after this went to quarry and stayed about a bit until 5.30 when we came home. Had tea and went to church after which came home had supper and made myself comfortable with the Boy's Own Paper until 9.0 when I went to Mrs. McKendry's for my trousers, stayed there until 9.30 when I came home had supper, washed my eyes, and went to bed at 10.00.

Aug 19th (Monday)

Rose at 6.30 and went to work. Did not bathe today. Went to breakfast at 8.0 and after breakfast washed my eyes, went back to work at 9.0 and at 1.0 came home had dinner read a bit and went to work at 2.0.

At 6.0 came home and had tea after which tidied myself up a bit and went to the shop at 7.0. At 8.0 Uncle came down and I had to write a letter to Messrs. Gale & Polden. Mr. Everard came down and stayed chatting a bit. I also gave him a few stamps.

After 8.40 Uncle let me leave the shop and after coming home with a book I went to the band. I stayed there until 10.0 and saw both Bill Edwards & vision. There came home, had supper, read a bit, washed my eyes, and went to bed at 10.45.

Aug 20th (Tuesday)

Rose and went to work and bathe (with G. Hall) at 8.0. Had breakfast and washed my eyes and wrote in diary. Went to work at 9.0 and got some postal orders for Uncle. At 1.0 had dinner (I forgot to mention yesterday that I received a pile of ... etc through the post from England, suspect it is from that young chap I saw about 8 months ago).

"Después de comer E. me tempto, pero yo no caye (Ella fuíso de sentar se en mí, pero yo no le deje)". [Translation: *After food, E tempted me, but I did not fall for it. She went to sit on me, but I did not let her*]

After dinner I went to Mrs. McKendry's with the trousers and saw Dr. O. Keefe who examined my eyes and told me to wash them in hot water and also to boil two heads of poppies in a pint of water and boil it down to half pint and anoint them with the solution.

After this went to printing office and at 6.0 came home & had tea, after which read a bit and went to shop. At shop finished Scully's letter altogether and counted out 300 Gibs.

At 8.20 Uncle came down and I went home (I would have gone up South but I had a pain in one foot. Read "Little Women" until 9.40 when after having supper I washed my eyes & feet in hot water without lead in it) and went to bed at 10.15.

Aug 21st (Wednesday)

Rose at 6.0 and went to work and bathe, had breakfast at 8.0 and washed my eyes, and wrote part of Tuesday's diary. At 9.0 went to work. At 1.0 had dinner and went to work. Executed several messages for Uncle, also, called at P & O Office for a parcel from Cowie.

At 6.0 had tea and went down to the shop. I intended counting out a lot of Gib stamps but just as I was about to begin, Mr. Everard called in and I stayed chatting with him until 8.0 when Bill Edwards called in and we had a lively discussion about theology and religions, Bill for Atheism and Everard & I for the Bible. I am glad to say that by 8.45 Everard had completely beaten Bill & made him retreat.

At 9.45 Mr. Everard went to the recital, as also, did Uncle & Mr. Pearce who came down about 8.40. When they had all left Fred Moore called in and stopping until I shut up shop, came with me for a walk, we went up to Frankie's and went with him as far as the New Mole. Frankie returned with me as far as home, and returning Ivanhoe I leant him '**300 years hence**' and the '**Wandering Jews**'. At 10.15 having had supper I went to bed after washing my eyes - time 10.30.

Aug 22nd (Thursday)

Rose at 6.15 and went to work and bathe, also had breakfast, washed my eyes and wrote in diary (I always write my diary of a morning).

At 9.0 went back to work. At 1.0 had dinner and went to work, coming home to tea at 6.0 made myself a bit tidy and went to shop at 7.0. Counted out 500 stamps and saw Mr. Everard.

At 8.15 Uncle came down and let me go (but with no good grace) and I went to the Rec Rooms until 9.0 when I went to the band (the Black Watch were playing) saw vision, and knocked about, going up twice to look at the pipers who marched up & down the parade. During the interval saw Bill Edwards at 10.15 and stayed with him chatting (no spiritualism allowed) until the band finished at 11.10.

I then came home and found that all but Uncle had gone to bed. There was no supper and Uncle seemed rather mad, telling me that if I could not come home earlier, I should not be able to go to the band at all!! (humph!)

He then poured out my water into a jug which, after I had washed my eyes, found out had contained some lemonade which had not been washed out (bravo tío) I went to bed at 11.30 feeling that the day had commenced well but ended badly.

Aug 23rd (Friday)

Rose at 6.30 and went to work. Met Uncle at the printing office who seemed in a tantrum (he met me again when I was bathing and indeed **regular "harassed" me all the morning**).

At 8.0 had breakfast wrote in diary and washed my eyes, and went to work at 9.0. At 10.0 had dinner and read a bit of the 1st volume B.O.P. At 2.0 went back to work and set 2 types of sticks of type/ first good quality for a long time.

At 6.0 came home to tea, and went down to the shop at 7.0. I thought I

154

should have to write a letter to Cowie, but Uncle said I should perhaps do it tomorrow. I therefore counted out 600 Gib stamps and shut up at 9.0. I had to barricade the shop again tonight as Uncle had taken the key away again. I met Fred Moore and went with him to Frankie's. We stayed on the seat at Armstrong's Building until 9.45 and noticed a great conflagration in the grass near Algeciras. We walked slowly down and at the Saluting Battery Frankie went home and Fred & I walked back.

I had supper, washed my eyes, and went to bed at 10.30 (there rose a great East wind at 10.0)

Aug 24th (Saturday) – Emily's Birthday, but no mention of it?

Rose and worked as usual, all the morning, also collected a bit for Uncle at 1.0. Rec. 1 postcard from Hope and a not from Peckitt, also as I had to take a good lot of bills up South (for Burnes) and had to take a lot of books for Mr. Smith (Scud Hill). I went up by the 1.30 bus. I finished everything by 2.45, when I went with Frankie to bathe. After bathing we went and examined several new streaming near the old cave and Frankie also dug away a lot of earth revealing to sight another cave that we intend exploring. After this we (I don't remember if we bathed again or not as I am writing this Sunday night (25th)).

After that I came home by 6.20 and having had tea I went down shop. When I got there, Uncle sent me to Balestinos for some paper and after that asked me to go with it (to Off. Mess. R. H.). When went to get my cap he asked me when was he going to have his tea. I then told him "when I get back." He then said, "you can take it tomorrow morning by 7.0 and give it to the Black Watch Cap down there."

After this I set to and counted out some Gib Stamps. At 9.05 Fred Moore came down and promised to take the parcel up for me as he was going that way. I was very glad at this you (dear diary) may be sure.

At 9.30 I closed up, went home, washed all over, had supper, washed my eyes, and went to bed at 11.30.

Aug 26th (Sunday)

Rose at 8.0 and did not go to bathe but went to market for the beef and posted the Guardians to Arthur.

At 9.0 had breakfast, after which dressed and went to church. At 11.0 came back and changed my shirt.

At 2.30 met Fred Moore and went with him up South to Frankie's. We then went to Camp Bay, and swimming after which we walked as far as the quarry, coming back we swam again and went up at sunset (6.30). I then went to Frank's and had tea with him, after this we walked down as far as the Alameda and sat on one of the benches in the promenade (coming along the Saluting Battery saw "Vision" with Sords).

We stayed chatting until 9.0 when I went home, had supper, washed my eyes and feet (for my cold) and getting in bed, piled clothes on top and perspired a lot. (I am not very satisfied at **Fred Moore's** language as it is a comic kind of swearing, (he doesn't mean harm, but I shan't have it).)

Received postcard from McAuslan.

Aug 27th (Monday)

Rose at 6.30 and went for arrivals, did not bathe this morning as my cold was very bad.

At 8.0 came home, had breakfast, and went back to work as usual. This morning while in the office I was told that I should have to go every morning to the Police Office to get the reports of prisoners. This I was very sorry to hear as it will curtail my time much further, indeed I determined to speak to Uncle as **it is not nice that I a mere boy should be made to go every morning and hear details of crimes that are not fit for anyone to hear**.

At 1.0 had dinner and went to work (nothing from post today for me).

At 6.0 I came home to tea and finishing by 6.30 I went down to the shop and spoke to Uncle about my work, he agreed to see about it but did not give me much hope by manner, as he did not even hear me out. I had to write a letter to Cowie which I finished by 9.0 when Uncle having come down, I left. I tried to see Fred Moore about the breaks, but when I went to 21 Bomb House Lane, he was away. Therefore, went home and read a bit of "**From Log Cabin to White House**".

At 9.45 I washed my eyes in the poppy water (I bought the poppies this evening) and went to bed at 10.15.

Aug 28th (Tuesday)

Rose at 6.30 feeling very unwell and out of sorts, went to printing office and did Shipping Gazette.

At 8.0 came to breakfast. During breakfast Uncle spoke up and said he didn't want me to do nothing but go about the streets, and therefore to send someone else for the Police Office (I cannot write this quite perfectly as it is written on Thursday and I have not got over my illness). There was a bit of a row, John telling me that if I worked harder I could manage a lot more (which isn't true).

After this upon going down to the shop Uncle told me to make up my mind upon what I should be.

At 10.0 I and Briton went down to the Port Office, to show him how to do the clearances. After this on going back, I worked all day distributing, etc (not going however to Police Court). At 6.0 I had tea and went down

156

to the shop. I went home with Fred. I leant him some **Boys Own Papers**, and stayed chatting with him (waiting until Emily & Harriett should come home) until 10.15when Harriett & Emily having come home.

I washed my feet and eyes and went to bed.

Aug 29th (Thursday)

Rose at 6.30 feeling a good bit better, went to work, at 8.0. Came home, had breakfast, and when I went down to the shop. Uncle told me to come there at about 10.0 as he had to go as a juryman to the Court House.

At 10.15 I went to shop and stayed there while Uncle went away. About half an hour afterwards, the cricketing goods (that we were expecting for some time). This I opened & put in their places. At 12.0 Uncle came & let me get back to the printing office.

At 1.0 I came to dinner but Uncle didn't appear, and at 1.45 the two youngsters of Mr. Hundery brought the key of the shop, saying that Uncle wanted me to go down there. I went down the shop, and stayed all the afternoon, reading a bit of some "**English Illustrated Magazine**" that were there to be bound.

At 3.0 I was very surprised by the postman bringing a registered letter in, upon opening which I found was from Buffer Bros. and contained £1.16.0 in postal orders. He said that through illness he had not answered before, and said he'd give 2/6 for old issue and 2f for present issue of Gib stamp.

Right up to 6.0 relock did not know what to do, having a dreadful "ennie" but at 6.0 Briton came with the guardian and I sent him for a bottle of cider, also asking him when he went to Digby's with the Guardian to tell Harriett to send down something to eat. At 7.0 Harriett brought me down a bottle of ginger beer and some bread & cake, after demolishing this I commenced the other letter to Arthur which I had not completed when Fred Moore came in, I left off then as Uncle came in at 8.30 saying he had been to Mr. Hundery's wedding!! (Mr. Hundery, boarding officer, is a widower)

I put away Arthur's letter.

At 9.0 we shut up & I went home, had supper, and commenced writing in my diary, but feeling bad again went to bed at 10.0 after washing my eyes. (I forgot to mention that I saw Chacha tonight, who says Dr. Keefe isn't very well).

Aug 30th (Friday) Arthur's Birthday

Rose at 6.15 and felt as bad as I did on Wednesday. At any rate, I went to work, but didn't do much as my head ached so much.

At 8.0 I had breakfast and went to work. At 11.0 I did several messages, but feeling my head ready to split I went home and lay down. I snoozed a bit until 1.0 when I had dinner, after which I kept up application of vinegar on my forehead, and went for a message for Harriett to Hernandez.

After that (4 o'clock) I commenced bringing my diary up to date, which I finished by 5.0, when I had to go again to Hernandez for some baking powder. After getting this, I looked at a few pictures in the Boys Own Paper, and at 6.30 I helped a bit in the kitchen with the tomatoes and eggs.

After this, I went down to the shop, and examined my stamps a bit, after which, at 9.0, shut up and came home. When I got home **Bella & Lucy Hume** had come down and were studying a bit with Harriett & Emily.

They however went home at 9.30 and I got to bed. Uncle told me to take four of Beecham's pills, but first I lost one, and then the others I could not get down as I was taking cold tea. Uncle then tried sending them down with treacle, but that failed, after taking eight spoonful's, so as Uncle gave it up as a bad job. I got a whole bottle of ginger beer and swilled them down with that. After this I bed.

Aug 31st (Saturday)

Rose at 6.0 and as I still felt unwell, got up, but did not go to printing office. At 8.0 had breakfast, after which I pottered about and settled down to clean the book shelves in the parlour.

At 11.0 I heard Uncle outside whistling and he told me to go down the shop as he was waiting for a gentleman. I went down there and after waiting half an hour Uncle came down and I had to go to the printing office with some letters. After that I went home and finished cleaning. After which I lay down until dinner.

After dinner read a bit and at 3.0 dressed up as I had to go with Emily to see the doctor (not for myself). We could not find him so I went home, but had a bit of "the leisure hour", which came today and which I got down the shop. After this I had tea, and went to the terrace for about 20 minutes, after which I went down the shop and let Uncle come up. When I got down Bert Pepper came down (can't say I was very pleased) and stayed chatting a bit until 8.0 when I read a bit of the Chamber Gl. And put any stamps in a bit of order.

At 9.30, I closed up, and came home (I forgot to mention that Chacha called in and said that Dr O'Keefe had given her only 7$ pay, as there was only one to attend to and not two as if Dr Charlesworth were there).

When I came home, I washed all over, washed my eyes and took two more of Beecham's pills, and went to bed at 11.0

September 1st John's 'Coming of Age'

Rose at 7.0 and didn't bathe but wrote a bit in diary, as I had promised to take down John's towel, etc. down to the bathing place for him. I went down at 8.0, (John had gone to Campamento for a walk). John asked me to stay there to mind his watch, etc, so I could not get some "hick" that I had intended giving him (as he walked back with me).

John Beanland

When we came back we had breakfast, after which I was rather busy, as the pills began to work; dressed and went to church at 11.0. Came back and had dinner (Mr. Clahworthy & Mr. Pearce were down to dinner today).

After dinner, I went up to Frankie's (I forgot to mention that after church I went up to Frankie's and borrowed his From Log Cabin to White House, we then went down Camp Bay and waited half an hour for Fred Moore. When he came down he brought Paddy Griffin with him, we all talked and fuimos a Rosia nadando vas otros hincamos en herrar ir después a Camp Bay otra vez.

Publisher note: The spelling is dubious, but translated it means... went to Rosia swimming and then to Camp Bay again.

We then went home it being about 5.15. I managed to catch the 5.30 bus and got down early. I had tea and went to church (Vision did not come). After church, I came home and read Boys Own paper and at 9.0 I went to Rec. Rooms, stayed there half an hour and went to bed at 10.15.

September 2nd (Monday)

Rose at 6.30 and went to work, as I felt a good deal better. At 8.0 had breakfast and wrote in diary. At 9.0 went to work, and did several messages for Uncle. At 1.0 had dinner and went to work. At 6.0 had tea & went down shop, opening of Christmas term University was tonight, but I did nothing but draw up my programme.

At 8.0 Uncle came down and I was going up South to see Frankie, when Uncle said that I had better go home instead & not go out until my cold was better, so I went home, and Harriet out (at the band). I went to bed at 9.30, but was a long time trying to catch a horsefly that was in my room. I didn't manage it, however, but Harriett coming home at 10.0 caught it so

I washed my eyes and went to bed at 10.30.

September 3rd (Tuesday)

Rose at 6.30 and went to work, at 8.0 came home & had breakfast, after which washed my eyes and went to work at 9.0. I posted my letter to Arthur, sending him 2f and asking him to bring out 3 or 4 ties with him, for the money.

At 11.0, I commenced taking out the bills (for town), these I very nearly finished by 1.0 when I had dinner. At 1.50 I went up South & took up the ones for there, these I finished by 3.0, when I went & waited for Frankie. He came soon, and after changing his clothes we went to Camp Bay. The water was very swelly, with a South wind. We swam but did not go so far as to see Rosia. We then dressed and went up at 4.30.

I then returned to town, finished the town accounts, and did several messages, until 5.45, when I went and asked Uncle if he wanted to go to the Circus, (Mr. Malin told me to ask him) and as he said yes, I had to hunt for Charles Malin, as he had the ticket. I also saw Mrs. McKendry, going to Boat House Lane. I also saw the new boy, but did not think much of him as though he is older than Fred Moore he isn't as tall as I am.

I went to tea at 6.0 and after tea tried to find C Malin again but as I couldn't I went to the shop and told Uncle. I learnt how to tie the long tie's tonight after a good lot of practice (I went down to Gamble's and after buying another 6d tie asked him how to tie it, he showed me so that was why I practiced at night).

I also stayed chatting with Chacha, who came in (I didn't study anything tonight, as I had no books yet and was very tired).

At 9.0, I shut up & went home, but finding that they hadn't gone to Bella's tonight, so I brought my diary up-to-date and I went to bed at 10.30.

September 4th (Wednesday)

Rose at 6.30 and went to work. At 8.0 had breakfast and washed my eyes. At 9.0 went to work and at 1.0 had dinner, and went to work. At 6.0 came home and after tea, went down to the shop.

I studied Arithmetic & Geography (of Arith I did practice). I also gave the circus ticket to Uncle who said he might be going.

At 8.45, however, he said I might shut up and go to the circus as he was going to the Organ Recital at the Cathedral.

I therefore went up and got there by 9.15, but found that I had missed 3 parts. I however enjoyed it very much, especially the 4 tame bulls.

At 11.15, it finished and I walked sharply home, and after washing my eyes, got to bed by 11.45.

September 5th (Thursday)

Rose at 6.15 and went to work. At 8.0 came to breakfast and at 9.0 went to work again. At 1.0 had dinner, and found a letter from Routledge in the post. I took it to Uncle and found he enclosed a B/f of the P. & O. co.'s ship Oriental. I went down the P. & O. office and got the case up on a truck (charged for boatage & storage).

At 6.0 had tea (before tea I tidied myself up intending to go to the band tonight as the Black Watch Regiment were playing).

I went down the shop at 7.0 and tidied up the novels, also had the door glassed "Shipshape & Bristol fashion".

Uncle came down at 8.0 and helped me a bit.

At 9.0 I was going to the band, but as there was a bad East wind (levanty) blowing Uncle told me not to go, so I came home and brought my diary up to date and went to bed at 10.15.

September 6th (Friday)

Rose and went to work at 6.0. At 8.0 came to breakfast. I did not do anything particular today, but when I went down to the shop I brimmed the glass case on the counter and looked at a few novels.

At 9.0 I closed up and brought up with one book of Dicken's novels – **N. Nickleby and "The Chimes"**. I went to bed at 9.30 after washing my eyes, etc, and read Nicholas Nickleby until 10.30, when I went to sleep.

September 7th (Saturday)

Rose at 6.0 and had to go to the shop for post. BB note for BM & Co. At 8.0 had breakfast and went to work. I distributed until 11.30 when I went collecting for Uncle. I got a considerable lot. At 1.0 I had a "snack" and after going to the post and doing one thing and another I went to Scholl's to collect his account, but was told to call on Monday.

I went up with the 2.30 bus to the South and saw Frankie, with whom I went to Camp Bay. We bathed and knocked about enjoying ourselves until 4.30 when we bathed again and after that went to the quarry.

At 6.0 we started for home, and went down the shop at 7.0. Down there I read part of "N Nickleby" and examined the novel. At 9.30 I closed up and got home, washed myself (not all over) had supper and went to bed at 11.45.

September 8th (Sunday)

Rose at 7.30 and went to bathe with John (rather low water). At 8.30 had breakfast and dressed for church. At church saw vision and G. Hall. At 12.0 came home and read a bit and after dinner went up South and with Frankie went to Camp Bay. On our way we met **Paddy Griffen** who went with us down Camp Bay. We joined **Fred and Harry Moore** who were down there. We swam and went as far as Rosie, where we saw a sucker caught. Coming back to Camp Bay we saw another sucker, which a man caught with a hook and line. We then went as far as the quarry and coming back at about 6.0 we swam again and went up home (during the time we were at the quarry Fred Moore shouted some more of his mala lengua (translated: *bad tongue, meaning rude language*), which I am sorry to say made us laugh, though we didn't want to.

At 7.0 I had tea at Frankie's and stayed at Armstrong's buildings until 8.30 when we walked slowly down. We met Fred Moore coming down and when I reached home they went up South again and I went home had supper (Mrs. Walker was at home) and read Boys Own Paper in bed going home to sleep at 10.30.

September 9th (Monday)

Rose at 6.30 and went to work. At 8.0 I had breakfast and went to work. At 1.0 came home & had dinner, and after dinner I got hold of a book Emily had borrowed from F. Adamson, and began to read it, when Emily asked me for it. I said she would have plenty of time to read it in the afternoon but she said she wanted it then. So **I got in a bit of temper, and went up on the terrace to calm down** a bit leaving her the book. I could not help feeling a little wild, as it did seem so selfish not letting me have to book for a little while.

At 2.0 I went to work and then at 6.0 came home had tea and went to shop. Down the shop I read a part of "Mr. Barnes of New York", and at 9.0 left Uncle in the shop and went to Rec. rooms, stayed there until 10.0 when I came home & found that Harriett had not put the poppy water on (I was nearly getting up steam for a blowing up to her when I controlled myself, and waited for it, instead. I had been rather thinking how going on I wasn't satisfied so I commenced another "half new leaf" by reading the portion of the bible set apart for everyday in the Schoolboys Christian Union Card.

At 10.30 I washed my eyes and went to bed.

September 10th (Tuesday)

Rose at 6.0 and went to work. At 8.0 had breakfast and went to work. At 1.0 came home and had dinner, and went back to work at 2.0.

At 6.0 came home and had tea after which went down to the shop where I found a registered letter from McAuslan, containing 19/8 for the 500 Gib stamps. I did a good lot of work, etc. At 9.30 I locked up & came home, brought my diary up to yesterday's date and went to bed at 10.30 after reading my "portion" and washing my eyes.

September 11th (Wednesday, Uncle's Birthday) [46th Birthday]

Rose at 6.15 and went to work. At 8.0 came home and had breakfast, after which on going back I wrote a postcard to Schenk of Rotterdam, telling him that I would send him the stamps upon receipt of cash and also that I should require 4/- for them in future. I also wrote to Frankie asking him to ask Fred Moore for the Creek and Boys Own Papers, etc.

At 1.0 had dinner and after dinner went to work, and at 6.0 came home, had tea, and went to shop. At shop, wrote return note to McAuslan, sending him 1000 stamps for £2. I also saw "Chacha", who is looking for a room as they are all leaving Mrs. Baglietto's house.

At 9.0 I came home and after chatting a bit wrote my diary up to date.

September 12th (Thursday)

Rose at 6.30 and went to work, had breakfast at 8.0 and went to work. At 1.0 had dinner and went to work. At 6.0 had tea and went down to shop.

I forgot to mention that I received yesterday the book I ordered called **"1000 ways to earn a living"**, it contains several good openings for me and I mean to study it.

I wrote a letter to Butler Bros. in which I am sending them 1000 Gibraltar obsolete stamps for 10f and also put those catalogues etc into order though I was not able to settle them altogether.

After nine a bit, Uncle being down the shop we closed up and I went home while Uncle went to the Oddfellows Ball.

When at home I had a bit of a chat with Harriett about "1000 ways, etc" and begun to think seriously of a sea boy's life.

At 10.0 I had supper, washed my eyes etc, and went to bed.

September 13th (Friday)

Rose at 6.30 and went to work. At 8.0 had breakfast, etc (I mean to "lump" putting in about meals etc unless something particular happens).

At 6.0 I came home, and after tea went down to shop. I was rather surprised when I went down there at Uncle's telling me that there was a stray cat in the rack for the cricket bats that I was not to chase away (I was surprised as I thought that Uncle would not have harboured an animal like that).

I was occupied until 8.30 with writing a letter to Cowie, after which I settled a little more of the stamps, catalogues, etc shutting up at 9.20 when I came home and brought my diary up to date (while did as Harriett complained a bit of not feeling well).

September 14th (Saturday)

I did nothing particular this morning but as I didn't go collecting I went up South. At 3.0 we went down Camp Bay and bathed twice.

At 6.30 I returned home, had tea & went to shop, where I brought up my books (at last). When I shut up at 9.30 I went home, washed myself all over and went to bed at 11.0.

September 15th (Sunday)

Rose and went to bathe with John. At 8.0, came back and had breakfast. At 9.0 when after breakfasting I went and dressed myself in my best and went to church, saw vision, and G Hall. At 12.0 I collected the offertory and came home, had dinner, and after dinner went up South.

Saw Frankie and swam after which Fred Moore came down, we went to the quarry and watched "Philip and Antonio" fishing after which swam again and came home at 6.0.

I had 2 cups of tea and some cake and went to church (vision did not come).

After church I went home, had tea, and read the weeks Boys Own Paper.

At 9.0 I went to the Rec. Rooms and at 9.45, came home, had supper and went to bed.

September 16th (Monday)

Rose at 6.30 and went to work. At 8.0 came home and had breakfast.

At 9.0 went back to work, helped with the shipping news (setting up) all days. At 6.0 I had breakfast (supper?) and went to the shop. Did a little bit of the stamps and at 9.0 closed up and after coming home for my jacket went to the band (where I saw Bill Edwards but not vision). [I here will say that although I occasionally see & speak to **Bill & Charlie Edwards** we never talk about or even discuss Spiritualism but only ordinary topics]. I stayed at the band until 10.30 when I came home, had supper, washed my eyes, went to bed, and read my "portion" at 11.0.

September 17th (Tuesday)

Rose at 6.15 and went to work. At 8.0, had breakfast and wrote in diary a bit and then went to work. At 1.0 had dinner and went to work.

At 6.0 had tea and went down to shop. It was not a good night being rather levanty. I did nothing much at the shop, but settled my foreign stamps and looked at one or so novels.

At 9.0 I closed up and went up South to see Frankie. I stayed with him chatting until 9.45 (he told me that he had not been able to see F. Moore, hope he turns up). When I came down there was a bit of thunder and lightning so it was not very pleasant when I came down. I had supper, washed my eyes, read my "portion" (when I went to bed, John had already gone) and went to bed at 10.45. I was however rather bothered as they were singing rather noisily down the Oddfellows Hall.

September 18th (Wednesday)

Rose at 6.30 and went to work, came home to breakfast at 8.0, during which Uncle astonished us greatly by saying that Mr. Rothe's little baby had smallpox. I offered up a prayer that if it should be true none of us should catch it.

I went to work at 9.0 and set to thinking about what Uncle had said and found, rather to my surprise, that I was not very frightened at even death, as I am glad to say I felt pardoned of my none to slight sins.

At 1.0 we had dinner, nothing more being heard of the truth of Mr. Rothe's baby's state. I have however, taken several precautions such as washing my mouth after meals and crossing Mr. Rothe's door without breathing.

At 2.0 I went down to the post and had to pay 4/d for a letter for Emily.

At 6.0 I went home, had tea, and at 7.0 went to the shop, studied a bit of "1000 ways" and examined the foreign stamps a bit more.

A woman called in and asked to see the cat we kept and upon hearing her and seeing her the cat ran to her and she got hold of it and said it was hers, but I said that I must have her name before she took it, this she gave me (**Pepa de las Alguhas**) but departed without giving a word of thanks.

Bye and bye Chacha called in stayed some time chatting. I did not tell her anything about Mrs. Rothschild as it would make her anxious.

"Me pregunto que ..." (No idea what this says in Spanish or how to translate it!)

At 9.0 I shut up and came home, brought my diary up to date (from Sunday 15th) and went to bed at 10.30.

September 19th (Thursday)

I did nothing particular today but at 6.0 on coming home to tea I noticed a guard of honour drawn up before the convent. I stayed a bit and found it was for **H.R.H Prince Henry of Prussia, brother of the German Emperor and grandson of Queen Victoria**.

When the carriage drove up I noticed very remarkable thing: - that the Queens colour (Union Jack) was lowered such a lot that about half, or nearly so, or it scraped on the ground (this seems very extraordinary, it reminds one of "the flag that braved a thousand years" it being trailed ignominiously in the dust. I did not catch Prince Henry's face, but could only see his "cocked" hat.

Publisher note:
Looking up Wikipedia, the Prince was on SMS *Irene* at this time. One of the ports must have included Gibraltar:
'Over the winter of 1889–1890, Irene and the II Division of the fleet went into the Mediterranean to escort the Kaiser's yacht, Hohenzollern. Prince Heinrich remained in command of Irene during the cruise. The Kaiser made state visits to Turkey and Italy, and called in ports throughout the region, including Athens and Venice. Irene and the rest of the squadron returned to Germany in April 1890.'

When I got home I titivated myself up, as I was going to hear the band (Black Watch) [I should here mention that it was the guard of honour (?) and band of the Black Watch Regt. that were at the convent].

After tea I went down to the shop but only looked through some of the foreign stamps.

At 8.45 Uncle came down and I had to make out some accounts, so it was ¼ past nine before I put up the shutters, leaving Uncle in charge.

I went to the band & paced up and down on the Saluting Battery, neither seeing Vision or Bill Edwards.

At a little after gunfire however, I found Bill seated on the stone wall opposite the benches on the Saluting Battery, also noticed that Sweetie was next to him although with someone else not him. We after a bit got up and walked up and down when I saw Vision seated also on the stone seat.

After 10.30 I left for home, had supper and was going to bed when hearing a row outside looked out and saw a **Highlander fighting with a Rifleman**. I stayed looking until the piquet came up and the combatants ran away, when I washed my eyes and went to bed. (11.30).

September 20th (Friday)

Nothing happened particular today except that on looking out this morning I found that the wall of the house was stained with blood (probably from that fight last night) [I forgot to mention that yesterday Uncle said that Mr. Rothes child had chicken pox not small pox, needless to say how thankful I was].

This afternoon there was a bit of a row in the printing office as I **having told John about the flag being lowered such a lot at the guard of honour, yesterday evening he made up rather a "strong" local bit about it**, but told one to go to the shop and show it to Uncle.

Upon going there he told us not to put anything about it. When I told John he got in a bit of a huff, and tore up the local and as he wouldn't put anything about Prince Henry in it I was forced to do it myself. Britton also told me that he was leaving tomorrow to work in the Grand Store (wonder if I shall have to do the arrivals)?

I went home had tea and went down shop but did not do anything particular. At 9.0 I closed up and went to the Rec. Room. Looked at the Graphic & Illustrated and at 9.30 went home had supper and went to bed.

September 21st (Saturday)

This Saturday was very like others except that Britton applied for a character (I do not know whether he is coming on Monday or not). I went collecting for Uncle late (1.30) as I was busy all the morning with setting up a poster, which I couldn't leave.

At 1.0 had a snack and went to the post (a letter for Harriett for which I had to pay 5d). After this collected until 2.30 when I went home with the letter for Harriett, and went to Camp Bay, bathed and went to quarry. When we came back we bathed again and I went home (just in time for a comfortable tea before I went down to the shop).

At 7.20 I went down to the shop and counted out some more of my Gibraltar stamps. At 9.30 I closed up when I went home, washed all over, had supper and went to bed, at 11.30 about.

Diary for the Month of September

Through press of work in having got off some more stamps to McAuslan, etc, I have not kept up my diary, for which I am sorry, _ I am now going to record the most striking parts of what has happened, in rather a desultory order, but "lumping" the minute & uninteresting details.

SUMMARY

On Monday 23rd

I resumed my old occupation of taking "arrivals" etc, as though Britton came down late today, afterwards he didn't turn up. On Tuesday or Wednesday (24 or 25) Mr. Everard departed in the Midlothian (a merchant steamer) for Liverpool, paying £3 passage money. I was on the wharf for nearly an hour with him, chatting, he being waiting for his call to arrive. On Friday I dispatched 1,300 stamps to McAuslan for £2. 12. 0 (I must mention that Harriett & Emily helped a good lot with taking off the backs of the stamps. I didn't ask them to help but they offered.

On Saturday (28th) I went up South at 3.0 and we bathed as usual having been thoroughly tired out last night. Determined not to do anything at all just rest; Bert Pepper however came down and I bought some stamps off a few of Bond's approval sheets he brought down. He began again with some "mala lengua" but on delivering a bit of a "sermon" to him he said that he would not refer to anything, and if he did I should give him a whack, I making the same stipulation (I hope this may be productive, some good).

On Sunday morning I went as usual to church, bathing in the morning with John) (water cold). I forgot to mention that I got a bath on Friday morning at about 10.30 paying for it down the market.

Further Summary

I am sorry to say that since writing the above I have not touched my diary since now (12th October) and as it has gone so far I have determined to "lump" all that has passed, and commence writing every night, what has happened during the day. I must not however forget a very important thing that has happened – namely – **Arthur's coming from England** – I shall curtail it as much as possible. Here it is –

Monday October 7th

Last night we received a postcard from Arthur, saying that he expected to sail so soon, that he would reach Gib on Sunday night (6th). We didn't hear of anything though but next morning when I went for the arrivals I saw that the S.S. General Eliott was the first vessel to arrive here this morning.

Upon seeing that I hastened up to the shop & told Uncle, and then went down to complete the arrivals, but during then Mr. Bassadone (one of the clerks at the Post Office) told me he had seen Arthur near the Post Office so I didn't hurry so much, but when I had finished went up to the shop but Uncle told me that he had seen Arthur who had since gone home. I then went home, not so much to see Arthur & seeing how eager I was for E.H & W.R. to come & then wishing they would go back, but when I got there I saw Arthur who seemed much the same & also a pair of Indian Clubs, which I thought very heavy since I have found they weight 2 ¼ lbs each club). I then went and completed arrivals.

2nd Incident

From Monday 30th September we commenced 8 o'clock to 7 working hours (I work from 8 to 6 (to let Uncle have his tea). I have found this better than 6 o'clock since not only does it let one go out a bit of night but I have commenced exercises with the Indian Clubs, which at the old rate of 6 o'clock I couldn't have done.

3rd Incident

Arthur told me that he will not be going to the Presbyterian Church any longer but to the "Established (?)" Church of England.

I am now the only Presbyterian minus Uncle.

Recommencement of the Regular Upkeep

Sunday (Oct 13th)

Rose at 6.30 after having passed a rather uncomfortable night sleep, through the mattress being all in lumps & with a valley in the centre. (I sleep with Arthur in the big bed. John sleeping in the parlour on a bed.) I & John then went to bathe (Arthur didn't care about coming) water very cold – the bathe being in & out again.

For the first time, I jumped off the diving board at low water, not touching – feet first after coming back. I had breakfast and then dressed for church. (Emily is "great" having Arthur to go to King's Chapel – thought I, "quite welcome").

At church saw vision (not been looking too much our way lately). After church I went home and read a bit, also after dinner went up to Frankie's and after that went to Camp Bay swimming and saw Antonio (Frankie's brother in law's brother) fish. At sunset came up, and went to Arm Strong's Building. After going with Frankie a message, had tea, eat a little, crab & shrimps (which I didn't much like).

(I forgot to mention that yesterday Frankie gave me a letter from Alf).

After tea we stayed chatting a bit with Frankie, brother in law's brother Compa, etc. After that practised a bit with a model steam boat (a real thing with boiler, cylinder, etc, not like the wretched things we got from Theobald). It worked admirably and Compa offered me it for 3f. I said I would think it over.

At 9.30 we walked slowly down, and I went home where I found Mrs. Walker (who left in a few minutes), had supper, and John gave me 2 letters, one from McAuslan with £2.50 & the other from Alf (one for Frankie & the other for myself). The curious thing about them are that in both letters (I read that one of Frankie's as we have agreed to read each other's letters & not sand on ceremony).

Alf requests us to write in Spanish sentenced (both different) that are in English.

At 10.30 I read my portion & went to bed.

Monday (Oct 14th)

I really must not write such a lot as I did yesterday, as it takes such a long time to write, so all I shall mention is that I practiced a bit with the club in the morning. In the evening I left Arthur in the shop at 8.10 & went to the Rec. Room until 9.0 when I went up South, going to Frankie's, to see him about the translation of the two sentences Alf sent me. After a bit I agreed to see if Mr. Hare would translate it for me. I left him at 10.0, got home & went to bed.

Tuesday (Oct 15th)

I have nothing particular to mention. I took the letters to Mr. Hare who promised to translate them. I had to go at 3.30 to the shop, as Uncle wanted to see John make some rollers. Down the shop, I tidied up a bit and read a part of "Japhet in search of a father" by Capt. Marryat. At night I stopped down the shop until 9.30, read my & c. When I got home I wrote my diary a bit and went to bed.

Wednesday (Oct 16th)

Going down the Post Office this morning I found out there had been a collision. Also, that the Chimborago the Orient Rine S.S. that is going on a Mediterranean trip. Coming up I left the arrivals and going back I saw a lot of passengers.

I also saw Bill Edwards & we noticed a girl who was dressed in a sailor's dress with a plain skirt and was verily the most beautiful person I ever saw. Also a young man who was about the finest chap I also ever saw.

I was a fool, but I could not help thinking about her (**not love at first sight as that is rather too preposterous, but still plenty of admiration**).

Upon looking afterwards at the list of passengers booked for the trip, I noticed a certain Admiral Gillett and the Misses Gillett of Woolwich, this I believe must be the name, it must be that or Miss Thomasson, as they were the only likely persons mentioned in the list.

I feel great regret that I have not been able to write in my diary before now and though I have plenty of things happening lately, that should have gone down I am forced to "lump" them, feeling however that the most important of them will remain fastened on my memory for a long while.

I therefore commence with "a good wind & flowing sheet with"

Thursday 31st Oct. 1889
"Being the" (Death of "the Gibraltar Guardian")

Rose at 7.0 dressed and washed my eyes had breakfast & went for the arrivals (for the last time!). I brought them up at 10.15 and noticed that the "hands" were very boisterous, it being their last day. I shall be jolly glad to be rid of the disgraceful lot. In the afternoon read proofs with John (as my head ached a bit, having a bad cold, he read & corrected and I listened).

At 4.0 everything was ready so I took the Guardians down to the shop, and delivery of several letters. I went home and then to the Rec. Rooms at 6.20. I went to the shop, found Uncle there, Arthur having gone to his tea, stayed there until Arthur came down, went up then, had mine, stayed reading and at 9.0 went for a pot of treacle, came home & went to bed.

Saturday 2nd Nov 89

Today being still not well stayed in bed until 10.30 then dressed and stayed reading all day.

After tea, Uncle and I had a small chat, he saying that I *"should put my shoulder to the wheel"* and *"study printing"* as it "would be too late to take up anything else"

(I don't think so and I know for sure that it is not for
1. Emigration to South America,
2. Either apprentice, or boy on board,
3. Weaver,
4. Valet,
5. Ship's Steward.
All 5 of these I am open to before Printing).

I however told him that I should set my mind fully this winter to printing, as at present though I did not care for it I should give it a trial – the above was his answer.

I have adopted several resolutions. To master the ins & outs of the 5 above trades, and also **keep up correspondence with John about them all**. Another is that I shall keep a journal not a Diary in future.

Sunday 3rd November 1889 - John's last day at home in Gib

Rose at 8.0, dressed and had breakfast, after which dressed in Sunday clothes and went on terrace intending to read the Bible. When I went up, saw the "Tamar" come in (time about 10.30), Uncle then came up & began to clean up, and as he began to send me downstairs for several things and as I didn't intend going up for that came down & read in the Fam Bible. I also read afterwards the B.O.P.

At about 12.30 John came home and surprised us by saying that the "Tamar" sailed at 4.0 & he would have to be down at the New Mole at 2.15, punctually Arthur asked him if he had seen Mrs. McKendry yet, & he said "no" and as he seemed to think that he would have to go off without seeing her, I determined if I could, that he should.

We were all pretty busy packing up, we finished by 1.0 or so, and I & John had a hurried dinner as I asked him to go & see "Chacha" before he went, and I would show him where to go, after dinner John went to Mr. Grimshaw and I went to wait for him about the Spanish Church.

I waited there for a little while and he came down at 1.30, and I went and told Chacha that John had come to say "Goodbye". She came out and seemed finely composed at first, saying "Goodbye" but just at the door she broke down saying, "Ya no le vere ma!" **[Translation: I will not see him again]** (I hope not chas) and began to cry, so John gave another shake of the hand and departed.

We then went to a cab stand, "Chacha" standing at the door to see the last (??) of John when we got into a cab & drove up to the house, the cabman however making several mistakes in the lanes.

We got home and trundled down John's box, etc. We put them into the cab, and Uncle told me to get in (I would have preferred walking up). I got

to the New Mole and I stopped there waiting until the others came up (Uncle, Harriett, Emily, Arthur) accompanying John. We got the box out & got a young Maltese to take it down. We then followed but stopped at the top of the drawbridge by Mr. Roscoe, who said no one was allowed to accompany people down so we said Goodbye, I getting the last handshake (which wasn't a very strong one).

We waited until John had got out of sight down the steps, then went back, Uncle to Dearce's, I to Frank's, and the others home.

I went to Frank's and chatted a bit, and at 3.25 or thereabouts went to the Circus. I went down the Mole at 3.45 to see if I could see John, meeting on my way Mrs. Walker who had been down town to tell John to get ready as she told him before he was to go on Monday. We went down and I met Uncle but we were not able to see John, not being allowed on board (we would have been had we come down earlier).

I stayed down until the ship sailed (4.5 o'clock). I watched it until it was about 1 ½ miles or so away & then went again to the circus, watching the Tamar on my way.

After a bit we left the circus (I & Frankie) and went through the Alameda Gardens on my way home. I went home, seeing the last of the Tamar at the bottom of the Alameda valley: - line wall → road to town → road to Alameda Road → Road to Suicide Place. The star marking where I believe I was when I saw the Tamar last like this on the water.

I went home and found B.O.P. had not come, had tea (asking the others to come home after tea). After tea read Chambers & B.O.P. (volume).

After that got out my diary & wrote about today's occurrences.

Publisher Note: The above is the last diary entry.

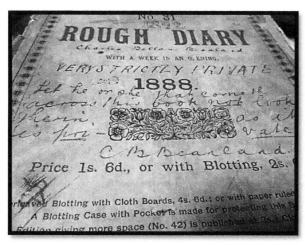

What follows are pages and pages of shorthand notes and a few sketches. One quote of note is:

"I may write to you 'ere long. Use your eyes in the right way. Use your time also in a right way so make it of value to you. Live a life of purity and so die a calm death."

Also, found amongst the notes is a practice letter in Spanish. It leaves me in no doubt that my Great Grandfather was a meticulous and hard-working man.

The last entry, as below, is a shorthand translation.

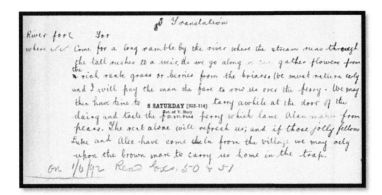

The remainder of the books holds many empty pages, this diary obviously abandoned.

Another interesting aspect of the diary is the number of sketches found throughout the pages. Some are funny, strange, or revealing of the attire of the period.

The last entry dates to 1892. Amazing this diary survived 125 years and has finally been brought back to life by the great granddaughter of Charles Bolton Beanland. Even though an orphan, from the age of two, Charles led a remarkable life and this diary gives an insight into the teenager who eventually became a pillar of the community of Gibraltar.

DIARY

of

CHARLES BOLTON

BEANLAND

(Aged 20-21)

1895

Tuesday 1ˢᵗ January – 6ᵗʰ January 1895

In afternoon being a lovely day and a hard frost, I asked off from work and had a bicycle run to Earby. They were skating on part of Toulridge. Came back when dark at 4.30 and after tea went to theatre to see Ingomas wk – was very good (A Greek play). In evening stayed in and finished bookkeeping. Frost continues.

Stayed working till 9.30. Snowing and Emma went skating at Car stall. Still freezing hard. Library in evening.

Indoors doctoring leg. Harry and the Wormwells and Jamie & Anthony came to tea and passed a pleasant evening. Harr is to stay home again being worse.

Stayed indoors all day feeling bad headache. Harry Watson and Harry (the comical) were in to tea.

Monday 7ᵗʰ – 12ᵗʰ January

Did nothing particular. Emma up at St Johns. Left work 8.30.

Library and home reading. Made up app shed and reading.

Have bad headaches every day. Colder and colder.

Stayed in bed till midday. Snow afoot deep. Afternoon saw doctor. Had a walk up to Walverden to see skaters. After tea library and went with Harry at 9.0 to Sefton street but slow do Jim not being there. In afternoon wrote letters. Evening reading &c. Thaw starting. Bath & fruit to bed.

Monday 14ᵗʰ – 20ᵗʰ January

Evening library post and Gdn Str (Aunt Harr being better) till 10.20. Thaw. Stamp counting rc.

Went with In to theatre to pantomime "Cinderella" very fair scenery rc. Work till 8.45. Leg still obstinate. Bed early.

Evening was out and with Harry all evening besides post & changing library. Stopped at Mes Hill 10.0 came home with Harry and Emma. Harr bitter.

Changed and at 4.30. Alice, Harr and myself went to Burnley Bks and spent a pleasant evening at Bella's some other friends being in. Anthony came out in quite a new light.

Rose 10.30. Feel poorish with my cold. In afternoon went to Gdn Str and to Willies to tea along with Jenna. Came home 9.0. Wet all day. Harriett improving.

Monday 21ˢᵗ – 27th January

Did not go to work but in morn was working correspondence rc and went out to buy shirts rc

Harry has gone to Blackburn to see abt match with "M/C City". It was a lovely day. In afternoon library and went with Mc to Burnley Bks and had a Turkish Bath. Came back to Nelson.

In evening stamp counting rc. And preparing to return Butlers skts.

Harr a bit on the improvement and counted stamps out for me.

Posted letters to Butlers returning sheets and stayed in the library til 9.30. Home with Alice at 6.0 and had tea with Mae, coming home at 8.30 and straight to bed. Parcel from Gib.

Great liberal meeting at Salem. Sir Ughtred and Earl Spencer.

Harr was downstairs for 1st time tonight.

Some working till 3.30 am at office but Jim & I were not on.

Library 8.30-9. Home rc.

In evening out a bit al Maco and coming home at 8.30 found Harry in having brought little Maud Wildman. At 9.30 at Gdn Street staying till 10.30.

Afternoon preparing stamps for Butler and bookkeeping. After to post rc. Stayed in all evening as Alice and Harr were alone. Emma being at St Mary's Cricket Social and M & J at Coop tea. What promised to be a dry evening mended alright however as Harry came in with grapes for Harr and stopped to play cards. Tom Deel also coming in. At 11.15 Harry left and I went up to Nelson with Emma.

Naturalmente sigue mi punto con el sitio, pero estaba ahí de la tienda de Mac sin esta acompañada por él. Parece que un lobo me come y yo tan alegre por afuera.

[Translation: Naturally, she follows my point with this place although she was at Mac's shop without his supervision. It seems that the wolf consumes me whilst I maintain a happy outside demeanour!]

Snowing all day thick. Stopped in doors till after dinner reading. At 3.0 went alone to St Mary's choir festival helped by Reedyford choir. Very good home tea and writing.

Monday 28th – 3rd February

Very cold in morn. Tried to inspect Witham's stock but missed. Couton poorly.

Witham's sale on. Couton is however trading for a few things I want.

Evening in library. Alice, Emma & Harry had gone to Walverden skating.

News of loss of German S.S. "Elbe" received with 380 lives lost.

Evening changed library book at Coop. Home book work, etc.

Stayed in afternoon reading. After tea at 7.30 went to dentist and had 6 teeth out preparatory for false set. Home and bed.

Frost continues very sharp. Alice and Emma are skating with Harry. After tea changed and went to Butter field who completed the job by 4 more extractions more or less painless.

Came home read until bedtime.

Stayed indoors all day having asked off on a/c of sore mouth/ painful gums. Good read of Conan Doyle's Book. Harr for company.

Monday 4th – 10th February

Felt unwell all day so visited doctor – bronchitis. Nothing serious. Harr is beginning to go out a bit.

Felt still unwell. Left work at 8.45. Frost most hard yesterday. 4 below zero. Did not go to till work till after brkfast.

Still rather unwell. Evening changed book at library getting one by Rides Haggard.

Came home bkfst with sharp aches in back. Could not go back to work. Stayed in all day.

Very keen frost. Had a walk during church/ time with Harr and after dinner saw Harry and had a walk with him and Harr round by Rendle Forest.

Monday 11th – 17th February

Frost still hard: Canal frozen: Being a fine sunshine day, after dinner Harr & I had a walk along canal to Toulridge and back by rail, Harr being tired. Evening changed library book for one of Galas and read till bedtime.

Another beautiful day though keen. After dinner was about with Harry calling in at office and getting paid in full; afterwards about 3.30 had a sharp walk together to Colne and round by locks and canal. After tea a long read.

Frost continues pretty much the same; afternoon Harr not wanting to come out walking anymore, passed the time at Reading Room.

Feeling much the same and being all the week off work and being rather hard up to kill time being extremely averse to writing.

Slightly damper but cold winds. Before dinner had a walk. Afterwards reading room and changed "Galas dream" for "People of the Mist". Harry came in during the evening.

Beautiful sunlight but cold morning had a walk up Barker House Road. Afternoon reading and went with Mac to football match. After tea read and visited dentist (doing nothing). Harry Watson was in from Burnley. Finished up at theatre half time to see "Coleen Bawn".

Morn church; Rev Edwards being away his substitute is a very indifferent speaker: After dinner went to school with Harr and Emma and after school a walk with Fred and Rennie. Tea at home after a muddy tramp through top of Rendle Forest: Bella Wormwell was in from Burnley. Spent evening indoors reading & c.

Monday 18th – 24th February

Started work again: warmer weather but dull. In evening post and saw Mrs. Jones of 106 Clayton Street about lodgings.

In evening library and Garden Street.

Went to dentist and got cast taken for teeth. Came home read. Coulton's baby girl died and we contributed a wreath.

Left work at 8.30 and at 9.0 met Pickover and went to see the Colne Amateurs perform in "Marituna" half time. Very good. Football Bazaar opened. Alice, Harr and Gerty went.

Changed book at library for J. Vernes Factory Ticket and at 7.30 saw Marituna again with Pickover. Emma and Annie at Bazaar.

Afternoon library and got my teeth. By evening went with Alice and Harr to Bazaar. It was very congested and a lot of ruffling. Came home at 10.30. Emma was at St Paul's dramatico.

Morn turned out damp and cold. In afternoon turned to snowing so stayed indoors. Harry and also Janie Belton came in and stayed to tea. Harry was to go to the Baths, so I went up with him and then to church going in with Eddy Wild as I was late. Came home with Harr and read.

Monday 25th – 3rd March

In evening went to see Span of Life at Grand theatre.

Indoors bookkeeping. Don't feel so well.

Evening letter writing. Felt pain in shoulder acutely.

Working till 9.30.

Changed and called in at Jerry's and dentist settled for teeth. Had a bottom one extracted so came home and read Til Bito.

Afternoon set off to find Harry but mixed Southfield Str for Vale Str so missed him. Watched Southfield ward election going about with Catbow for voters. Called in at Gdn Str but found it was a shut-up question when they found out I was looking for lodgings. After tea Alice & I with Harry Long went to Burnley and passed the evening at "Williams". Alice stopped the night with Bella, but Harry and & came home 11 p.m.

Morn went to church with Harr & Emma. After dinner went up to Harry's, 57 Vale Str, and settled to come on the 6th. Stayed in reading till tea time as Harry Long didn't turn up. Church & met Alice from Brnly train at 8.30. Came home and bed early.

Monday 4th – 10th March

Evening home work with stamp sorting.

Evening making up sheets. Harr continues going to work but is very shaky on her feet and need bandaging & rubbing.

Evening counting Gibs pricing sheets. Library 9-9.30.

Work till 9.30.

Evening mostly at library.

Afternoon Harr, Pickover & I went to Burnley Baths (Turkish) came home and stayed indoors. Harry Long came in at 8.30. Emma had Miss Elliott in to tea.

Morn clearing up room. After dinner went to Brnly Farm with Alice finding Maggie Hartley ill. But went on to Jane Alice, Starkies, 56 Plumbe Str with Geo. Riley and Alice and had tea & spent the evening coming home by tram.

Monday 11th – 17th March

Evening busy homework writing.

Working till 9.15.

In evening went to Circus to see the Steene's American mystififiers.

Shifted quarters to 57 Vale Str Parade. At 3.30 with full kit Commisaried from Clegg. Returned for tea and visited library rc till after 8.0 when I stopped at home till 10.0 with Alice Hulstead also being in splendid weather. Returned Vale Str and bed at 11.30.

Rose in morn and had a read in bed. Beautiful morn. After bkfst went to St Mary's - no one else there. After dinner called at Chapel Str and found water had thawed at last. Caught 2.15 tram to Brnly. Mr. J also going by it. Spent afternoon in Park. Had tea with Mr. Leaves who was alone and evening to St Peter's Rev Eddlst. Came back 8.17 and spent rest of time at Chapel Str. Harry Long also calling in for a while.

Monday 18th – 24th March

Day passed fairly comfortably. Good meals. Mrs. Md is rather poorly with a cold which makes her rather quiet. Library and post at 8.30 to 9.0 after writing to Butler. Chapel Str to 9.45. Harr improving.

Alice rec letter from Harr saying she wld sail on 4th prox. Visited Chapel Str and W. Rileys (card playing) till 10.30.

Bkfst at office. Evening went to Chapel Str. Harry Long also came in a bit.

Very wet day. Stayed indoors tidying up luggage & reading till after tea. Went to Chapel Str and stayed in. Alice Long poorly.

Monday 25th – 31st March

Evening went with M to the "Grand" to see "Dorothy". Just fair.

Evening went to see Mae about changing my machine & fitting another but don't think I will. Also Chapel Str and up home. Stamp work, McAuslan sheet rc

Left office at 5.30 and met Emma & H. Long at station and went to

Burnley Victoria to see "La Cigala". Very good. Got home by last train. Wet very.

No sirve: lo quiero todo lo mismo y más que tengo que está a su vera para poco tiempo para sentir más pasión lo mismo que siempre. Dios lo haga.

[Translation: It will not do. I want everything the same, and only have to be at her beck and call for a short time to have to feel more passion than normal. God do his will.]

Left work at 8.45 and went with Pickover and Jim to see Dorothy half-time.

Evening wet: visited library reading room & Chapel Str. Harr still much the same if not worse. Joe poorly also home all week.

Afternoon stamp work wrote & posted to McAuslan. After tea went to Sanders Circus. Cold & uncomfortable didn't like. Called in Chapel Str I found Harry Long in playing cards.

Morn church. Showery. No one else there in pew. Afternoon called for Harry but found him at Chapel Str. Had tea there and then a walk to Burnley Lane with him instead of church. Chapel Str and home till 10.15.

Monday 1st – 7th April

Evening bookkeeping indoors all evening.

Went with Barnsley to stamp down B'field to get Rules for Uncle Emmett. Spent rest of evening in Chapel Str till 10.0 when I took a note to Harry Long about a vacancy.

Evening bookkeeping went down to Chapel Str finding Mc a bit better (Uncle still off work). Some snow fell and cold.

Late do 9.10 office. Chapel St & home

Made up with Harry to go and see "Charley Aunt" at Burnley but he missed train so we went to Grand to see "Greed of Gold" or "Dumb Man". Very good.

Tidied up and bookkeeping: After an early tea wen to Chap St and found they had bought the table. Alice agreed to accompany me to Burnley. Harry missed train again but came on later to the theatre. Came home at 10.35. Enjoyed it very well.

A parece que no puede hacer nada mal Enrique y no quiere más que su compañía.

[Translation: It seems that Enrique can do no wrong and wants nothing more than their Company].

Morn church. New curate there. Afternoon wrote to Uncle Emmett. Visited Gdn Str and had my tea there and then church. After had a long walk with Alice down B'ford.

Evening bookkeeping &c

Nothing particular.

Evening work at office till 8.45. Chapel Str till 10 then home.

Left office at 5.30 changed and was down town looking around. Visited St Joseph's. Alice and Harr are getting ready for Southport. Met John's train at 10.30 and helped him with box up to Gdn Str.

Rose at 6.0 and saw Alice and Harr off to Southport at 7.10. Had bkfst and changed to cycling suit, saw John and had a ride out on bike to Moor Creek. After dinner went with J to Burnley on bikes visiting Aunt Mgts. Had tea there and came back and came up Vale Str changed and stayed at Chapel Str reading. Came home early turned in.

Rose early and went to Chapel Str Found a letter from Harr saying she wouldn't come until Monday so I got my bkfst and took 8.52 train to Southport. Arrived in about 11.0 leaving my coat at Mrs. Bramwells. I had a stroll round till 12.30 when I came across Alice and Harr. We had dinner altogether and went out in afternoon to Berkdale for a drive with Susannah and husband. Saw cemetery and got back. Had a look round & after tea went to Opera House to see Richard III. Uncomfortable place but good acting. Home to Talketh Str and bed.

Morn on pier. Feel queer in my light clothes on a Sunday. Afternoon wrote to Nelson 3 letters and had a walk out till tea time. After went with Alice & Percy Bram to Christ Church and then a walk with Alice till 9.30. Harr stayed in. Two very nice young likeness fellows staying in Bramwells called Ottley & McCallum. Also a pseudo invalid & a couple from Manchester.

My mate has gone for a row before bkfast. Find I've a bit of a cold. Got shaved and bought some collars & c. Spent morning on Prom. After dinner we took tram to botanic Gardens and saw round there. After tea Harr being too tired Alice and I went out and had a long walk round by new carriage drive and stayed out till 10.0. Southport was fearfully crowded and rather rowdy.

Sufre tentación de piensa miento con a sobre tontería.

[Translation: Suffer temptation of thinking about nonsense]

Got up early and was first out on lake. Had ½ hour row. Also a long walk before bkfst. After bkfst on pier till dinner time; then a look around shops & c till 3.0 when we had tea and started for station. Left at 4.8 and landed at Nelson at 6.30. Got down to Chapel St and found our Harr is looking much the same as ever. Had tea and stayed till 9.30 when I got back to Vale Str and bed. Though quiet time at Southport I enjoyed it very much

& liked Bramwells very well.

At work again. Evening getting Gibs ready for Butler. Also saw Harr down at Chapel St. Bought music at Eastwood. Vale Str 11.0 and bed.

News day till 8.45. Visited Chapel Str and tried to see Harry Long but failed.

Evening busy all time getting 5000 Gibs ready for Butler. Finished by 10 pm.

Opening of Technical School. Posted a parcel to Butler. Was down town till tea time when I came back to Vale Street and had a read till 7.0. Saw John who came hath on my machine at 6.30 and at 8.30 visited Chapel Str and played cards till 11.0. Vale Str and bed.

In morn went to see Harry Long & church. At dinner time called to see John at Garden Str but he was out seeking me so we didn't get. Afternoon **Emma celebrated her coming of age by a tea to which numerous no of friends came and Harry Long also came in**. Stayed in all time as it was rainy but Emma & her friends went out.

Monday 22nd – 28th April - Emma's coming of age

In afternoon began to feel ill and at tea time had high fever, called in at Chapel St on way home to leave chocolate. Also got some nitre. Went to bed early well wrapped up. Symptoms of influenza.

In bed all day except getting up for dinner. Very weak and pulled down. Rec letter from John.

Felt better so got up but after tea to which H. M. Stopped having come up to see me. I felt return of the fever and had to turn in early.

Felt a lot better and did not go to bed till 10.0 was reading playing cards & c

Encouraged by my feeling so much better. I went out in the afternoon and saw Emma & Gladys on their way to M/C. Had tea at Chapel St & came home at 6.30. Rapidly began to feel feverish again & turned in as bad as ever at 7.30.

Feel low spirited at again being down. Can't make out why Arthur Gib doesn't write. Pottered about reading rc and at night had a return of the fever. Doctor came at 11pm.

Fine warm sunny day. Thought I'd have to stay in bed by doctors' orders but he came up at 11.0 and said I might get up and go out a bit. Jolly soon got up and after dinner went out for a bit but found myself very shaky. Harriett M came up to Vale Str to tea and went with Mrs. Mtford to St Mary's. I stayed in with Harry and read till bedtime.

Monday 29th – 5th May

Morning writing rc. Harry was playing in afternoon so went fishing; I called in at office to see Coulton and sever my connection therewith except perhaps for casual work. Saw the hands rc. Had tea at Chapel St and home early.

Fineish day was busy in morning with corresp &c and in afternoon saw doctor and visited Chapel St. After tea it came on to rain a bit. Spent part afternoon and Garden Street and saw Mrs. Mather.

Rainy in morning; after dinner went out and stayed in Coop Library a bit. Also had an early tea and went out and saw Harry Long. Home early and played crib.

Grand sunny day. Morning out by 10.0 and had a walk by Park till dinner time. After dinner got machine out and spent a lot of time getting it fitted up at Macs. Also new saddle. Rode to Colne & back. After early tea visited Chapel St and came home by 7.30 thinking Harry Long would call, but he didn't so played cards & read till bedtime. What a contrast to other Thursdays!

Morning grand day again. Smooched thro' the morning and after dinner went to Brly on machine and had a look round. Came back early and had a walk up Walverden. After tea had a walk down town till 8.30 home and read rc.

Grand day. Morning shaved and went out. Bought shoes at Coop and stayed in Reading Room. Met Willie Riley and went down to Mather's shed with him. After dinner changed for cycling but found I wasn't going out staying in at Chapel Str an hour or so and then rode to Laneshaw Bridge & back. Had tea at Chapel Street and then took matching up home. Went out and came across Harry Long and Harr and then stayed at Chapel Str playing crib with Tom Peel re till 11.0 came home.

Grand sunny day. Got up at 7.30 and dressed for cycling. Met T and Greenied and were at Colne by 10.0. Got to Skipton by 12.30 and took back by Over t'Moss. I was to be in Nelson early so left them behind and reached Nelson by 3.0 very dusty and thirsty. Had a complete change and dinner and went down to Willie Rileys to tea, Bertha & Jeanette also being there. Went to Salem Chapel. Mark Knowles was to preach but didn't after staying at Willies till 9.0. Went to Chapel Str and found Harry Long there. Harr M came in from Brly shortly and I left at 10.0 for home.

Monday 6th – 12th May

During breakfast they were taking new boiler up to the Valley Shed. After bkfst set to and brushed my clothes and cleaned machine. Wanted to go and have a bath but was advised against it. Stayed in Macs till dinner time calling for my jacket at Evan's. After dinner changed and tried to see doctors but he was out. Took 3.15 train to Brnly. Aunt Harr & Bertha going too. Had a look round Brnly and tea at Aunt Margaret's and home by 6.25 meeting Harr & Emma at station. Just going to Brnly Baths. Met Harry Long and had a walk to Bfield and home by 8.30 played crib.

Fine day but windy morn. Afternoon too windy to ride. After tea Harry came up and we went down town. I stayed at Uncle Joe's till 9 so then home.

Publisher note: Joseph Beanland, three years older than his father, Bolton

Morning fine but very windy. Got my things ready and after dinner Harry M helped me to station with box, which I got from Garden Street. At 2.30 I called round at Werby Str but Harry Long had not found the maps so at 2.50 I made a start on machine from Chapel Str. I reached Acarington at 4.15 and Bury at 6.0 where I made a very good tea. It was fine and sunny but roads dusty and windy. I got to Man. by 7.45 and up to John's in 5 from Nelson. I found John & Emma in the midst of their spring cleaning. Stayed up pretty late. Gladys is looking very well.

Morn went down town with John and had a good look round. Brought up my box from Station and after dinner went down to Miller Street on bike and bought furniture cream. After tea went down to Theatre Royal to see "Chieftain" comic opera. Fine day.

Friday 10th May 1895 – Am 21 today!

Was down in city morn and ordered suit at Noble's. In afternoon went to Altrincham, Cheshire on machine. About 24 miles there and back. Grand day. Up home by 6.30 tens and then letter writing. John busy cleaning.

Morn City and bought different things in. Covert coat at Lewis. Dinner at 2.0 and then got up Middleton way with John & Gladys and Arthur Catling. Had tea at Catlings and then went down town to Exhibition. Arts & Crafts that and huge still market kept us pretty late.

Morning was out a bit after making "Rosto" for dinner. It was very fair but rather sharp with cayenne. Afternoon reading & c feeling sleepy. Dull day turned to rain. Evening Harpurby Church (very low) and chatting & c

Monday 12th - 19th May

Finer day morn library rc afternoon rode to Middleton evening down town to try on at Nobles. After tea went out again, library rc

Dull day. Thought I'd ride to Bolton so made a start at 10.30 and met Mr. McCallum & Otley in Beansgate to my great surprise. Exchanged addresses. Found it stiff rough road. Arrived at Bolton at 12.50 and found the Nightingale's home at Conservative Club and not gone elsewhere as I thought. I stayed right to 10.5 so as to see them all and passed a very pleasant time. Hamos & Ethel are grown a lot, "Georgie" and Eliza much the same. Took train back cost ¼ with bike. Borrowed lamp in Bolton.

Morn busy writing rc afternoon was out with Gladys! And also walked down to Fivesay Street. Wrote & posted letter to CJC and played cards with John.

Fine day but brisk breeze from NW increasing in evening. Set off after writing to Seully for Knutsford but at Wothington came a cropper owing to a hansom and was delayed from 11 to 2 o'clock having nowhere to go or anything. At 2.0 started and had a pleasant ride to Knutsford through Wilmslow & Mobberly. Came back via Alfrincham having bad head wind all way. Very tired and stiff from my fall. Got home 7.10 and did nothing particular. Elliman's.

Morning in town. At 12.0 met Willie Riley and had lunch at Lewis; then a good look through Royal Exchange (market) which I much enjoyed. After tea called at Nobles but couldn't get my things. After tea at home I walked to Cheetham Hill and hunted up McCallum & Otley and went down town & had a look round. They were rather busy also. Home by 10.15 but found clothes were a bad fit.

In morning went down town to get clothes altered. After dinner John not having come up and Emma out to see a wedding. I left the keys and went to meet Mr. McCallum but found them just gone being 3 mins late. I followed on to Belle Vue but not liking returned to town, had tea at Lockharts and went to Prince's Theatre to see "Go-Bang". Very fair.

Morn smooth and walk. Cold raw day. After dinner read & c. After tea went to Irish Presbyterian Kirk which was like old times and walked home. John went with me.

Monday 20th – 26th May

Morning being dull but not rainy. Smooched. At 11.0 had a ride to Bury and back down Broughton at 3.30 came home cleaned machine & had an early tea and went down town and saw "Derby Winner". Very good but not finishing till 11.20 had to walk home.

Turned to rain. Patched up in morn and after dinner went down town; got my clothes also a few gifts and up home early. John was unfortunately late & kept at office. Saw Mr. Bristol & Arthur. Gladys has been rather cross. Evening chatting.

Day dull & rainy at times. John helped me with box after bkfst. Left it at Vio and went up home. After dinner at 1.40 mounted & rode carefully down to station; very slippery; Took 2.20 fast train. Bike cost 1f: arrived Nelson 3.50 changed and unpacked: After tea went down Chapel Street found them very jolly seemed quite glad to see me! Gave me a jolly present of a set of links K. Stayed till 10.0 playing begeque with Alice rc.

After bkfst was about town on machine. Called in at Chapel Str & Garden Str. After dinner to 6.0 busy writing & stamp work. Post & Chapel Str after tea and half time to theatre to see "Old Guard". M & Emma being there: saw H Long & Pickover.

Friday 24th May 1895 – Harr Birthday

Morn Stamp work to 10.30. Out on machine rc till dinner. After dinner letter writing and changed. Visited office selling Coulton back his type. Bought Harr a brooch and after tea took her to see "Pepita" at the grand stalls. Liked very well. Nada feo.

Morn library & afternoon library & after tea. Theatre "Talka" just fine. Went with Alice & Emma. Met H Long there. Came home late.

Dull in morn. Rain in afternoon. Fine in evening. Burnley Sports & Whalley meet. Morn new to go and went to church. After dinner, finding out H Long had gone out, went round & took Alice out for a walk round Noggarth. Had tea at Chapel Str & then went with Harr & Emma to church. Harr M was at Brly. After church Alice not caring to go out, met Harr at station & took her round Bottoms. Home by 10.0.

Morn church fine day all thro'. Afternoon took Alice out round Noggarth. Evening tea at Chapel Str & church with Harr & Emma. Harr M at Brnly but met her coming back & had walk out with her.

Monday 27th – 2nd June

Grand day all through. Round about in morn did nothing particular. After dinner at 2.0 started for Gisburn & did the North Round stopping at Whalley for tea (6.0) and visited the Abbey ruins. Permission from Ms Kay c/o Miss Pye. Stayed ½ hour at Aunt Margaret's and came home 10.0 after calling in at Chapel Str.

Discarded wearing pants. Grand day. Morning stamp work and writing; afterwards at 11.0 went to Baths & had a swim. After dinner dressed & joined tradesmen in their run to Worsthume Show; Came back at 6.0 with Mr. Croft had tea & visited ruins finishing up till 10.0 at Gdn Str.

Day very warm & close. Morning reading in park. Feel rather too stiff for much. After dinner went out with Jim & Mulch and library. After tea went down, post and went on to Willie Rileys staying there till 11.45 had supper. Came home.

Very warm & sultry. Reading **"Two Clippers"** all morning. Before dinner cleaned machine and had a short run till 3 pm with Jim Croft. Called in at Chapel Str and library & Macs till 4 pm then home and writing. After tea went down Chapel Str taking machine with one but finding Arthur had come from Lancaster and that it was stormy I did not go out beyond library.

Morning round town with Arthur. Harr M received telegram from Mary Scott saying wld arrive that afternoon so we went to Brnly to meet her and coming back had tea together and in the evening was out viewing the decorations and saw Pickover, H Long, rc. Home rather late. Fine day on the whole. Mary is very dark but I could recognise her and she is very chatty and nice. Repaired machine in morn.

Rain at intervals. Fire Brigade Day. Morning round town going out rather late. After dinner watched parade of Fire Brigade & Mayors from every Str and later with the rest from New Inn (Willie Harry Bower). Had a good number down to tea inc Rupture with Rileys through refusal to allow Mary thro' mill after promising H Long. Passed a very pleasant evening with music contributed by Arthur & Emma and songs all round. Mary giving "Wid better beds a wee" & c. Went out during evening to see about train for Mary and broke up quite late 11.30 or so.

Morn damp & showery during day. Church morn, Mary going also. After dinner cards and saw Arthur B off to Lancaster. Tea & chat at Vale Str and packed up. Chapel Str for an hour and they all saw me off at station at 10.30. There was very little time to spare to catch my train but Harry Long looked after my bike. Changed compartments at Accrington and arrived at St Pancras at 6 a.m. I managed to doze off once or twice.

Monday 3rd – 8th June

Arrival in London to stay with **Charles Saword**.

Left my luggage at station and rode to Gascoyne Rd. and Emma came down and opened to me at 7.0. After bfkfast I changed and went to St Pancras for my things going as far as Kings X with Wally amid Oceano of Trippers singing and carrying on. Made it up to go with same Wally & so the Walthamstead but they left us in the lurch so Sally & I had to go alone to Homerton to Hampstead 5d and looked round; good view from the Heath, of London. Got lost trying to find the Home but made for Sta and got to Broad Str 4d by 6.30. Had tea in Cheapside and went on to Globe Theatre and saw Charley's Aunt – 2f pit. Very very good. Home by last bus at 12.0.

Rose at 11.0; took it easy all day and spent the evening in the Park; went out with Lottie Wally and Sably but eventually Sarah and I had a long walk together and reaching home at 9.30 found Uncle C in; stayed chatting till 11.30. Fine weather mild.

Rose at 8.30; morn was round about Mare Street. After dinner changed and went into City by bus. Had a view from the top of the Monument 3 and met **Alf** across London Br at 5.30. I find myself to have grown taller than him but otherwise we are much the same and soon fell into old ways. We took train to New X and (having had a drop of tea in the City) we soon went out after seeing George, Frances & Mrs. Scully (who looks better if anything). We walked to Greenwich Theatre and saw the "**Grip of Iron**". Home to Brockley calling in at a pub.

Rose at 8.30. Saw Bert Scully at bkfst. We walked to Greenwich and looked through the Museum; then taking the boat to Westminster 4 we had a couple of hours in the aquarium (after a comical dinner). We voted the Acq.

Slow so went out and visited Alf's Aunt, Mrs. Petit and saw Fred Scully who is a shop man. Had tea there and then Alf had to visit dentist again. Train to New X and spent the rest of the evening indoors and a long stroll round with Alf. Fine but cold at night.

Rose at 8.30 and after bkfst visited Goldsmith's Institute. Walked to Greenwich and boat to London Br. Left Alf there and made my way to Broad Str. Changed into my cycling things and had dinner after which I went to Days and got photo'd! (Attached?!) Had a short run and in to tea after which I had a 8 to 10 mile run to Woodford and Walthamstow through Epping forest: splendid roads.

Home 8.30 and at 9.30 went out for a long walk with Sarah till 11.0 to Clapham Common. Fine all day: warm.

Very warm day. Did not feel inclined to go down to the land so in morn did a bit of cycling in afternoon. Lounged about and after an early tea set off with **Sarah** to go to Olympia but getting rather late changed it to the Savoy where I saw opera "**Hansel & Gretel**" German fairy opera. It proved rather childish in plot but very good music & singing in fact superior to anything I've ever heard. 2/6 pit home last bus but one. Beautiful evening.

Very warm & close. Did not rise till late & annoyed by slight cold in the head. Morn read & c. Could not wake up my mind what to do but finally decided to go down to Caterham, **Uncle expecting me yesterday**.

Dinner at 2.0 and at 3.0.

I started and had a warm but pleasant ride thro' the city which was very quiet and thro London Bridge, Brixton, Streatham and Warlingham reaching Longhurst about 6.30, but had an hour to wait before Uncle turned up. Had some work to do & tea rather late. Turned in early.

Monday 10th – 16th June

Rose at 6.0 and was busy till 8.15 with Uncle on tryclcle (tricycle) & I left the land together as far as the lodge; here however Uncle found he'd not left the key behind so I took it back & went on towards Oxted.

The path was very precipitous down to Godstone and then good roads thro' Turner's Hill and Lindfield to Brighton which I reached at 4.45. I had only had a lunch of bread & cheese on the way so I made a good meal. Tea and then had a look round the place. I went to the Royal Pavilion (Gio IV's palace) and stayed to the promenade concert. Very nice night and good bands & illuminations. Feel it grand to be at seaside.

Rose at 7.0 and had a walk on prom before bkfst. Then went round town, Styne and Pier till noon. Had dinner, cleaned machine & took the 1.25 train to Haywards Heath 13m avoiding the 8 mile rise out of B'ton. The day tho' a lot more sunnier was cooler and a nice breeze. I made good progress thro' Crawley to Red Hill where I met the Miss Browns returning from seeing **Alf off at the station**.

They asked me to tea so I consented and saw the Browns bar, Ralph & Harry. Lilian looking as charming as ever. Made a good tea & start for Longhivist via Caterham thro' Merstham at 7.05 and landed in at 8.45. Nice road but hilly.

Rose 6.15 mad bkfst & helped rc. At 8.0 made a start on trike to Croydon from whence I went on alone to London via Brixton & Vauxhall Embankment and Clerkenwell and Old Street rc. Arrived after only walking the merest trifle at 11.30 and found letters waiting. Had dinner, a good wash & change & started correspondence rc. After tea took trains to Brockley where I arrived at 8.0 Saw Alf who was going to tea at the Joanes' and then had a stroll out with Bert. Alf came in abt 11 and we retired.

Rose at 8.0 went up to town with Alf at 10.0 and saw thro' the Guildhall picture gallery. At 12.30 were down at New X again and had dinner.

Alf came to station and saw me off to Woolwich Arsenal Sta from New X Sta and I arrived at the Arsenal to 2.0 where I met Mary and her brother, a very tall strapping fellow. We among a lot of others got shown thro' the Arsenal and process of making guns, cartridges rc, and then we saw Mary off to Charing X and I had tea with Sergt Scott and watched a cricket match. Caught a train the Charing X went to Covent Garden "II Trovatore" by Miss Macintyre and tenor Famagno.

Morning rose at 7.30 and just managed to catch connecting trains to Charing X so as to arrive at Waterloo by 9.50 and saw Alf and Bert off to Southampton Fred Scully also being there. I strolled around town and looked in at the Bishopsgate Institute. Was up to dinner by 1.30 and then changed and got down to New X again to tea. Met the two Miss Browns Ada & Lilian there and went out a bit with them & Mrs. Scully and then Bert came in from Southampton. Had a long chat with Mrs. S while Bert went up to London Bd to see the Miss Browns home then turned in by myself.

Rose at 8.30 and after bkfst at 10.0 took George up to town and had a look round the National Gallery and then on to Kensington and thro' the museum till 2.0 when we had tea and I saw him off at 3.0 from Cannon Str going up myself to Hackney afterwards. I had coffee and changed into other clothes and at 6.0 got down to city and to Covent Garden opera, a great crowd being there by 7.0 even; had a fair seat and heard Madame Adelina Patti in "**Traviata**". She is good, very; but I did not care much for the opera. Home by bus at 12.15.

Morning correspondence & c. Continued into afternoon when I had a short walk into the park and after tea **Sarah & I had a visit to St Paul's Cathedral to evening service 7 p.m**. After which a walk on Embankment & a visit to Tower Bridge then home by bus.

Monday 17th – 23th June

Morning correspondence & cleaning machine & c. After dinner at 2.0 started for a run and had a cheerless dusty road thro Bow, Barking to Rainham (n. Woolwich) then striking across country to Romford. I had pleasant but heavy roads to Chigwell (saw Maypole Inn) and Woodford, down Clapton & home. Had a chat with Mr. G. Longcroft. Uncle C came in later. Weather still grand.

Oppressive but fine day. In morning got dressed and took the 10.0 train to Brd Str. Had an interview with Ed Healey & then visited Bishopgate Inst till 2.0. Had dinner at St. Paul's and went up to Br Museum to see Sapling wel. From there bus to Hyde Park, walk thro' Park & St James Park to Westminster, boat to London Bridge and home by train. At 7.30 felt tired and so, tho sheets had come from Healey did no work. **Jim Saword & Jinnie (refer to p.270)** came up but Uncle didn't.

Rain at last. Found it raining hard in the morning.

Was busy correspondence rc. Reading Dombey & son. After dinner changed and took train from Coborn Road for Loughton at 13.45. Arrived Loughton about 5 and found Nellie, Maggie & Gertie in. Had tea and then Miss Butcher (Nellie) showed me all over the place, which is very pretty indeed. Gertie seems about the jolliest and best looking also youngest.

Mr. Butcher came in at 9.0 and we had supper & chat till 10.40 when I took train home.

Rose early and went to Ed Healey and after waiting a good while did some business. Afternoon visited Bethnal Green Museum and White Chapel and train Aldgate to Victoria. I met Jim and saw Drake & Gorhams offices. At 6.30 we went down to Thornton Heath and had tea with Jim. Also saw Fred & wife and Mr. Reid. Spent an enjoyable evening the weather being splendid and came home latish.

Fine day. Morning had a long spin to Waltham Cross, Waltham & Chingford till 1.30 when I came home to dinner. The sun was very strong and hot. I made an error and got to Camden Town before I was aware of it. After dinner I changed & got down to City. Saw Healey & then took train to New Cross. Had tea with Mrs. Scully and went out. Met Bert at Institute & watched a Polo match. Spent rest of evening pleasantly. Two letters received from Alf.

Dull to fine. Left New Cross 10.49 and **rambled round City where I came across Uncle**. Had drinks. Came up to Homerton & **brought present for Aunt Emma**. Had dinner, correspondence. Packed up.

After tea rode machine to St Pancras & came home by 9.0. Had supper and a **very affectionate parting** and started with my luggage.

Got to St Pancras by 11.15 but a lot of time was taken up with booking rc from the National League. Left St Pancras 12.25 and had a pleasant ride in fair company.

Day broke fine and sunny but after leaving Leeds it got cloudy.

Had an incident here thro' coupling bolt of engine breaking which delayed us. Started Scotch Mist when we got to Skipton. To my surprise & pleasure I found Harry Long had come to meet me on F's machine. Started back for Nelson together leaving luggage to follow but on nearing Earby it started to rain and we did not land into Nelson till 10.0 wet through. I had to change & get my things from Station Road by 12.40 train. I then changed again & went down to Chapel Str. Had tea and then went out with Alice for a walk. Felt all day rather sleepy & tired.

Monday 24th – 30th June
Fine day. Very warm. Rose at 8.45. Morn spent in tidying up room and correspondence. After dinner letters and went out Chapel St and library till tea time. After tea, Chapel Str and met H Long, had a walk and home at 10.30 a read & bed.

Shed on Fire!

Very warm. Morn corresp & Gib sorting. Went out before dinner after cleaning machine and task wheel to be repaired (spoke out). After dinner Bookkeeping till 4.0, changed, shaved and had tea at 5.0. Went down Chapel Str was rigged out a' la Henley Regatta so got changed.

Went down to Sports Nelson CC and at 7.25 fire bells rang for shed on fire at Kerkel field Road. Left sports and got splendid view of fire from railway embankment. Had a look round and home by 10.0. Saw some of the Rileys & spoke to them.

Fine morning. Wet after tea. Rose in morning. Bookkeeping rc. Brought wheel up home & called in at Chapel Str. In afternoon was 2 hours fitting machine. Washed had a read & tea. At 7.30 went out tho' it was raining and called in Chapel Str & library till 9.30. Home early & to bed.

Started making up stamp album. Turned out a lovely evening so having an early tea I went down to Harry's and together had a walk to Burnley Lane.

Continuing my stamp work. After dinner changed & went down Chapel Str. Met Miss Elliott and Miss McDonald & acc by Emma went thro' Someshaye shed. Fine afternoon but showery. After tea at Vale Str. I went out, met Harr & Alice Glover and together rambled round with many a joke & just about "Jim" FC.

Well to fine. Morning stamp album. Afternoon dressed & Alice was going to Bella in Brly asked me to go too. Spent the evening so so. Anthony also being there. Back 10 pm. Am reading Baring Goulds **"Rennico me quicks"**.

Wet at intervals. Morn Sunday Sch (O what a surprise). Also, church being school sermons. After dinner read a bit and then Chap Str for half an hour. Had a stroll out but did not see anybody except Ard Robinson. Had tea at 5.30 and attended evensong but Harr & Janie also being there. Fairish good singing. Went to see Harry Long who has a sore throat met Alice Glover but did not go out with Harr & that lot.

Monday 1st – 7th July

Well at intervals. Was busy all day with stamp album. In evening was at library and Chap St also Garden Street.

Well now & then. Confined indoors with stamp album which I finished by tea time. Went down Chapel Str rec letter Uncle Emmett. Library till 9.15 saw Harry Long at 7 to 8 o'clock. Saw Jim & Fred Wainwright. Chap Str till 10 then home.

Wel (well) day on whole. Fine evening. Rose at breakfast morning post & library also called in Coultons and saw Gad on ruling machine. After dinner reading and wrote to Frank. Changed and had tea. An old ex-lodger was also in to tea. Called in at Chapel Str and went out with Harr and Alice Glover round Someshaye park and M/c Road. Put in time very pleasantly and at 9.30 called in at Derby Street to see how Harry was accompanying Alice most of the way home. Harry was no better & had gone to bed.

Morning getting bike seen to ce cocter pin. Library afternoon stamp work and reading. After tea went out at 8 to Willie Rileys till 10.15. Heard about Pritchard getting job in Natal.

After bkfst and read went out on bike to Burnley and back via Aunt Peggy's who I stopped to see. After dinner library and at 3 started for

Rendle Hill it being a grand clear afternoon. Got to the top by 5 pm and started back a different way at 5.30. Landed in to tea 7.20 rather tired at Vale Str. Had a wash and change and went out to change book at library and saw Harry Long and Harriett and A.G. But it was then quite late. Came home 10.30.

Morning was out round town and before dinner went out with Emma and Bertha Barker round Carr Hall way. First time I've been out with Emma for ages! They wanted to go to Pendle but we thought we'd leave it to next Saturday. After dinner I went to Cleveges on machine and watched result of **cricket match Burly v Nelson** not going in field but to the park. Had tea at Aunt Margarets Greeme'd having joined us. Rode back to Nelson by 8.0 and had a walk round Park seeing Jim fish and Harry L. Came home with Harr and did job for Tom Peer. Not getting to Vale St till 11.45.

Grand day. Rose at 8.0 and after an early bkfst went down Chapel St where I had left machine and as I did not care about coming too went on to Croft's from where we made a start for Brnly and Nelson by 1 p.m. Had dinner and an hour in bed to cool off and then dressed and shaved. Harry L came up and we had a walk up Walverton going to tea and Chapel Str. Alice, Harry and I then had an hour in the Park and a walk up Noggarth calling in at Janie's who I asked to go to Gib. Chapel Str & home by 10.15.

Monday 8th – 13th July

Grand sunny day. Morning read and visited office to see if there was any work (Call on Wed). Went to baths and had a swim and did some messages for Harr M. After dinner cleaned machine. Correspondence rc had an early tea and visited Chapel Str and Harry Long. Went down cricket field Nels on 2nd v Colne 3rd till 8.0 then round library rc with Harry. Stayed at Chap Str till 10.0 then home and read Julius Vernes Begums Fortune.

Morning writing to Lurra & diary rc. Post and town on bike. After dinner met the tradesman at top of Nelson and at 2.0 started for North Round. There were two waggonettes and about 20 cyclists. We took very easy stages to **Clitheroe** it being a fine sunny day. At Clitheroe, Harwood & I who were on the front missed the others so had tea by ourselves and then went on to Waddington and Brungerley Bdge. I left at 7 as it had turned windy and threatening and arrived in Nelson at 9.30 just as rain started.

Rose at 7.30 and after bkfst went to office but could not get anything to do being slack so went to Chap St and library and Macs till dinner time. After dinner correspondence diary rc. Changed and went to Dyson's and stayed a bit with Alice Glover at her looms. Rode to Burnley on bike and back before tea after which was out with Harr & Alice G. And at 8.15 met H. Long and went with him to Salem and heard Sir Ughtred. Came home

10.30.

Went to work 6.30 on news all day. Quite like old times. Good lot of excitement in office over elections. Left at 8.30 and as it was raining hard went with Pickover halftime to theatre Variety Co.

On lists and handbill circ bill. Left at 5.30 and being a fine evening had tea and changed and went out with Harr. Emma being out with Remie. Also saw Bertha & Jeanette and stayed ½ hour at Garden Str.

Work till 12.0. Paid at 6 an hour. 13/6 for ½ week. Had drinks with Pickover to celebrate same. After dinner changed and at 3 o'clock went to cricket match where I saw the Beanlands & H. Long. Stopped to tea at Chapel Str and Miss Elliott was also there. After tea library and hunted up H. Long and went to Tom Peels to see about pension paper. Stayed chatting till 11.15 home. Match v Rishton Nelson (74 Rio). Turned to rain after ten.

Parece que el padre de E la vio el domingo pasado con el srto y lo saben en casa. ¡Padre lo tomar con calma! Pero madre no lo mira con favor, pero la consecuencia es que se van juntos ahora sin miedo ninguno. Escribiendo lo arriba puedo decir que lo miro con calma y sin pasión porque enteramente se ha desaparecido el amor que la tenía y me encuentro satisfecho y contento, pero sin amores.

[Translation: It seems that E's Dad saw her last Sunday with the man and everyone knows at home. Dad is calm, but Mother is not in favour. At least they do not have to hide anymore. After writing the above I am calmer and without passion since the love I had is gone and I am satisfied, if without love!]

Turned to cold and very windy. Even sleet during day. Went to church in morn. Read election news after dinner and then visited Mrs. Mather along with Harr & Bertha & Jen being there had tea. Went to S Mary's with Harr M and then visited Beltons. H Long also passing by came in teas. It seems Janie isn't going to Gib, Alice isn't either and Emma keeps it up thick with Rennie.

Monday 15th – 21st July

Dull morning. Rose at 8.30 and after bkfst read J. S. Winter's "Stranger Women" and then dressed & went down town library & c. Bought some fruit as I was feeling dyspeptic for dinner after which started corresp. & diary rc. Went down town calling on Caffry and at office and came up to tea after which went to library to change book for "High Heavens" by Ball and took 7.30 train for Burnley with Harrison Arnold & the others. Had a look round fair & treated Harr & Emma whom I met & came back with at 9.45.

Morning reading **Ben Hur**. Wrote letters to Uncle Emmett went down town and came upon a letter from Arthur rc. After dinner wrote letters to Arthur & Mrs. Mac. Diary & c till 4.30. Library till 6.0 had tea and went down Chap Str till 8.30 came home and played crib till bedtime.

Well in morn early. Went to work at 6.30. At 6.0 had a quick tea & borrowing F's machine Jim & I had a run to Greystone it having turned out a nice dry evening but dull. Got back at 9.0 and had a look at library & Chapel Str.

News day at office till 8.30 after which, Pickover, Harrison & myself went walking to Burnley arriving just in time to hear polls declared Stanhope fitting in by 321: Came back by 10.50 train. Great excitement.

On voters' lists & a handbill. At 5.30 called round at Chap Street and found Arthur & Agnes Rogerson had come. After tea changed & went out with Arthur & the others till 9.0 when I went up Gdn Str till 10.15 then home.

Left work at 12.15 (18/6). As it is wet the Derby is ruined. Took it easy after dinner & wrote diary rc. Went down Chapel St at 3.30 and finding Arthur, Alice & Agnes going to cricket match went off with them and met Harry Long.

The match was a farce and ended. Either after Derby match at Nelson or Sunday to Reedyford chapel & on Tuesday 1/2 day to S Port or else Sunday rode on bike to S Port. Work of post rest of week in a draw. At 6.30 I came home to tea at Vale Str and after a read, went to library till 9.30 when I went to Chapel Str and had a musical evening till 11.30 when I came home.

Arthur B being in Nelson changed my plans. Rose in morn at 9.30 & was too late for church so had a stroll. After dinner **played mandolin** and went down town at 3.0 calling on Harry who wld not go out. Went round Récré there being a sacred concert in cricket ground. It came on to thunder so went home to change my straw hat & then had tea at Chapel Str. Alice Glover & A Halstead being there. M & af at Padcham & Arthur at Annie's. It came on to rain but we went to church. H Long also going. After church had a reunion at Chapel Str till 10.0 when Harry & I left.

Monday 22nd – 28th July

At work again. After tea it being a finish evening went out & posted letter to Cooks I had written. Also went round town with Harriett & H Long I came across. Visited library till 9.30. Chap Str till 10.0 then home.

Fine day. Rose before bkfst at 6.30 and went out on bike a bit. Work again on lists. After tea **wrote to Uncle Ch**. saying would probably go down to London on Sept 2nd for a couple of nights & offering bike for 6/10 f or £6 without pump light & bill. Went out to post & library and called at

Chap St till 10.0 then hence.

Evening spent part time in shaving & c and also called in at Garden Street for a while. The evenings seem to pass and nothing done. Home 10.30.

Left work at 8.30 and spent an hour or so at Chapel Str before going home.

In the evening went round to post and also went round with little Harriett round Btms. At nine I called in at Dr. Robinson's who says he is going out to New Zealand this winter. Coming home I had to treat Walter & Harry at the Engineers it being awfully stormy.

Afternoon being well I did not go to Cricket Match but went smooching round library &c. Tea at Vale Str, Mrs. Mtfords mother having come from Keefhley: Open unless we did not go to Rford last Sunday when you can go to this Blackpool Sands to if Scarb for holiday or else Keethghley wkend. In evening turned dry and went to Barrowford with Alice for a walk. Chap Str till 11.0 then home.

Morn rose 8.0 made tomatoes & eggs. Shaved & changed and then wrote to Uncle saying that Ullmer did not seem very obliging & that I left choice of machine to him & would go to Caffry after Nelson feast. Also asked for cash for passage to be sent me. Probability of Alice going.

After dinner I went down to Chapel Str and Emma & Harr not having yet gone to school I went on also. Afterwards I took Harr M round by Noggarth & we had tea at Willie Rileys after which church again & then I dodged round seeking Harry Long & Harr who has had a split with Alice Glover.

Monday 29th – 4th August

Dull day. Fine evening. Evening posted letters to Uncle & Arthur and then spent an hour teaching Pickover on machine red Baly road. Finished up with a run thro Burnley forest. Saw H Long & called in at Chapel Str.

Fine day. Evening wrote to John & Wilmer. Mrs. Mtford father down from Keybty. Both went back at tea time. After tea I wrote to John & Wilmer and went out at 8 meeting Pickover and gave him another bike lesson till 9.30 on Old Burnley Road. At 10.0 came home after calling in at Chapel Street.

Fine day. Cooler. Rose at 6.15. Work 6.30. After tea corresp diary rc. Went out and gave Pickover another lesson on bike this time on Colne rd and Chapel st. He is getting fairly proficient. Came home at 10.0 after being in Chap St from 9 o'clock.

Work till 9.0 then had a walk to Bfield with Pickover and home at 10.30.

In evening changed, shaved and went out round town calling at library and Evans but not finding a suit to my liking. Harr was not out tonight. Saw Alice Glover for a minute or two.

Fine in morn. Very well afternoon. After dinner spent afternoon at library calling in at Chapel Str where I had tea. I met Pickover at 7.0 & walked in to Burnley and had a look round town till 10.35 train to Nelson. We took Harr to Brly and S. Peters and open called in at a couple of pubs and I also bought a suit. 37/6.

Well most of day cleared up a bit in afternoon. Went to St Mary's in morn & after dinner (rec letters from Arthur). I read till 3.30 and then went to Garden Str where Harr M also came. Had tea there & then Bertha, Jeanette & myself went to Rdyford chapel. We were going for a walk up Higherford but coming on to rain we turned back to Gdn Str and then I went out with Arthur & met Harry Long having a walk altogether. Alice & Janie met us too.

Monday 5th – 11th August

Well morning. Fine afternoon. Morning busy corresp & arranging answer to Butter. At 3.30 knocked off & went to Chap Str & post. Bought shoes & went walk with Emma up Hard Plat! Till tea time. Saw Pickover. After tea went to library on machine & changed book then gave Pickover some lessons on bike, he managing quite by himself. At 9.30 I called in at Chapel Str for a bit & home by 10.35.

Rose at 8.0 and after breakfast arranged answer to McAuslan counting 3300 Gibs. Went to post & Chapel St before dinner. After dinner stamp work & **wrote to Emily & Arthur**. Diary at 5.0. Went out to post and at 6.0 Harry helped me home with bike crate. At 7.15 I went to Garden Str till 8.0 then Chapel Str till 10.0 and home. Very wet at 9.0 or so. Rec letter from Mrs. Scully saying that Alf arrived at Para July 12th.

Dull morning. Fine moonlight night. Morning corresp & stamp work till 11.0 when I called at Chap Str and Garden Str and had a wash all over. After dinner I tidied upstairs and cleaned bike going out after tea to top of the Moss for a ride. Saw H Long who called in at Chap Str with me.

Grand morn. Afternoon dull. Rose and went to library to see weather forecast which was so poor that I almost abandoned straight off projected ride. Smooched about and after dinner changed and thought of going to see Burnley Scott Park opened but went walk to Bford & Colne with Emma instead. Had tea at Chapel Str afterwards went to library till 9.30. Grand read thro' Strand & rc. Came home 10.0.

Dull rainy morn. Rose at 8.0 and after bkfst & read went to Chapel Str finding letters from both Arthur £5 & Mrs. Mc. Had to give up cycling though on a/c of weather and now think of going to Sport & then on somewhere. Came home 11 and wrote diary & c. After dinner went down town and got tickets & c and called in at office as there were losing. After tea spent the evening about town; and on fairground everybody being busy and holiday making. Saw M & HM off to Edinburg at midnight & slept at Chapel Str; Mr.& Mrs. Mtford having gone to Brum.

Weather beautiful. Rose early and got to station in good time with bike. Got into carriage with Rennie & Harr & Maly Wood; arriv at Sport at 10.30 and after a wash and bkfst went out with H & M till dinner time. After dinner had a run on machine round cemetery & St Lukes. After open being holidays. Tea went to opera house. Derby Winner. Most of them cried. Came home 10.30 and sleep in small room with Rennie.

Rose early & went out with Rennie before bkfst. Went to St Philips Church; good choir, alone. After dinner went with the others carriage drive to Crossens & Banks. Came on to rain. After tea having gone to see Jim & failed I went out with H & M and met him (Jim). Came home 9.30 and had singing & music till 11.30.

Day fine & showery.

Monday 12th – 18th August

Day fine on the whole. Monday after bkfst went to market library & Picture Gallery. Coming back at 11.0 found Mary's friends waiting for her. After dinner we 5 went to Botanics & had rather a slow do (some dancing) returned in a landau and after tea I was out on new prom on bike but it was very windy so at 7.0 I went up to Station with the others to see Mary's friends off Alice Broham & Eliza Smith (?). Met Tom Barton & Ed Whitehead & stayed on prom till 10.30 then had music till 12.0 at home.

Morning dull to fair. Morning met Ed & Tom & the two girls and walked round Cemetery and St Luke's till dinner time. After which we had 2 hours sail Lpool way. Jim had gone to Llandudno. After tea Tom, Ed & myself had an hours bike run to Crossens & Banks which being 12 miles was very good in the time. We then met the girls at 9.0 on prom & I made the acquaintance of two from Bradford Clitheroe as Tom & Ed monopolized the others. Lizzie & Naomi! Good gracious!

After breakfast Tom having gone to Blackpool, Ed & myself with H & M went to Hesketh Park; at noon Ed & I had a swim in baths.

After dinner was busy writing and had a run on machine. At 4.0 met Jim & Mitch & Berry with Ed & the girls went to opera "**Mikado**". Rennie & Emma & Mac & Annie also going. A walk on prom after.

Modern Day Blackpool, 2015

Dull and raining in evening. Rose at 6.0 and after brkfst Ed, myself, the girls & Jim, Mitch & Berry took the 8 o'clock boat to Blkpool.

I taking luggage & machine also played cards on way; very smooth sea. Found Blkpool very busy but leaving things at Mrs. Ficks where the Rileys are staying. We all had a walk around and into the P of W Baths (fun) and after dinner Jim & mates went to **Winter Gardens** & we to the circus under tower. I saw them off to Sport at 6 o'clock & then met the Rileys and went to see the "**New Woman**" at Grand. Very good.

Emma & Gladys also thro tea. I went alone to Winter Gardens where I met **Mary of Halifax, a charming girl**! We were together all time and had a walk on prom afterwards till 10.30 when I agreed to meet her in morning off Adelaide Street.

Morning on prom. Saw Arthur off to Sport but Jim & c didn't turn up. Visited South Shore by tram & at dinner time saw picture "Flave Mort". Saw Mr.Dutton who served drinks (9d ea). Afternoon we all went to Tower and I went to top and got photo'd. After had tea 6d at Garstang and then met Mr. Fred Smith of Sanwrk. Nuisance Inspector of the NCK & a young lady Miss Emily Hamer riding tandem. Went to Lancaster together where I put up at Hamers. M Smith showed me round Lane & the club where he tried to teach me billiards. Had a ride on tandem & I left him at 9.30 and spent the evening chatting & music with Emily.

Morning fine. Great influx of visitors. On prom before brkfst at 9.45 met Mary and were on Central Pier till noon. Then changed to cycling suit and after dinner at 3 o'clock made a start, having had spanner & c stolen had to buy fresh ones. Road via Poulton & St Michaels. Dist 25 miles in 4 hours.

Saturday go to Brly Wormwells & c if back from Holidays if not next week.

Fine and very hot.

Rose at 8.20 and after bkfst walked to Asylum only to find Arthur and Agnes out for the day. Stayed in the Park till noon. After dinner went to school to see Mr. Smith & then made a start for Kendal via Milathorpe. Stayed at our old shop the Dolphin OJC for an hour 5-6 and had good tea. Reached Windermere at 7.30 over grand Switchback Road. Scenery fine, put up at Mrs. Christophersons. Walked to Bo'ness (resembles Hampton Court) and coming back made friends with Emma C & two gentlemen from Ashton under Lyne. Agreed to rise at 6.0 and mountaineer.

Dist run 30 miles in 4.5 hours.

Publisher note: My husband took 4.5 hours to run the London Marathon, which is 26 miles! He must have been a pretty decent runner.

Monday 19th – 25th August

Morn dull to fine. Rose at 6.0 and went to top of Forrest Head with my two friends. Grand view of the whole of Winere from the top. After bkfst I walked to Buness Stork Steamer for Lake side. Walked to Newly bridge. Steamer was very crowded coming back. Made two friends. 1 cyclist one commercial at Mrs. C who tried to mash Emma. Grand Road but warm to Ambleside 6m and amid plenty of turnouts & tourists started a stiff climb via Grasmere, Thistmere & passing Skeddaw & Helvellyn to Keswich & Werwentwater. Beautiful in the extreme! Tea & a long dark ride to Penrith.

Dist **39miles in 7 hours**.

Penrith dull place; saw Mr. Alt Barmly at Post Office. Getting out of the hilly district now and over broad moors to appleby & had dinner at Mrs. Hunns CJC at K Stephen. Very little sun wh made it cooler over good roads thro Seabergh, Lonsdale to Ingleton; put up at Mrs. Lumbs, Ingleton. Nice pretty place very dark night. Machine keeps making a clanking noise.

Dist 54 m in 9 hours.

Fine day, very hot. Had a 2 hrs walk up Beaugley falls after bkfast. Then rode to Lutle and had lunch at "Commercial" CJC and then to Long Preston and Gisburn. Where I spent my last copper on a drink. Entered smoky Nelson at 4.30 after very warm work. Came up to Vale Str and had tea & a change then down town to Chap Str & c. Saw H Long and walked round with him & then Garden Str till 10.30 for my luggage.

Dist 31m in 4 hours.

Total distance 179 miles in 28 ½ hrs. Av. 6 ¼ miles per hr.

Day rainy, fine but dull after. Spent most of day rushing about settling things, cleaned bike and took same to Mac for repairs. After tea wrote to Jus Moss & Arthur & post. Went out with Alice, Emma & Harr round bottoms. Home q. Soon.

Showery. Well at night. Morning corresp & c library. After dinner shoemakers, haircut, took 3.15 train to Brnly to get crank repaired of bike. Had tea at Aunt Mgts and came back 6.30. Finished meline at Macs and after took round town, saw Mac & Willie Widdup off to France and came home at 10.30.

Morning corresp & round town calling in at shed.

Afternoon walking round with Emma & went to Brly with Alice. At 4.30 had tea at Bella's and walk round Scott Park with Anthony. Alice was rather unwell but Emma & Rennie turned up and we played cards, rc. Came home 10.30. Vale Str at 11.30. Open being last sound perhaps in Nelson.

Cold & dull. Wet at night. Rose 8.30. Went to church in morn. Rev Edwards away. Saw H Long. After dinner called in at Gdn Street & Chap Str & went out with Alice & H Long up Marsden Height. Had tea along with Harr (little), Mary Wood & Alice Halstead and the others at Annie's. Afterwards went to church. Alice & Harry not going. Saw Fred Wainright. Stayed at Annie's till 9.30. Very wet. Abe Scott is down from Keighley & sleeps with me.

Monday 26th – 1st September

Well on the whole. Morning round town with Abe. Afternoon library &c. Evening after tea Chap Str and went with Alice up Nelson wrote 4 letters in afternoon.

Well again. Morning one thing & another afternoon saw Ed. Wild & library evening up at Annie after going to Garden Str &c. Saw Harry Long.

Wet in evening. Before dinner weather being so poor jacked up cycling & started taking machine to pieces and packing up. After round town, it having dried up. Saw Alice Talstd and Mary Wood. Spent an hour or so with Dr. Robinson chatting. He goes to **New Zealand** this year.

Turned to fine but cloudy morning read Til Bits, and walk round town; library &c. Afternoon working carpentry &c After tea called in at Chapel Str and to Willies staying till 10.30.

Morning buying in iron for box also strengthening same. Saw Git at office. After dinner was packing &c "Pudding" photographed us. After tea was round town till 8.0. Came up to Vale Str and had drinks round. Met Alice at 9.0 and went up to station after a bit of supper. Got a thro train to M/c arriving there about 11.30.

Got acquainted with Mr.& Mrs. Ireland who **thought Alice & I were wed and even asked her how many children she had**!

Left Vic at 12.30 via Stockport. Arrive Birmingham, Northampton &

Iring arriving at Euston about 8 o'clock, went by Metro rlwy to Westmr and found our diggings very handy & good frontage on bridge end.

Had brkfst and then saw The House of Lords, steamer to London Bdge, subway, Tower Brdge. Tower.

Alice & I were both tired & sleepy tho' and had a long rest at Tower Gardens. Then walked to Poultry and took bus to Hyde Park, Marble Arch, walked across to Albert Memorial & bus thro' Piccadilly to Trafalgar Square.

Had tea and then took bus to **Adelphi** to see opening season with **Saword and Daughter**. Had over an hour standing outside. Saw H longs bro?! Beautiful moonlight night, got home about 12 by Thames Embankment.

Rose at 8.0 bkfst at 10 after shave. We're going to Westminster Abbey but being late went on to St Paul's 10.30 service. Left before sermon and took bus to Hyde Park. Saw the "Church Parade" and dinner at a French restaurant, took Putney bus and boat to Kew 4d.

It was a beautiful day & very warm. **Kew Gardens** were very nice and we enjoyed well. Two hours ride home by bus and got look in by a pirate after all charging 1/6 to Liverpool Str. Train to Hackney arriving 7.15.

Saw **Aunt Sarah, Wally (refer to p.266), & Uncle C** soon came in. Lottie had a little boy yesterday night and may call him Charles. Left at 10.45 and train & bus to Westminster getting in by midnight.

Pidió que la a compañía en el cuarto hasta que justo el cabello. Sufrí tentación, pero sin ser tonto y la bese nomas. ¡Dejará de ser la más completa tentación!

[Translation: She asked me to accompany her to her room and she even released her hair. I suffered temptation, but without being foolish, I kissed her all the same. It will be the most complete temptation!]

Monday 2nd – 8th September

Another fine day & terribly warm. Left Westminster at 9.50 and looked thro' Nat Gallery and then up Strand to St Paul's doing business with field & Color photo firm on way wh lost us a lot of time. Train to Farringdon Str and saw Harrilds abt ruling machine.

At 3 had dinner at ABC Cheap Fleet Str and then bus from Holborn to Oxford Street walked down Regent Str and thro' Westminster Abbey. Steamer after collecting luggage to London Bdge. Underground from Monument to Gower Str. Left luggage & went on to Earls Court wh was very nice. Went on wheel and saw the lights of London dimmed however by the full moon. Left at 10.0 and made our way to Gower Str and Euston and for a third class to ourselves to Stockport leaving Euston at 11.30 and arriving m/c.

At 7.0 it was rather warm on way & we didn't sleep much. Took bus up to Harperby and saw **John, Emma & baby** who can now both speak and walk well. We had bkfst and short sleep on sofa & then leaving Alice asleep I went down for our luggage.

After dinner and a rest we took tram down to City but it started a regular storm so we only had a short run round getting back to tea by 6.0. Saw Catlings & left at 8.55 catching the 9.35 train. Both Rev Fry & Parker Taylor (drunk) were in same carriage & darker who knows. Alice sang a bit. Arrived Nelson 11.30 and after a bit of supper at Chapel Str came home.

Rose at 8.0 and busy finishing crate. I got it down to station after dinner and then passed time at Chap Str. Back at 5 and wrote up diary. After tea went to H Longs and stayed till 9.30 then town and Chap Str.

Morning busy packing & Chap Str. Bought Mrs. Macs books & rc.

After dinner still packing and met Alice and went to Brly 4.15 train to Aunt Margaret's back via Brly Lane and Maggie Hartley's arriving in Nelson 8.0. Harry Long was at Chap Str and we spent a pleasant evening till 9.45. Maggie gets moves on 14th. All day on the rush. Got box packed by afternoon. Had a bath at Garden Str at 11.30 and stayed to dinner. Had tea at Vale Str and got 2 boxes taken to station. Visited Coop library & got my release from Coulton. Saw Pickover at club & stayed with him till 9.30. I had visited in morning. I then took parcels from Vale Str to Chapel Str and visited Willie Riley & Mac getting in at 11.0 pouring rain.

Rose at 4.20 had woke at 3.0 dressed said goodbye to H & wife. Took 2 parcels to station & called Annie going on to Chapel Str had a snack and got to station with HM Alice, Emma. Harry Long soon came but couldn't got to Lpool as he hadn't a weaver. Rennie turned up & we had a fast train to Lpool getting out at Sandhills station.

It was wet & gloomy & we were all rather in dumps, **Alice especially**.

I missed the tea crates wh went on to exch so after, a look at the vessel which looked very dirty. We went on overhead railway to town & got parcel & had breakfast at Oriels. Got back to Huskesoon docks and at 12.0 they left for shore having a kiss all round.

Alice had tears in her eyes.

They kept in sight till we got out of docks by which time it was turning out a lovely day. Watched the coast, had a read & chat with Boyd. Lunch at 1.30, dinner 7.30 (poor) & a lovely moonlight night. Reading in saloon & semi-concert. Turned in at 10.0

Good night but x.

Beautiful day. Off the Scillies in the evening.

Monday 9th – 15th September
Back to Gibraltar

Beautiful day and grand moonlight in the Bay.

Well in morning. Fine after. Sighted **Cap Firmaterre**.

Fine day but rougher. Righted the Burlings. The fellows still keep very distant and conceited.

Morning sighted Cape St Vincent. A lot warmer. Turned in during the afternoon have got so tired of the voyage.

Morning rose at 5.0 to find ourselves off **Cabrita Point**, a dull Levant. Anchored by 6 but had to wait for luggage so it was 9 when Boyd, myself and luggage landed; found Uncle waiting, he having come out to meet me.

Cart took things up and we followed afoot. Streets look awful narrow and bare. Saw Arthur on way up. Unpacked after breakfast and seeing Emily and Mrs. Mc.

Had a look down town shop and office & returned to dinner. At 2 I met Boyd at the Calpe and we walked to Caleta Bay and saw all the works in progress. Coming back we called on the Torries and had refreshments. I telephoned up to Frank at 4.30 but only had a few words as he was so busy. Walked home and had tea and then at 8.30 I went to Central and saw Frank. After a good chat, Scullard, Arthur & Rosere came up.

Left at 10.30 and Arthur and I had a long chat. Agreeable to 8/- a week rent free.

Saturday morning posted letters to Alice and visited office besides putting machine together in the morning. Went up South before 12 on bike and leaving it at Deareco went down Camp Bay and bathed; didn't see Frank but did Mr. Murphy. Saw Frankie's mother & the others at Armstrong's Buildings and again al Deareco to tea and rode home at 6.30 finishing up at Mrs. Mes and shop.

Warm East wind. Morn rose 6.30 in boat with Arthur & Willie Roscoe. Afterwards hunted up Boyd and went to St Andrews. Saw Lottie Torrie there who only lately returned from England. Afternoon, Mc and Central, walk with Frank to Alameda & tea upstairs. Then to Cathedral with Arthur & Em then walk on Saluting Battery. Walk to St Josephs and stormy meeting on reflecting Frank's play he resigned. Band La Independencia plays for last time. Was there for a while with Frank.

Monday 16th – 22nd September

About 8.0 and Levant. Started shop after bkfst and rather slack. Learning prices &c and in evening saw Lucy Hume and at 9.30 went out on machine with Ch Eds & Maxten up New Mole till 10.30. Very hot work.

Still as hot Levant. It blew great guns last night evening. Left shop at 8.0 and visited Rec Rooms till 9.30 when I wrote to Harr M chatting & diary.

Doing some stamp work and bookkeeping at shop.

Patty coming down at dinner time and stopping to tea I went up South with Emily and her at 7.30 intending to take John's shots to Miss Walker but coming across Rearees we found she was at Rosia so went there and spent a pleasant evening coming down at 10.30. A bit rainy.

Am reading and doing my own bookkeeping at shop. Went to band after closing up with Arthur & Willie R but left them and saw Frank at 10.0 staying till it finished. Afternoon bathed with F at Camp Bay coming back in bus.

Evening was a couple of hours upstairs chatting. Came home after closing up. Arthur was boating in afternoon with Bob Hume.

Afternoon Arthur & Em were out boating. After tea I was at lodge & played billiards. A short walk came across Frank afterwards. East wind all week Levant.

East wind freshened to gale & rain in afternoon. Morn went up South to St Joseph's School and bathed at midday. Dinner at 1.0 and went with Arthur in boat to Camp Bay. Walked to Franks house & back to Camp Bay. Arthur then left for town alone & Frank & I walked to Wind Mill Hill. We had tea at Franks along with Manuel & then music on at Miss Stillwells. Home by 10.0.

Monday 23rd - 29th September

Morn in shop. Afternoon in shop. Evening met Boyd & friend and went to concert on Casemates Sq. Finished up by torchlight tattoo. Also met Frank & Manuel & took them home to see photos & c

Afternoon **Arthur went to Algeciras** with Boyd. Evening at Rec Rooms and stroll with Frank.

Afternoon went to Rosia with Frank who had come to town to meet me. Saw Acquatic Sports. Bathed at Camp Bay and back by 5.30.

Afternoon went out to North Front to see Gymkhana, band of Cameron's. I met Mr. Pearce, Patty & the Miss Nivens there. Came back together. Rather dull day but cleaned up after. After tea shop and with Emily to band (Yorks). Took her home 10.0 and was with Frank till close.

Morning dusting bookshelves. Afternoon shop and at 4.30 had a short run on bike to New Mole & back in 20 Minutes. After tea went with Emily to Torries & saw Mr., Mrs. & Yothee. Pleasant evening chatting. They're none of them altered.

Rec letter from Alice. Morning diary & c. After dinner went up South by bus taking some bills to collect. Watched the aquatic sports at Rosia. Came back & let Arthur go to his tea and at 7.0 changed & went up to Pearces (I had taken the presents in the morning) with Jenny & Emily in a cab. Found Mr. Stewart, Mr. & Mrs. Finlay. Rosere, the Miss Nivens & others there. Had a good blowout & had singing & music in the yard it being a nice night & evening. Changed to West. Came home 12.30. I gave two songs.

Wind West & calm. In morning went out in boat with Arthur for short pull and then bathed at Devils Tongue. Breakfast & went to St. Andrews intending to meet Boyd but he had gone out somewhere, which made me indifferent to what he choose to do. In fact, the fellow is very lame, almost a fool. After seeing Mrs. Mc and having dinner and a read Arthur and I went over to Algeciras at 3.10 and saw the new pier. Had a stroll Los Barrios way and back by 5.10 steamer. Had tea & went to Cathedral with Emily. A short walk on Battery and then at Central till 10 o'clock.

Monday 30th – 6th October

Shop as usual wind turned to West still. After tea changed & went to **Zarzuela at Theatre Royal**. "Rep Chambra" good the rest indifferent. The intervals were so long allowed me to have supper at home & visit Frank at Central.

Wind changed to East. Grand but very warm. Evening shop till closing. Was at office a lot siding shop goods. At 9.30 went to Central till nearly eleven. Then read Reade's book till past midnight.

East wind. Took Mrs. Mc again to see Doctor Triay who tried her successfully with glasses. Evening shop till closing then Central.

Morning had a swim at Camp Bay going up High Rd on machine to school. Evening went up South to Pearces with Emily & stayed at band (Highlanders) on way back till the finish.

Afternoon **Arthur & Emily went out in boat**. Started to answer John's letter. Evening shop & central to see Frank.

Morning went up South & had a bathe at noon on machine. Afternoon started to write to John. Evening shop and at 9.30 went out on machine with C Eds & had grand moonlight ride to Gov. Cottage.

Morning boat. Tho' E. wind it warm's strong enough. Bathed. Church in morn. After dinner saw Mrs. Mc and Frank and Central; went to Alameda saw Mary Pritchard, Emily Niven, Patty & Lilla were down to tea, Mr.& Mrs. Pearce being at Granada.

Afterwards Cathedral & then went up South & had musical evening with Frank & Miss Stillwell & then came home at 10.30.

Monday 7th – 13th October

Fine & warm. E to W wind. Morn shop & went up South on machine to collect Ugametts a/c. Had bathe at Camp Bay with Frank & & afternoon there was a big fire at Cayes. Evening spent an hr at St Andrews Scripture

Club & then shop till closing & Rec Rooms till 10.15. Hot still E Wind. Am writing to John.

Wind W. cooler & breezy. Temp 70. Mrs. Mc unwell! Morning Orient liners in & some passengers ashore. Boyd left in the Orient at Midday without calling in to say goodbye. Sent letters to John, Evening shop till closing & Rec Rooms for a read.

Wind East. Cooler Temp 70. Morning 6.15. Boat with Arthur & Julius. Bright morning cool & row out to HMS Leander. Work non-particular. Dinner. Mrs. Mc a bit better today. Afternoon reading "Poor Jack". Tea & shop 9.0 went to band with Arthur & met Emily & the Miss Nivens.

East wind. Calm & sunny. Temp abt 70 to 73. Morning 7.30. Work cleaning photo album shelves. Dinner & change. Afternoon reading "Poor Jack". Saw Frank at Central. Tea, music, & shop 7.30. Diary stamp work. Arthur went up South & I stopped to close & then went upstairs & played cribbage.

Shop till 9.0 then got ready and went out with Frank & Manod in boat to Carthei. East wind took us there in an hour, but we took 5 hours to return tacking. It was enjoyable but rather slow. After tea I attended meeting at Oddfellows & then home. Read & bed.

East wind. Morning rose 8.15 & dressed for church, St Andrews. After dinner read & saw Mrs. Mc & then met Frank & went up South rather latish. Had walk, town, New Mole & Buena Vista & then tea at Franks & played cards Ronda. Didn't have music as Miss Stillwell RA is rumoured dead. Home 10.30.

Monday 14th – 20th October

Levant & then clear. 70. 9 boxes came up from S.J.S. Morning bkfst at shop. Very busy with the goods. After tea changed and went to S. Andrews meeting. Stayed at shop till closing & then home. Montegriffo's servant threw herself from the window.

East wind dull & threatening. Morn cleaning inks stand cupbd. After dinner stamps & c. Called at office to see bike wh Bro reported to be crooked & found to my dismay that the forks are cracked. In evening shop til 9.0 then up to Mount with Arthur & brought Emily home.

Morning saw Frank at Central to say couldn't go tomorrow to Rivers. After bkfst settling the 6d novels & parcel of more books from Sampson Low. Evening Arthur went up to Rosia and I closed shop and visited Aunt & played crib.

W. Yorks band. Morning ordinary. Afternoon took bike out to Lorries for repairs but had to fall back on Ballantyne who took it home. Had a run round Eastern Beach however. After tea went to Universal and at 9.0 to band being with Jose who came home & had supper with me.

Foggy in morning. Morning stamp work also in afternoon when Arthur & Em went out in boat. Made up 5 appshts. After tea, shop and cleaned out window.

The sad news rec of Mrs. Pauleans death while on her way out to Gib in Anchor ship SS Bolivia. Buried at sea 2 days out.

Levanty all week, abt 70 degrees. Morning finishing out windows, then diary & c. After dinner walked to Camp Bay & embarked in boat which Frank & another fellow had taken out there. We tacked about & then got down to wharf by sunset enjoying the out very well. Leaving the boat there came up to the shop & tea after. Went with Jose to the cafes a bit & then helped to close & went home & to bed early.

Rojelio debe 67 run por navajas o'sea 10f Inglese y 1.50 ademas

Morn fresh from E. went out with Arthur sailing to Campo. After bkfst St. Andrews & upstairs before dinner. After dinner went out with Arthur for a walk to Victoria Park & North Front, calling on Margarita on way. Came across the Torries of RF. Home to tea after putting boat in her berth. Then went with Uncle to St Andrews. Poor congregation & then Central stopping with Frank till 10.0 who is being chaffed abt Zammitts sister! Home & read till 11.30.

Monday 21st - 27th October

Shop as usual. Evening saw Ballyntyne about mehne & was at shop. Arthur going up to **Buena Vista**. Closed up & went home & wrote to H Long till midnight.

Grand day but foggy. Morn shop as usual & cleaning out dictionary shelf & c. Evening Pearces were down at Aimts so I was up & played whist.

Turned to wet at intervals with a strong SW wind. Morn nothing particular except reading Lynns Galon. Afternoon smooching. After tea changed & shop till 8.30 then café with Jose and to theatre to see "**Rebohea & Duo Africana**". Came home 11.0 very wet.

Very wet. J Chamberlain came yesterday. Slow business all day. Am reading "**Mdme Crysantheme**". Evening preparing essay on Luke X v.38. Also went upstairs a bit after helping to close shop as the Mc Clouds were there.

Still wet. My eye is troubling me so I tried to see the doctor but failed. In evening visited Rec Rooms & shop till closing.

Wet at intervals and stormy. Heavy sea running. After dinner saw doctor and got some eye wash. Also had a bath in Market Str and after tea, shop and central till 10.0 home and bed.

Communion Sunday. Rose late & feel eye worse. Got to church & stayed to communion, being over 2 yrs since last time. Afternoon writing out essay; vis Mrs. mc & Central going up with Frank at 4.0 had a short walk & back at home to tea going with **Uncle & Jinny** to St Andrews. Watched 2nd communion & may prove to be Mr. Murray's farewell sermon. Walked to Battery with Rennie afterwards & then up to St Josephs. Met Frank & Manuel & young Andrews & went round past Gov. Cottage being grand moonlight. Home 10.30.

Monday 28th – 3rd November

Grand clear day, cold. Visited Signal station. After dinner changed to knickers and went Willie's from where after meeting Frank & ADay we went to signal station. Nice walk & good view. Wind changed to East. Got home after 5 and changed & had tea, then at 7.0 went to vestry and gave my paper on Luke X 38-42. 6 of us there. Rennie, Fraser, Campbell & Piper (2 more)! It went off fairly well but agreed to bring it up a bit.

Shop till closing & Hall for dance till 11.15, quadrille, schottische, waltz, & lancers.

Very wet & colder. Shop all day and after closing went on writing to Harriett. Rec letter from Alice. Took bike back home. Cost $1 for repairs.

Fine day. 64 degrees or so. Morn shop. After dinner shop. Mail parcels. At 4 I had a run out to Torries, North Front on bike & back at 5.0. After tea shop as Arthur was going out to Roscoes with Emily. Closed at 9.45 and went up on terrace till 10.45. Mrs. Slather, Lottie & Evan & Charlie being there too.

Estar tío con la idea de cambiar el nombre a E.A.B. mientras que estar pintando la tienda y Arturo y yo contra la idea. También quiere que tomamos un salario de £10 semanal. Que es lo que quiere (?) el guardase la tienda por el mismo. Yo quiero que Arthur o yo y Arthur hablamos para saber si novamos a tener parte con él o que sepa bien como es la cosa. Dios cuiden nosotros.

[Translation: Uncle has the idea of changing the name of the shop to E.A.B. whilst it is being painted. Arthur & I are against the idea. He also wants us to take a weekly salary of £10. Does he want the shop for himself? I would like Arthur, or both Arthur & I to chat the situation over with him. God look after us.]

Nice day but dull & rainy at night. Nice and cool. Arthur went out to **Spain for day with Bob Hume** so I was alone. Gas turned crazy and had to call repairer. At 7.0 I went up home with Frank & Manuel and had tea together & played games. Miss Park also being down.

Lucy Hume's Wedding Day. Rainy warmer. Could not see the ceremony as Arthur came back from dinner too late. Afternoon saw Dr and got more med for eye. After tea at 6.30 played mandolin & changed.

Shop till 8.30 when Arthur & I went up to Humes and had refreshments. I played sev. airs on mandolin and sang "Tommy" le dumno & several others. Span & English. Came away 11.0.

Fine day. S W Wind. After dinner took machine out for a run to Rosia finding Pearces out and owing to the death of Mr. Arthur of the Castle. At 4 Arthur had vestry meeting to attend. After tea playing mandolin & shop. Called at Mrs. Mc on way home.

Colder W wind. Keen fresh morning. Cool thro the day. Rose at 8.0. After bkfst church St Andrews, Uncle going too. Saw Mrs. Mc and stopped at Rec rooms. At 2.30 went up South but found Frank was on duty so went alone to New Mole and Alameda. Tea with Frank & Manuel and then singing & music at Miss Stillwells till 9.30. Walk to Gov Cottage. Home 11.30. Locked out. Grand moonlight.

Monday 4th – 10th November

W wind fine & clear, cool. Prepared to get shop painted by Stewart's man. After tea at 7.0 had a continuation meeting at the vestry when **I again took the chair**. Stopped in the shop till close and then was at Hall dance till 11.30. Didn't do much.

Shop in a mess with painter. Evening shop till 8.0. Went up South with parcel along with young Scullard. Met Frank & Day at St Josephs & then had a walk to Europa. Home 10.45. Moonlight but waning.

East wind. Evening writing letters. Arthur went up South with Emily on a message leaving me to close and then I went home for correspondence.

Afternoon visited Torries NF and had good run on bike finishing up on alameda to hear band. Now changed to afternoons. Evening visited Humes with Emily.

Evening visited Theresa & Carlotta with Mrs. Mc then shop till closing. Painter finished.

Afternoon was out on North front seeing Highland sports going out on bike. Shop till closing and home reading "**That Frenchman**".

Rose in morning at 7.0 and was out on bike at North Front with Beleno who can ride alright now. Also got into Spain with it. Home to bkfst by 9.40 much enjoyed the spin. St Andrews and after dinner down to Dockyard by 1.15 and on board "**Skipjack**" to see Street; were shown round the boat thoroughly and had tea in mess. Came ashore to Cathedral with Street & picked up Emily at home. After church the four of us a long walk round Europa. Home and supper. Street seems a very nice all-round kind of fellow but not as jolly as H W Long.

Monday 11th – 17th November

Fine and warmer. Am worse with eyes so saw Dr again. Finished reading

"**Frenchman**". Shop till closing and then Rec Rms till 10.0. Did not feel up to going to Vestry meeting or dance.

Evening ac. Emily up to Hume's and saw her home at 9.30 and then Central. Frank on duty putting in part time at shop.

Evening Mr.& Mrs. Kirkwood came down at 7.30 and I saw them till 8.0 and shop till closing; then they left at 10.0 or so and we were upstairs a bit Pearce's having come down.

Grand day. Warmer. Saw J Pauleson. Afternoon Mrs. Evans was in at 4.30 to say Jim's ship the anchor lines "California" was in so asked permission to go on board in the launch with Micklereid, but just as we were leaving Jim with his father & Ms Whalley came ashore. Bought serge from Street. We all went up together to Mrs. Whalley's and had tea & then walked up town to the shop. Jim looks very well in uniform & is even **taller than in 1894**. Stayed in shop till closing then central till 10.0.

68 degrees. Dull day. Damp no rain. Eyes still bother one. Shop all day till closing time, then Rec Rooms till 10.0 home bed. Intend to start a private philatelic collection again.

Dull day. Afternoon shop. Left shop at 8.30 and home changed & went out cycling with Chase & Maxted till 10.30.

Morn went out in boat with Arthur & W. Roscoe as far as Nio being good sailing but dark Levanter. After bkfst smooching till dinner. Mrs. Mc visit & c. After dinner was upstairs chatting with Uncle till 3.30 when I went to Central up South at 4.0 with Frank and had a walk. Went to St Joseph's evensong then tea with Manuel & Horatio for company. Had thought reading & music till 10.0.

Monday 18th – 24th November

East wind. Levant. Morning Mr. Mosley came into shop and I agreed to give him a few lessons. After dinner & a change went out to North Front and went out to North front and met Frank & Manuel and leaving machine at Torries watched the races till 5.0 when Mr. Mosley had a go on bike till gunfire. Rode to shop and after tea changed. Shop till closing & supper with Uncle. Dance till 12.0 dancing 4 or 5 times. Annie Moon, Taylor & others. Arthur & Emily up at Pattips birthday party.

East wind, dull. Evening in shop alone. Arthur going to Rec Rooms concert. Closed at 10.0 making up Gib sheet. Home & bed.

East wind, dull. Afternoon saw doctor and after tea went to Theatre. Mrs. Salacroup's juvenile concert which was very good comprising zarzuela & Spanish dancing. To bed at 12.45. Italians from wreck ashore. Also plenty Austrians from Man-0f-War.

Wind dropped for change. In afternoon took meeting to North Front and got chain tightened at Torries. Gave Mr. Mosley another lesson and had a run round with Fromow. Evening shop till 9.45 making up Gib sheet & c. Arthur mandolin.

Change of wind. Fine and sunny. Saw Pitman in morning about collection of stamps. Afternoon shop also at night till closing. Home and bed.

Fine and sunny. Afternoon was out at 2.30 with Mr. Mosley and machine. Got another spoke loose. Had a ride round with Fromow and sister. Evening shop very busy till 9.30. Home and stamp sorting till nearly 11.30. Bed.

Young Street was down to tea. Morning out in boat with Arthur to watch the Malabar till 9.15. After bkfst changed and wrote letters to Harry Mtford and started one to Gitty. After dinner at 3 went up South and on New Mole with Frank going on board the Malabar to see Campbell of the Cameroons who goes home. Had a walk round Buena Vista with Frank & Day seeing Carmen & Rosa. Tea at home at 5.15 and the Cathedral. On battery with Emily & chatting with Street. Saw him as far as Battery then finished letter. Bed at 12.

Monday 25th – 1st December
Rain at intervals. Evening shop till closing then Rec Rooms till 11.0 or so. Evening stamp work on Leafs sheets. Up to late. Closed shop myself Arthur being out. Rain to fine. Dull evening as I had catalogue covers, not go on with the stamps so went to rec rooms.

Rain all day. Busy with first 5 of Leafs shts which took me all day and up to midnight to square.

Nada particular. (Translation: Nothing particular)

Busy with stamps. Short walk with Arthur & Emily after supper being nice night.

Morning up at South Chapel 9.00 service. Then met Frank & went to school & saw Mrs. Jones. After dinner & a read, Patty being down and as usual behaved like an earthquake. Saw Mrs. Mc & a read after tea then Central till 10 o'clock. Raining hard most of day.

Monday 2nd - 8th December
Mrs. Mc caught chill while washing. Evening after closing home. Stamp work was intended but after missing seeing Lucy who goes to India tomorrow. I feel too unwell so went to bed.

Evening after closing stamp work. At Central till 10.45.

Evening shop till closing & then central till 10.45. Stamp work.

Evening at 8.0 left shop and went on with stamp work. At Central till 10.45. Mrs. Mc only mending.

Busy all day being fine but levanty. Evening went to see "**Rey que rabio**" at **Royal**. Free ticket. Serg to mess with Jose.

Grand day. N W wind. Morning St Andrews getting up late. After dinner & a read at Rec went out in boat with **Arthur & Willie** sailing up to **La Linea**. Went up South at Sunset and met Frank outside St Josephs and attended service being a grand procession of Daughters of Mary. Then tea at Franks & a chat on geography till 9.30 then a walk up the hill where we discomfited young Manuel then home to tea.

Monday 9th – 15th December

Evening did not go to dance below but went on with Leaf's sheets.

Finished working on Leaf's sheets for a bit having got a lot on sale.

Caught cold today in head so had hot foot bath at night. Very busy all time at shop. Improved shop by removing fan light over door. Evening hot water bottle in bed.

Feeling a bit better of my cold.

A lot better of my cold. Did not close shop till 10 o'clock.

Poor **Chicardo** died this morning. **Charlie Stacher** came out in boat in morning but was too rough to be pleasant with fresh W. N W wind. Morn church. After dinner Mrs. Mc and South going behind Rock with Frankie for walk. Home to tea and then letter writing to **John and Uncle Charles**.

Sunday 22nd December

Morn dull. Rain all day after. In morn, went up S. Chapel & reform service. Mr. Murray lending me his waterproof to come down with. Afternoon Mrs. Mc & Rec Rooms. After tea St Andrews Church & then Frank at Central.

Monday 23rd - 29th December

Nothing particular except fine day. Dr in afternoon – ointment this time. Evening after closing stamp work at Central.

Nothing particular. Very busy.

Very busy in shop. At 8.0 Frank called for me and we went up to supper at his house along with Frederick. Fermin also came in. Frank to go away in a hurry at 9.15 to go on duty so I stayed on till 11.0. Music in Miss Stillwells then I went to Central and with Frank at 11.30 to St Mary's in the organ loft with Stopgood to the **misa de gallo**. Very good music but we were in a bad place for observation.

Wet all day. Morn went with Arthur & Em to Cathedral to service. After dinner stamp album. At tea **Uncle & Aunt (Uncle Emmett is now married)** were down & Mr. Stewart came in after so we had card games. I went to Mrs. Stewarts and Central afterwards. Quiet Xmas but pleasant on the whole.

Morning reading and after dinner stamp counting. Met Frank on Saluting Battery and walked down with him going on to Wharf. Mrs. Torrie & Lottie were up to spend the evening & Arthur & Willie P came in too. Emily & c accomp Torries home.

Fine day. Got back to shop but fell slack set up. In afternoon went on board "**California**" with Carnduff and spent a couple of hours with Jim Paulesen on board. Shop & Central after closing.

Morning did not feel so well of cold so stayed indoors. After dinner went with Em down Main Street, she going to Torries, and then met F at Central. Went up South in bus and then walk up hill. Church at St Joseph's **agua bendita (holy water)** then tea at South. After a walk round to Monkey cave with F and Horatio. Home 11.0. Grand moonlight.

Monday 30th – 31st December
Fine moonlight. Work at shop again. Evening short walk on Saluting Battery with Frank 8 to 9.30 then stamp work till 11.0.

Jinny of a Son at 5.10 p.m.

Evening being very busy in shop. Left at 7.0 and after quick tea went up South meeting Frank & crowd outside church. Albert came down with us to tea at Franks then music at Mess Stillwells and at 11.0 Frank & I came down town. Saw the new Jcas in opposite Convent. Home 1.30. **Jinny doing well so's baby.**

Commenced with illness and indecision as to my stay in England. From Easter to end of August one succession of holidays on bike &c at intervals and from my return to Gib, hardly able to form an opinion.

With Arthur I maintain a **cordial yet rather distant intercourse.**

With Emily **reserved tho sympathetic** & with Mrs. Mc **the best of relationships.**

Find I'm keeping very fond of Alice as a cousin. Rest rather forgetful of. Frank again my bosom churn & long may he remain so.

Slight flirtation with Leonora...

***

Several lists for each month of letter written.

Letters Received & Sent

Alice, Nelson
Andrews, J.D.
Annie Widdup
Arthur, GIB plc
Arthur Lane
Aunt Emma, London
Auslan Mc A
Butcher Mr
Butler (£5)
C Pickover
Cook & sons
Dr Robinson
Ed Hedley
Edwin Healey
Emily, GIB
Emma B, Nelson
F. Ullmer
Frank
Guardian Off
H Mountford
Hall Gio – Inland Revenue
Harr GIB
Harr London
HW Long

JB Sport
JB M/c
J. A. Palfrey (Mrs. Harrian)
J Paterson
J Moss Liverpool
J. Sierra
J Sierra, Seville
John M/c
John Nelson
Mac Mrs.
Miss M Scott, Scotland
Mrs. Mae
Mrs. Saword, London
Paulesen J
Riley, Nelson
Saword C.E.
Scully
Stanley Gibbons
Sydney Saword, Ireland –
June 16th
Uncle Charles
Uncle Emmett
Weller Mr

N.B. There are some Beanland names in the period mentioned at Burnley Cemetery.

LETTERS

OF

ALBERT BEANLAND

1942 ~ 1951

**Charles Frederick Beanland, Albert Beanland
& Malcolm Beanland**

11th June 1942

My dear Hortensia & Charles,

Your letter of the 9th has arrived very quickly and I am so glad that the pram has pleased both you and Charles as well as the other things.

I am not surprised that you found the letter very short and I was very sorry that it was so but **I was feeling rather depressed** on that particular day due to some business worries which I have been having, and by the copy of my letter to my dad you will get an idea of what it is all about and I can tell you darling as time passes **I am finding it more and more difficult the burden which fell on my shoulders in 1940** and though you know me well, as you know how many difficulties come my way I try never to lose heart but always look at things on the bright side, but **there is a limit to human endurance** and believe me darling if it was not for my father I would not mind throwing the towel in and give it up as a bad job, but unfortunately my nature is not like that and when I promise something I try to carry it out no matter how hard same might be, and the more sacrifices I have to make the better I like it, strange don't you think when it is the **habit nowadays for people to find the easiest way out**.

With regard to going over, I think I shall have to leave it till the third week in July as at the end of June we have all the work of stock taking to do which is rather a lot (if not ask Wilfred who helped me last year) and so I want to leave everything ready by the time I go.

I hope Wilfred & Scullard are enjoying themselves. I hope Wilfred does appreciate that it is through my efforts that he is having a fortnight away, though I must agree he deserves it, and both Willie & Johnny are now beginning to realize what he does every day as they have to do it while he is away.

I am very pleased with my bonny boy **for the kisses he so nicely drew in your letter**. I am looking forward very much to the day when he will be able to give me a hand with the correspondence.

I heard very sad news yesterday for the little boy that was in the pram if you remember when we were at the Paris Café, died suddenly. He was the son of a friend of my school days, Frank Sant, he was one year old on the 29th May. What a terrible thing for both parents, especially for her who is completely alone, how she must feel it.

I am going to the Algeciras fair with Ted and thinking that Dolly might be coming over. I asked for permission to stop in Spain but I now hear from Frank, who I saw yesterday, that she has left it till the La Linea fair. I wish you had bucked up and come over.

Well my darling the wool you asked I cannot find it but I am sending another shade. Actually, the stock the shops had a few months ago had all gone and they do not anticipate receiving more.

Well, dearest I don't think I have any more news for the present and also till my next one with fondest love to you two as well as all the others,

Your loving & affectionate hubby,
Yours forever
Albert xxxxxxxxxxxx

Hortensia & Albert Beanland

Beanland, Malin & Co Ltd.
Established 1884
Printers, Lithographers, Stationers and Booksellers
76, Main Street and 2, Bedlam Court

Gibraltar, 1st December 1942

Dear Sirs,

As the year draws to a close we cannot fail to look back and recall the momentous events which have marked its passing, and thank the Almighty he has been pleased to allow us to bear witness to such historic occasions.

The passing of 1942 brings to an end another year of business association with you and we would like to take this opportunity of expressing both to you and to all the members of your staff our deepest and most sincere thanks for your loyal co-operation, and for the splendid service which you have dispensed to all the orders we have been privileged to place with you.

To use such splendid service came as a pleasant surprise, for we knew very well all the difficulties with which you had to contend, but believe us Gentlemen, we always knew that you would do your very best to "Carry On". We have not been disappointed!

Your continued support has been very gratifying not only to us but also to our thousands of clients, who are very often surprised to see that we are able to meet most of their requirements. We claim no credit for this, but we are pleased to give same where it is due, and we can safely say in this case that the credit is all yours.

It appears now that the War has entered a new phase, and it is with confident hearts that we face it. Just now the latest moves have been very near the Fortress, and Gentlemen we can say **Gibraltar has seen history in the making**. The famous "Rock" has been a witness of these events and we can safely say that we have both witnessed and felt that which we are pleased to call "Sea Power", as no other part of our great empire has yet had the chance.

When the History of this Great War has been written it will be found that Gibraltar has more than lived up to its name of "**The Key of the Mediterranean**".

Lastly, we wish to take this opportunity of repeating our most sincere thanks for your loyal co-operation, and also to wish you and all the members of your Staff our very best wishes for a very happy Christmas and the New Year.

Assuring you of our co-operation at all times.

We remain, Yours faithfully,

For Beanland, Malin & Co., Ltd.,
A Beanland, Acting Director

Charles Bolton Beanland, at 74 Main Street, Gibraltar

10th March 1951

My Dear Auntie,

We were all so glad to get your letter of the 22nd February and to hear that you were feeling much better and that you were receiving treatment which we hope will prove very satisfactory and that very soon it will have completely disappeared.

How very right you are in all you said in your letter with regard to my Dad, and you cannot imagine how empty this house is without him, and on many occasions in these past weeks I have come up from the shop thinking to see him about the house but alas it was only a dream.

He has left **such happy memories** that at least it is a great consolation to remember all those very happy times we all had together, and especially we were all so glad that he managed to **celebrate his Golden Wedding Anniversary**, a thing he had looked forward to so much, that it was a real treat to see him then in such good health and so happy to have us all with him, of course except Charlie and family who fortunately enough have been here in April and spent a nice holiday with him.

We can indeed all be very proud of having had such **a loving father who had devoted all of his life for us**, and there are **very few people who having started with so little are able during their lifetime show so much for their hard work as he has done**, and now it is up to the three of us to continue the good work but no matter how hard we might try I do not think we shall be able to accomplish as much as he did for he always seemed so tireless.

I am glad to say that my mother is bearing up much better than we thought at first, for at the beginning she was eating and sleeping so little.

At last we have been able to persuade her to go out in the car and for the last two Saturdays she has gone out with Johnny, Isabel, and Leonie to Los Barrios where we get our supply of fresh eggs.

The weather this Winter has been simply awful, and we have not had a fine day since the middle of January, so Hortensia has been obliged to keep the children indoors all the time.

You will be glad to hear that **little Albert**, who is now 9 months old, is getting on fine and Malcolm too is growing into a big lad and **shows signs of being very intelligent**. Charlie who is now nearly 11 years goes to the same school at Castle Road that his Grandad used to attend, as the building has now been handed over by the Military authorities to the local education department. All the children miss their dear Grandad very much and **especially Malcolm who used to spend most of the day playing in his office and who is too young yet to understand his passing away, keeps asking for him**.

We are very glad to say that we had very nice letters from all our **Lancashire relations, Emma, Harriett and Ella**, they were all so fond of him.

He was buried in the family vault with his Parents and Uncle Emmett and we are having the inscription on the marble stone done and when it is finished we shall have it photographed and send you a copy.

I am glad to say that Willie has started to take much interest in my Dad's stamps and so he shall be able to continue with a hobby which meant so much to him and at which he had worked so hard from the age of 9.

Last week we also had another very sad event as a workman in the Printing Works names **Charles Aspery** who had been with us for 41 years in fact since he left school died. This poor man had been very ill since July 1949 but some months ago he seemed better and so returned to work. Though he was not very well he insisted on coming to my Dad's funeral and he seemed **very upset with my Dad's death as he considered my dad as his second father**. It is very sad to see people who one is so fond of passing away especially as he was only 54 years old.

We have been very busy the past week with having the fleet in but they left yesterday which is a pity as without them business will be rather slack.

Well Auntie we look forward very much to another letter from you soon and hope it will give us better news about your health.

With fondest love from my mother and all of us at home,
Your very loving nephew,
Albert

Beanland & Malin Stationers

Summary by

ALBERT VICTOR BEANLAND

Typed account, believed to be written around 1960

My name is Albert Victor Beanland, I was born in Gibraltar on the 7th November, 1914. After finishing with the Line Wall College, when I was 17 years old, my father sent me to London to Pitman's Commercial College where after a two year course in Commerce I obtained a post with the Petrol Firm of Shell-Mex & B.P. Ltd., in London. There I was very well liked and I kept the job for six years, but in January 1940 my father's firm suffered the loss of his Printing Works Manager, Mr. Joseph Reyes, and my father decided to recall me from England in order to help him as he could not cope with so much work, he being in charge of the whole administration of the business, Mr. William Malin by then being over 80 did practically nothing in running the business, my father always having borne the brunt of all the work.

Though it upset my future plans of eventually having obtained a post with the Shell Co. in America, I immediately resigned from my post, sold my furniture in England and left London in February 1940 in order to come to Gibraltar to help my father. My pay was only £2-16-0 per week.

My job for a few months was only getting to know the ropes, then in July 1940 a very important thing happened for Gib. The Evacuation.

Both my father and Mr. Malin left with only 24 hours' notice, my Dad left for England July 27th and Mr Malin for Madeira.

I all of a sudden was made Acting Director for my Dad, my brother Willie was the Secretary and Cashier, and my brother John with also slight knowledge of the Printing Works found himself overnight in charge of the Printing works. Of a staff of 26 employees no less than 14 were evacuated including the shop manager, Mr Trinidad and Senior Shop Assistant, Mr Axisa, both who could have remained if they had so desired, also Miss Cole our Accountant left, I had to undertake her work, my father's which consisted of doing all the correspondence and at the time serve at the shops counter.

The first few months were hell for us working under such terrible War conditions, not knowing from one minute to another what would happen.

At the beginning, when we were so shorthanded, some friends of ours seeing our difficulties used to help us in the evenings but getting no pay and thanks to them we were able to carry on. In 1941, in May, to my great surprise my name was down for evacuation, but Mr. John Malin who was very keen that I should stop in Gib so that I could continue to direct the business dictated the attached letter which in the end saved me from being evacuated and the business not withstanding all the great difficulties continued to prosper.

In case I should have been evacuated and the business ceasing to function, I advised that as by now there was already money available to spare that Mr. William Malin and my father should each receive the half of all the accumulated profits which existed from the formation of the Company till May 1941 each receiving £450.

The firm continued to do very well and on my dad's return and the Malins in 1944 the firm was in a very sound position having been able to invest £7000 in War Bonds, with this money which was then declared as a dividend it was agreed to pay off the mortgage on the house which had existed since the house had been bought in 1919.

***

History of Firm (Handwritten)

Business started as stationery in 1873 by Grandfather. He died nine months after this. Continued by his brother on behalf of widow and five children. He dies without leaving a will and grandmother died two years later, also without will. Business then put in uncle's name.

In 1884, Mr. Malin forms business and forms a printing works.

Uncle marries when over 50 years old and dies in 1899 leaving two boys and leaves will in favour of widow and two boys, nothing to my father who had meantime worked in printing works.

Widow sells to Malin and ½ share of business is offered to my father and it is arranged that he pays in weekly instalments of £2 and same is paid in 7 years.

From then on partnership between Mr Malin & my father prospered, though my dad being 18 years younger always bore the brunt of the work.

By 1920, with profits from the 1914 War, our property in Main Street is bought (though mortgaged for £8000 which existed from 1920 till 1945).

By 1936, when Mr Malin was 80, it was decided to make Partnership into a Limited Company.

FINAL THOUGHTS

By Malcolm Beanland

Marie-Carmen & Malcolm Beanland

For the past 15 years, I have been researching my family history and thanks to my wife Marie-Carmen finding a book at 74 Main Street called "The Letters of Bolton Beanland and Abraham Emmett Beanland to his parents" was able to establish that my great grandfather, Bolton Beanland, together with his wife Emma, nee Saword, baby Harriett and brother, Abraham Emmett Beanland, arrived in Gibraltar on the 23rd January 1867.

Since then, I have published articles in The Gibraltar Heritage Journal about the family. These are "The Diary of Harriett Beanland" (2003), "How Bolton Beanland and his family came to Gibraltar" (2005), "Beanland Malin Gibraltar Printers and Stationers" (2010) and "Memories and Memorabilia from the 1950's and 1960's" (2012).

Apart from writing these articles, I have built up the Beanland family tree with the help of my cousin, Peter Beanland, a distant cousin in Australia, Graham Beanland, and my daughter, Vanessa Wester nee Beanland. It now shows that the family can be traced to a **Matthew Beanland, born in 1455! Apparently, a knight.**
This means that the Beanland family in Gibraltar has lived from 1867 spanning six generations and 18 generations from 1455. The extraordinary aspect is that all information can be verified from various records.

I would like to pay tribute to my great uncle Abraham Emmett Beanland (1843-1899) who found himself with the great burden of having to raise five orphans, three nephews and two nieces, whilst he himself was a spinster and for that he deserves our most heartfelt thanks.

All five children lived through to adulthood.

Harriett emigrated to Australia, as did Emily, in 1915, after living in Bolton's birthplace of Burnley, England, for a few years. It is clear from Charles diary of 1895 that the connection with Bolton and Emma's relatives was retained so it is unsurprising.

John eventually emigrated to South Africa from Gibraltar and had a daughter, Gladys.

Arthur, who had married and had two children, Sydney and Edward, in Gibraltar, ended up raising his family in England.

Children of Edward Beanland: Gillian, John & Jane

His great granddaughter, Claire, now lives on the Isle of Wight, as does Charles's great granddaughter (my daughter), Vanessa.

Talk about coincidences.

Visit to Gibraltar by great-grandchildren of Arthur Beanland

Charles, my grandfather, was the only one of the five children who stayed with his family in Gibraltar. They raised six children. Only Charles Percy, his eldest son, left Gibraltar for a life in England, but his son, Peter has always maintained his relationship to The Rock.

I can recall my grandfather, by reference to the following photo, taken in 1950, when my grandparents celebrated their 50th Wedding Anniversary. I was only 4 years old.

TOP: (Left to right) Charles Frederick Beanland, Albert Beanland, Hortensia Beanland, Charles Percy Beanland
BOTTOM: (Left to right) Eleonora Beanland, Charles Bolton Beanland with Malcolm Beanland, Norah Beanland, Peter Beanland

My grandfather comes through as a gentleman, who went through a most difficult childhood, but managed to be a successful businessman and loving father. He was a founder member of the Mediterranean Rowing Club, Librarian of the Exchange and Commercial Library, Elder of the Church of Scotland and Director of Beanland Malin & Co Ltd.
I only wish I could have known him for more years.

My dad, Albert, was a very hardworking man, loving dad and person. He always made friends easily. At work, he treated everyone with great consideration, looking after his staff and ensuring that stationery, toys, typewriters, etc, were purchased and ready to be sold.

I remember when he took us on a Cruise to Italy in 1952. We sailed on the Union Castle to Italy and spent 3 weeks visiting Genoa, Pisa and

Viareggio where my mother had family, the Santini's. I remember that visiting the Leaning Tower, my dad did not allow me to go up the tower. But I remember staying at a house in Viareggio where a photo of Stalin was hung!! On the way back, we sailed in an Italian Cruise Liner 'The Americo Vespucci'.

During Christmas, he always placed all our Christmas presents in a sack at the edge of our bed and we pretended to be asleep!

My father was Secretary of The St Bernard's Catholic and Social Club that was located opposite 74 Main Street, our home. He also owned a small boat called the "PARGO Kid" and I remember going fishing with him and my brothers, Charles and Albert, inside the Harbour.

Together with my mother, Hortensia, we would go up the Rock, Camp Bay and Catalan Bay. I know that my parents loved each other very much, as can be seen by his letter to her in 1942.

Beanland Family, circa 1951

I further recall an incident in Spain, at Buller's Beach, when my sister, Dorothy, had to be rescued from the waves and Dad was helped by a friend Koko Gareze who later became my boss many years later.

My father was a great organiser and in 1963 he celebrated their 25th Wedding Anniversary at home with many family guests and friends.

I remember how happy he was to have met my wife, Marie-Carmen, and her family in the knowledge that he had taken that famous photograph of us at the Colonial Hospital when we were born just three weeks apart in 1946.

He died when he was only 49 years old. **Too young to see all of us get married and meet his grandchildren.**

I believe I take after my granddad and father, being interested in history, especially about Gibraltar, and in being an easy-going and friendly person, who has a knack for organising events and family Rock tours! There is nothing that I love more than to discuss matters that are close to my heart... and football, of course. A passion also shared by my brother, Albert.

I am so happy that Vanessa has taken a great interest in the family history and is writing a historical novel about the family.

In that regard, I consider that Marie-Carmen and I are very fortunate to be alive to see our three lovely daughters, six grandchildren and extended families.

Finally, I am so pleased to have organised, with support from Cousin Peter and my brothers and sister, the family reunion held on Wednesday 25th October, 2017, at Kings Bastion.

Beanland Family Reunion 2017

FINAL THOUGHTS

By Vanessa Wester (V. J. Beanland)

Robert & Vanessa Wester (nee Beanland), 2000

The last diary recovered of Charles Bolton Beanland, of 1895, mentions Leonora (the *"slight flirtation"* at the end) who became my great grandmother. Charles married her in 1900, 100 years before I married my husband, Robert.

Eleonora & Charles Beanland, 1900

The letter written by my grandfather, Albert, talks fondly of his father, Charles, on his passing, honouring his name and the man that he became.

Charles was obviously a wonderful man, like his father, Bolton, before him who is talked of so lovingly by his wife, Emma, in her letters to her brother,

> *"Alas! What a sorrow it is to lose such a good husband*
> *as he always was to me – such peace & happiness I had*
> *the whole nine years we were married."*

It is no surprise to me that they were such highly regarded men, since my father has always been a role model for me in every way. My father, Malcolm, has always inspired me to be the best I can be, and funnily enough, my affectionate son, Michael, seems to take after his grandfather in many ways – even if one of them is his love of football!

Charles and Leonora had eleven children. Sadly, five of them did not survive past their first year.

Eleonora, Charles, & children, circa 1910

My grandfather, Albert, was born on the 7th November 1914 – just four months after the start of WW1. My father, Malcolm, was born in 1946, a year after the end of WW2.

In the space of those tumultuous years the world was changed forever. Luckily, I have never experienced war or had to endure suffrage, as Harriett Beanland did when she fought for the rights of women in 1913!

The extensive research undertaken whilst writing these letters and the historical novel I am working on has taken me on a journey to the past. My ancestors have enabled me to understand, to some extent, how the world has changed and yet, through these letters, I have felt many times as if nothing has changed at all.

We all experience the same emotions, fears, regrets, and hardships in different ways. It is my opinion, the past is not something we should run from, but embrace. Through developments and shifts in society, we adapt and change how we interact with each other, whether on a local or global scale.

I personally believe we must never forget the sacrifices of those who lived before us. Neither should we take for granted the advancement of science in combatting illness. During the 19th Century, approximately ¼ of people died of consumption. Sadly, my great-great grandparents succumbed to this horrendous illness.

Finally, I must thank you for taking the time to travel back in time with me by reliving the words of my ancestors. I am indebted to my father, Malcolm Beanland, for planting the seed that led to this tree. I know that I have more stories to tell and hope one day I will finish the Beanland Saga I have begun. Bringing these letters to life in this book was certainly a labour of love.

The eBook publication year of 2017 marked the 150th Anniversary of the arrival of the Beanland name on the Rock of Gibraltar. Hopefully, the Beanland name will have left its mark on the famous Rock and be remembered for many years to come. I hope the pictures that follow help to visualize many of the people mentioned in this book.

As always, thank you for reading.

BEANLAND

FAMILY

PHOTOGRAPHS

19th Century

20th Century

&

beyond...

Bolton's Lancashire Family

A huge range of photos, but most seem "staged".

In most, if not all cases, these were taken in studios since people did not own cameras!

Bolton's Lancashire Family

We are unsure who all these family members are,
found in a family album.

Charles's Family

Charles's Family

These pictures show some of the relatives in England, as well as Charles's children and the Beanland Malin shop.

Albert's Family

BEANLAND FAMILY IN GIBRALTAR

Grandchildren & spouses of Charles Beanland (b. 1874)

Granddaughters of Albert Beanland (b.1914)
Daughters of Malcolm Beanland – Allison, Vanessa & Catherine

Great granddaughters of Albert Beanland (b.1914)
Granddaughters of Malcolm Beanland

Great grandson of Albert Beanland (b.1914)
with his grandfather, Malcolm

Granddaughters of Albert Beanland (b.1914)
Daughters of Malcolm & Charles Beanland

Granddaughter of Albert Beanland (b.1914), Daphne,
with family, and grandsons of Charles Beanland

Son of Charles Percy (b.1906),
Peter Beanland (& Grandchildren) – Catalan Bay

Great grandchildren of Charles Percy Beanland – Upper Rock

Wedding of Dorothy Beanland to Manuel Durante

Granddaughter of Albert Beanland (b.1914), Eloise, daughter of Dorothy Durante (nee Beanland)

Granddaughters & Grandson of Albert Beanland (b.1914) Children of Malcolm & Charles Beanland

Beanland Family, 1996

The naming of the Vanessa-C in 2003. A first for Gibraltar.

Beanland & Olivero Family in 2003

**Arthur Beanland, b. 1870, & Jeanette in U.K. & Gibraltar
with sons, Sydney, b. 1902, & Edward, b. 1907 (both born in Gibraltar)**

**Granddaughter of Sydney Beanland.
Nicola & family visiting Gibraltar.**

Beanland Family in Gibraltar, at 74 Main Street – around 1950

BEANLAND FAMILY IN UK

Son of Arthur Beanland, b. 1870 - Sydney Beanland & Family, b.1902
TOP: Arthur Beanland, Doreen Beanland
BOTTOM: Barbara Beanland, Ann Beanland, Sydney Beanland

Jack & Doreen Marsh   **Ann & Maurice Everest**

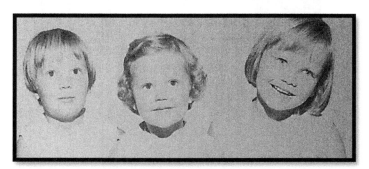

Daughters of Jack & Doreen Marsh – Nicola, Wendy & Lynne

TOP: Arthur, Doreen, Barbara (Sydney's wife), Jack, Ann, Barbara
BOTTOM: Nicola, Sydney, Lesley, Wendy, Lynne, (little) Claire

Wendy & family   **Lynne & her son, Matthew**

Nicola & Family

BONUS MATERIAL: THE SAWORD HISTORY

By Clare Kirk, April 2018

Ancestors of Diane Brenda Kirk née Saword, b. 1947

Saward is an ancient name - a rare Anglo Saxon survivor - derived from the personal names 'Saeweard' (sea guardian/coastal warden) and/or 'Sigeweard' (victory guardian). An early example is recorded on an Anglo Saxon grave marker in Norwich.

Saward with an 'A' is by far the more common spelling, and other variants and mis-transcriptions include Seward, Sayward, and Sawood, but Diane's ancestors have been spelling their name consistently as 'Saword' as far back as we can trace them (~1700). The rarity of the name has made it easier than usual to find historical records about the family.

The earliest parish records of Sawords (with an 'O') are from Essex and Hertfordshire, starting 1569. However, spellings may have varied, and these may simply be the places where records have survived.

Our Sawords are a fascinating family of merchants and travellers from the south east of England - who have frequently crossed oceans, emigrated, and sometimes returned to England!

Sources

I have been very fortunate to have several letters written about the Saword family tree by Diane's father, **Alfred Charles Saword** (1906-1996). My genealogical research has been undertaken using parish records, census records, the GRO, newspaper archives, wills, etc. Other notable sources, including books and archives, are included in the footnotes. I have striven for accuracy, while occasionally imagining our ancestors' feelings and actions, for which no records exist.

William Saword (b.~1708-unknown) & Deborah Wheatley (unknown)

We begin with William Saword and Deborah Wheatley, who would have been born in the first few years of the 18th century.

William and Deborah married in 1729 in St Nicholas Church, Deptford, Kent. She may have been his second wife (a William Saword also married nearby in 1722).

We know of five children: Mary, buried in 1731/2, Elizabeth, who was buried 1733, Mary c1735 and buried 1736, Susan, c1737 and William Gunton, c1739. So far, we don't know where the middle name Gunton comes from; however, a Frances Gunton was christened at St Nicholas, Deptford in 1700 so there is probably a connection to a Gunton friend or family member.

The children were christened in St Paul's, Deptford. St Paul's was consecrated in 1730, and has been called 'The finest Baroque Church north of the Alps'. Prior to the building of this new church, St Nicholas was the parish church for Deptford, and William and Deborah's first-born children may have been christened there.

Deptford is next door to Greenwich. Until 1900 it was in Kent, but is now a London borough. From the mid-16th to the late 19th century, Deptford was home to Deptford Dockyard, the first Royal Navy Dockyard. Baptismal records from 1730/1 show that William was a Shipwright living on New Street. However, William was probably working on the business side of shipbuilding, rather than engineering. In 1734-5 his occupation was 'Stowage' - so possibly managing the storage and transportation of cargo. By 1736 William was living on Butt Lane and in 1737 he was a 'Clerk in the Store Office, King's Yacht'.

William's father may have been in the same line of work; a record from 1707 shows that a Mr Sawords had drawn up a contract for Sir Henry Greenhill - who was the Commissioner for the Navy in Portsmouth. In 1702 Sir Greenhill was promoted to the Navy Board in London as comptroller of storekeeper's accounts. Perhaps Mr Saword(s) went there with him.

William's father may have also been called William; a marriage of William Saword, widower, b~1640 to Mary Coles, b~1660, was recorded in Woolwich, Greenwich, in 1698.

The time and place of William and Deborah's deaths is unknown.

William Gunton Saword (1739-1812)
& Frances Raggett (1737-1779)

William's son William Gunton did not initially follow in his father's shipping footsteps; in 1756, at the age of about 16, he started an apprenticeship as a draper. At the upper end of the draper trade were cloth merchants, traders, and financiers. Perhaps in the Deptford area there was also a connection to sail making? William was apprenticed to Charles Carne on 18 May 1756 for 7 years, with a premium of £21 paid by his father (about £4000 today). Charles Carne was a glazier and rose to become Master of the Company in 1772.

However, William Gunton didn't stay in the drapers' trade. The Worshipful Company of Drapers confirmed that William did not take up the Freedom of the Company and they have no information on him after

1756.

In about 1760, aged 21, William, a Gent, joined the freemasons - Crown & Sceptre Lodge. They met at the Black Lyon, a tavern in Greenwich.

In 1761, 5 years after the start of his apprenticeship, he married Frances Raggett in Kensington, signing the marriage document with an intricate flourish! Frances was the daughter of Edward Raggett, a Master Joiner of His Majesty's Dockyard in Deptford.

In about 1764, William started working at the Clerk of the Cheque's office in Greenwich Hospital. In this role, he managed one of the royal yachts, which were moored at the hospital. 'The presence of the Royal Dockyards at Deptford and Woolwich - both largely closed in the 1860s - made Greenwich Hospital the London base for the royal yachts from the 17th century to the end of the age of sail.'

Greenwich Hospital was founded in 1682 by Queen Mary II as a home for retired or wounded sailors (more like a workhouse than a retirement home as we understand that today). It was a hospital in the 'hospitality' sense of the word, not a medical centre, though by the time William was there it had become an infirmary. The Greenwich Hospital charity still exists, though the beautiful building - partly designed by Christopher Wren - became the Royal Naval College in 1869.

The National Archives at Kew hold a document from Deptford, 1772 regarding timber for the *Augusta* yacht, for which William Saword (most likely the younger) had been paid.

The *Augusta* was in fact a royal yacht! She was rebuilt from the *Charlotte* and renamed the Augusta in 1761, and then rebuilt again in Deptford in 1771. The yacht weighed 184 tons and was armed with 8 4-pounder guns. Royal Museums Greenwich hold a contemporary painting of its launch at Deptford in 1771, purported to be by the king's son, the Duke of York.

The Augusta was renamed *Princess Augusta* in 1773 to mark the occasion of the King reviewing the fleet at Portsmouth. Then, George III himself used the Princess Augusta to review the Fleet off the Nore in 1778, and again that year with Queen Charlotte aboard, to review the fleet at Spithead.

In 1772, after the launch of the Augusta, William became the Butler of Greenwich Hospital! William's job as Butler was to oversee the provision of food and drink to the >2000 pensioners who lived there. It must have been quite a prestigious position, but a huge responsibility, and relentlessly busy. Two 'Butler's Mates' assisted him with his responsibilities.

What was life like for the Greenwich pensioners?

'Seamen contributed sixpence a month from their pay towards the upkeep of the hospital. Pensioners were admitted from 1705 and originally wore a uniform of dark grey with a blue lining and brass buttons. The colour of the uniforms changed to brown and then blue. Pensioners who broke the rules were forced to wear a yellow coat known as the 'canary' and make amends with extra chores.

Those former sailors and marines who lived in the hospital were known as 'in-pensioners' and those who drew a pension but did not live on site were known as 'out-pensioners'.

Almost 3,000 sailors were living in the Hospital by 1815. According to recent research by the Greenwich Maritime Institute, the average pensioner entered at 56 but they ranged in age from 12 to 99. Younger pensioners had been injured at sea.

By all accounts the 'Greenwich Geese' as locals referred to them were a rowdy bunch and barely resembled our modern image of elderly pensioners. Records show frequent fights and other behaviour shocking to the public morals of the time.'

The National Maritime Museum has inherited and exhibits many objects from the old Greenwich Hospital. One of these, a ceramic jug, has this ballad, '**The Greenwich Pensioner**' printed on its sides:

Yet still I am enabled
To bring up in life's rear
Although I am disabled
And lie in Greenwich tier
The King, God bless His Majesty
Who saved me from the main
I'll praise with love and loyalty
But ne'er to sea again!

Greenwich Hospital was not only a home for Seamen, but also received visitors who came to see the fine building and art within. In 1773, one visitor was Phillis Wheatley - a 'negro' poet from Boston, who had been received by eminent members of London society.

That same year, 12 years after getting married, William and Frances had their first child (that we know of), a son, Edward William, who was christened at Greenwich. Three years later William and Frances had a daughter, Ann. Ann was christened at the Royal Hospital, Greenwich in July 1776, and may well have been born there. It must have been a noisy and not very private place to raise a family.

The **Court & City Register** - a who's who guide to London - reported in 1776 that William Saword, Butler at Greenwich Hospital, earned 25 pounds/year. This was a decent wage at the time, though the organist was making 60 pounds a year! Of course, William would have most likely received free accommodation as well.

In the same list of employees at Greenwich Hospital there was also a William Wheatley - likely to be a relation of William's mother, who was born Deborah Wheatley.

In 1777, Frances's father died. He left her a number of valuable items, including a coat of arms cut into a wainscot, half of his books, working tools and instruments and wood of all sorts, a large silver salver, silver tablespoons, and an equal share of his estate, along with Frances's two siblings.

In 1778, the lieutenant-governor of the hospital, a naval officer called Thomas Baillie, published accusations of corruption in the management of the hospital - including claims that *'landsmen have been appointed to offices contrary to charter'* and that the pensioners were *'fed with bull-beef and sour small-beer mixed with water'*. Baillie was taken to court over the allegations, and a rebuttal, the **'State of Facts Relative to Greenwich Hospital'**, was published in 1779.

Publications of the trial contains testimony from William Saword, who was called in to answer questions about the provision of meat, cheese, and money. He refuted the insinuation that the men had been forced to accept payment in one form or another, and said that it was *'always by choice'*. Another cause for complaint was the idea that staff without sailing experience had unfairly received appointments at the hospital. However, that was not the case for William:

'Go on to the next?

They are the butlers; the present one is William Saward [sic], who has been at sea.

When was he appointed?

On the 25th of February, 1772.

Had he been at sea before his appointment, or afterwards?

Before his appointment, he was clerk of one of the yachts, and had been [on] many voyages, I believe.

Who was the head of the Admiralty when the last butler was appointed?

Lord Sandwich.'

The **Statement of Facts** describes the 'Butler's List' of daily provisions - so that the butler could ensure that a suitable portion of each man's allowance would go towards food, not beer. Additionally, pensioners could only sell their provisions to the butler, and noone else - again, to control spending on alcohol. However, beer problems dominated the butler's job! Apparently, beer flowed through subterraneous pipes from the brewhouse to the dining hall, but for a while it was extremely watered down. Eventually, the butler sent his assistant to the brewhouse to find out why the beer was so weak. However, the foreman would only respond with an 'insolent sneer' that the butler would never know the cause!

In January 1779, a major fire destroyed the interior of the chapel of Greenwich Hospital and caused extensive damage. Five hundred pensioners had to be temporarily rehoused.

Sadly, William's wife Frances died in June 1779, the 'wife of William Saword, Butler of Greenwich Hospital'. Edward and Ann would have only been about six and three at the time. William managed as a single parent for more than four years (perhaps with help from a matron or other staff), until marrying again at St Paul's, Deptford in November 1783, to Ann Hall, a spinster.

In 1781, King George III and the Prince of Wales arrived at Greenwich Hospital, and were received by the Earl of Sandwich, First Lord of the Admiralty, the Governor, and principal officers of the hospital. He then immediately boarded a barge, which was accompanied by the *Princess Augusta*. This was the first of several news-worthy royal visits to the hospital where the *Augusta* played an important role.

On 5th April 1795, Princess Catherine of Brunswick travelled by Thames to Greenwich Hospital on her way to marry her cousin, the future King George IV.

'Met by massed ranks of Greenwich Pensioners it was on this occasion that she was overheard to remark (in French), "*Are all Englishmen missing an arm or a leg?*"

And which vessel brought the princess? None other than the Royal Yacht Augusta!

In 1797, King George III, along with his Generals, Admirals, and the Controller of the Navy, arrived at Greenwich Hospital ready to embark on the Royal Yacht Charlotte, 'which, with the Augusta and Mary yachts, were moored off the hospital for their reception ...The admiralty flag was displayed on the Princess Augusta yacht. ... His majesty never looked better, or appeared in better spirits. A profusion of strong beer was ordered for the Pensioners at Greenwich on the occasion.'

By 1801, William was still Butler of Greenwich Hospital, and still earning 25 pounds a year (no pay rise in at least 25 years!) However, his son Edward William, known as William, was now, at about 27 years old, working at Greenwich Hospital too, and as one of two Steward's clerks, he was earning 50 pounds/year - twice that of his father!

It doesn't seem that William senior and Ann had any children of their own, but they enjoyed 20 years of marriage, until she died in December 1803.

Ann asked to be interred with her 'dear mother and sister'. She left various amounts of three percent stock in south sea annuities to her step-children Edward William and Ann, as well as other beneficiaries.

In 1805 William's address was given in **Holden's Triennial Directory** as 8, Cold-bath-row, Greenwich. Cold Bath Rd still exists.

On Christmas Eve, 1805, **Lord Nelson's body was brought to Greenwich Hospital by yacht, surrounded by a mass of ships**. His body lay in state in the Painted Hall there for three days before his funeral at St Paul's. **Thousands of mourners came to pay their respects** at the lying-in, and to watch his funeral procession as his body was conveyed along the Thames by barge.

"Of all the pageantry that Greenwich has witnessed since it became a town," writes Charles Mackay, in his **'Thames and its Tributaries'**, *"this was, if not the most magnificent, the most grand and impressive."*

'The body, after lying in state for three days in the hospital, during which it was visited by immense multitudes, was conveyed, on the 8th of January, 1806, up the river to Whitehall, followed in procession by the City Companies in their state barges. The flags of all the vessels in the river were lowered half-mast high, in token of mourning, and solemn minute guns were fired during the whole time of the procession.

The body lay all that night at the Admiralty, and on the following morning was removed on a magnificent car, surmounted by plumes of feathers and decorated with heraldic insignia, to its final resting-place in St. Paul's Cathedral. From the Admiralty to St. Paul's the streets were all lined with the military. The procession was headed by detachments of the Dragoon Guards, the Scots Greys, and the 92nd Highlanders, with the Duke of York and his staff, the band playing that sublime funeral strain, the 'Dead March in Saul.'

Then followed the pensioners of Greenwich Hospital and the seamen of Lord Nelson's ship, the Victory, a deputation from the Common Council of London, and a long train of mourning coaches, including those of the royal family, the chief officers of state, and all the principal nobility of the kingdom.'

In April, 1806, when William had been Butler for 32 years, there was another enquiry into the running of Greenwich Hospital. William was interviewed in detail, and amazingly, pages of the examination with his answers have survived in **The Fourteenth Report of the Commissioners**

of Naval Enquiry. Royal Hospital at Greenwich.

The Examination of Mr. WILLIAM SAWORD, Butler of the Royal Hospital at Greenwich; taken upon Oath; the 10th day of April 1806.

'What situations have you held in the Hospital, and how long have you been Butler?
I have been Butler thirty-two years, and was before that time ten years in the Clerk of the Checque's Office.
What duties do you perform, as Butler of Greenwich Hospital?
I attend to the issuing of provisions, and the payment of money to the Pensioners in lieu of provisions. The butter, cheese, and salt, are in my charge, and I attend the weighing of the butter and cheese at the time of receipt.
By what rule are you governed in making your demands for meat?
The quantity of meat to be supplied daily is fixed by the Steward and Clerk of the Checque, and continues at that rate until there is occasion to alter it.
What is done with the meat provided to the Pensioners, if any remain, after the supply of the tables?
I take it in my charge, and it is generally kept till the next day, and served out.
Why was the daily expense [sic] of meat increased on the 6th of February last, from 860 lbs to 972 lbs, and continued to the present time?
Because the Chalk-Off lift was decreased, and the number victualled increased, that the broth might be made better.'
William described the very complicated system of distributing provisions, or money in lieu of provisions, to six different classes of men, as well as the nurses. He had two stewards to help him. A custom called the 'chalk-off lift' or 'butler's lift' meant that the Butler could mark certain tables with chalk, indicating that those men would receive money rather than meat. When asked if the men liked to receive money rather than provisions, William answered, "*Very much so.*"
William was also asked if he received any perks on top of his salary. It's hard to know if his response was said with pride or disappointment!:
'Do you or your Mates receive any allowance of provisions from the Hospital?
None.
Do you receive any fees, gratuities, or emoluments, in money, or kind beyond the salary and allowances made to you by the Hospital?
Never a farthing in my life-time.'
The following year, after four years as a widower, William Gunton

Saword, Esquire of Greenwich, ~ 63 years old, **married for a third time**. His bride was Jane Hodgkin, daughter of the Rev. Joseph Hodgkin, Vicar and Clerk of Elmswell in Suffolk, which was about 90 miles from Greenwich. She was probably 30-40 years younger than William.

Later that same year, William's son, Edward ("William"), got married too. It seems that after his marriage, William Gunton finally retired from Greenwich Hospital (perhaps after the gruelling examination!) and the couple lived together on Cold Bath Row. Two years into the marriage Jane lost her father, and after five years she lost her husband too. However, during her short marriage Jane had a personal triumph - as a contributor to the Royal Academy of Arts.

A miniature painter, 'Mrs Saword' exhibited from 1808-11; her 'Portrait of a Lady' was exhibited at the **Royal Academy Annual Exhibition in 1811 (work #597)** and she also showed a miniature of Shakespeare at the British Institute. Greenwich Hospital had a number of paintings; the National Collection of Naval Art was established there in 1824. Could the artworks at the hospital explain how William and Jane met, even though they lived 90 miles apart?

William Gunton died in April 1812. At the time of his death he was living in Bury St Edmunds, Suffolk, and he was buried in Elmswell, Jane's village. In his last will and testament he left several hundred pounds, as well as bank stock, to his wife Jane, son Edward William (his executor), daughter Ann (still a spinster at 36), niece Deborah Wates, his daughter in law Sarah, and Harriet Hillier, a '*spinster now residing with my son*' - whether as a servant, friend, lodger, or lover - we don't know! (The Hilliers in Greenwich had strong connections to the Navy and Greenwich Hospital).

Jane remarried less than a year later, to Thomas Pryor, a wealthy Suffolk gentleman farmer and landowner. Hopefully she continued her painting, though sadly I've found no record of a 'Mrs Prior, miniaturist'. Jane and Thomas Pryor lived in the White House, Stowmarket (the farm still exists). After '*a long and painful affliction, borne with truly Christian fortitude and resignation*', Jane died in 1828. When her husband died the following year, his executors sold the luxurious contents of his home, his livestock, and his property - comprising the '**White Elm mansion of modern erection**', with farm and cottages on 50 acres, two other farms - 76-acre and 75 acre, and a double tenement and garden. Unfortunately it's unlikely that any of this wealth found its way to the next generation of Swords!

Edward William ('William') Saword (1773-1815)
& Sarah Benwell (1781-1872)

Edward went by 'William', like his father and grandfather. By 1801, in his late 20s, the younger William was one of four Steward's Clerks at Greenwich Hospital, where his father was the Butler. He stayed there until at least 1805. He joined the freemasons in Greenwich aged 21 (a Gent). The lodge met at the Crown & Sceptre, a tavern in Greenwich. In his 20s, William was one of the Steward's Clerks at Greenwich Hospital, where his father was the Butler.

In September 1807, at about 34, William married Sarah Benwell in St Mary's University Church, Oxford. Sarah's late father and grandfather had been prominent tailors and community leaders in Oxford, and her father's shop was across the street from the church. Their marriage was reported in Kent and Oxford papers.

I'm curious about how William had met Sarah. In 1815 he took out an insurance policy as a Merchant with the address of 16 Garlick Hill, London (close to the Thames and to the Bank of England). Mercantile business may have brought him to Oxford, and perhaps he did business with the Benwells. However, Sarah's death certificate, decades later, states that she was the widow of Edward Saword, 'Clerk of Greenwich Hospital'. Perhaps she was most proud of that position.

William and Sarah probably lived in Kent, where they had a son, Edward William Turner Saword, in August 1811. (The reasons for 'Turner' are unknown. However, the name stays in the family for one more generation, with Edward's son Henry Turner). Edward was baptised in St Alfrege's church, Greenwich - where Thomas Tallis is buried.

Sadly, when little Edward was just over 4 years old, his father passed away at just 42 years of age in the autumn of 1815. We don't know the cause, though he created a will in January, so he may have already been in poor health then. Curiously, he was buried 170 miles from home in East Budleigh in Devon - was he traveling to or from Exmouth or other local seaports? Or could he have died at sea? 35 years later, his son stated that his father had been a Mariner; was he confusing merchant sea voyages or a position as Clerk of the Yachts with a career in sailing?

Edward William's will left all of his possessions to his *'dearest friend and wife'* and at her death to his *'dear and only child Edward William Turner Saword'*. He also left assets to his *'dear sister'* Ann (still a spinster, residing on Butt Lane) - as well as to Anne Wates (a relation), and Harriet Hillier (who had, as his father's will revealed, lived with him, but now resided on Sloane Street).

The will is somewhat unusual, in that it names the testator as Charles Benwell (relationship as yet unknown), and Sarah Benwell, William's mother in law, who came from Surrey to testify to the 'manner and character' of his handwriting. With her testimony, the will was proved.

Unlike William, Sarah, a widow at 34, went on to live a very long life! Unfortunately we don't have any records of her between 1815 and 1841. In 1836 her son Edward married a woman from Lancashire, and in 1841, she was living very close to her son's family, on Rathbone St, Liverpool. By 1851, both Sarah and Edward had moved to the other side of the Mersey, and we find them in Birkenhead, about a mile apart.

At the age of 67, she was a fundholder - meaning she could support herself financially. It's not at all surprising therefore that she had a servant, a 16-year-old from Wales. However, she also shared her home with a 35-year-old unmarried solicitor from Rochdale. George K Deardon was an 'inmate' in Sarah's home - a term used for lodgers and hotel guests as well as people within an institution. Six years earlier, George Kenyon Dearden had put up £4000 to help fund a new Scottish railway. He was clearly a very well-off young man. It seems that his landlady, Sarah Saword, although living near her son, enjoyed her independence.

In 1861 Sarah lodged on Tottenham Court Road with her oldest grandson Charles. She was a 'Shareholder' - in which businesses we don't know. In 1871, at age 89, she finally gave up some of her independence, and was living with her daughter in law Sarah and grandchildren in Hackney, and also next door to Charles's family. I imagine that Sarah and her grandson Charles were close. Sarah finally passed away in 1872, at the impressive age of 90, 57 years after her husband.

Sarah's sister in law, Ann Saword, was also an independent woman. A beneficiary of her father and brother's wills, she did not marry until she was almost 50, to George Griffyth, 18 years her junior! George or his father (also George) was a Deptford shipwright.

Edward William Turner Saword (1811 - unknown)
& Emma Edwards (1815-1849)

Edward was only three or four when his father died in 1815. He was an only child. His mother had inherited his father's money, so presumably his childhood was comfortable, but we don't know how much wealth she shared with him during her long lifetime.

By the age of 25, in 1836, he had left Kent behind and was living in Liverpool. Liverpool was booming in that period, and the Lime Street station (now the oldest grand terminus mainline station still in use in the

257

world) had just opened two months earlier.

In October 1836, Edward, a Clerk, married **Emma Edwards** at St Oswald's, Winwick, Lancashire (now Cheshire), where Emma was living. Winwick is about 18 miles east of Liverpool. They were married by license, avoiding the need for banns to be called - a convenience for those who could afford the fee. All we know for sure about Emma is that she was born in about 1815 in Cheshire. She was most likely the daughter of John and Mary Edwards, christened in St Peter's, Liverpool, in February 1815.

In 1841, Edward was a bookkeeper, and was living in Liverpool's spacious suburbs, on Rathbone Street, just beyond the brand new Wavertree Botanic Gardens. That same year, a fashionable house was built on Falkner Street, 2 miles closer to the docks - which was recently featured in the **BBC's** *A House Through Time*.

Edward lived with his wife Emma, 3-year-old daughter Elizabeth (**Emma Elizabeth, b.1837**) and 1-month old son, Charles (**Charles Edward, b.1841**). They also had two servants, Bridgit and Catharine, both from Ireland. In 1841, twenty percent of Irish people living in England and Wales lived in Merseyside.

At a glance it looks like a picture of middle class domesticity. However, Edward and Emma had already lost two babies - Edward aged 3 months in 1839 (convulsions) and an earlier Charles Edward in 1840. The first Charles Edward died at just 6 weeks on Valentine's Day 1840. The cause of death was 'debility' (a vague term indicating failure to thrive). His mother was with him when he died at their home on Washington Street.

After the second Charles was born, they lost three more children before the age of 1 - Sarah Ann at 11 days (dysentery), Frances Anne age 1 month (convulsions), and Henry Turner.

Adding to their woes, in June 1845, a fire broke out at their home on Portland Place, started accidentally by a servant who had dropped a piece of burning paper into the chip cellar (woodchip storage container) under the kitchen stairs.

Edward and his daughter Emma (about 8 years old) were **unable to descend the stairs, and had to climb out through the roof to escape**. The servant managed to get out through the hall door, by which time the house was completely filled with smoke. In newspaper reports of the fire, there's no mention of Emma or little Charles.

The fire police arrived but were not required, as some nearby labourers had quickly put out the flames. Thankfully, the only damage was a few broken windows and a severe fright to the family.

Edward and Emma's eighth child, Fanny, was born in 1848, but before

Fanny reached her first birthday, **Emma died after having consumption (TB) for 3 months**. She was **only 34**. (It's tragic to note that this is the 3rd generation in a row in which a parent died when their children were very young, and that there was more of this to come...)

When Emma died she was with Margaret Byrum, an Irish labourer's wife the same age as her who lived nearby - presumably a friend.

Of Edward and Emma's eight children, only three survived. When Emma died she left behind **Emma Elizabeth (age ~12), Charles Edward (age ~8), and baby Fanny**. Edward must have been devastated at the loss of five babies and his young wife. He now needed help caring for his family.

Edward soon moved to Oxton, Birkenhead, the other side of the Mersey. Within a few months of Emma's death, banns were called for a new marriage to **Sarah L. Gibson**. More than 6 months later (an unusually long waiting period) they married; Edward was 38 and Sarah was just 20.

Sarah, who was illiterate, lived in Oxton as well, but came from Droghedon, near Dublin. Her father was Sergeant Robert Gibson. That is all we know about her background.

Edward and Sarah soon had a daughter, Mary, b.1850. In March, 1851, the family of six plus one servant were at a new address in Birkenhead. Edward was a Clerk to a Commission Agent, and 9-year old Charles was a scholar, but 12-year-old Emma was not at school (unusual for a girl in a middle class family). Edward's mother lived close by.

Since 1840, Ireland had been in the grip of the great potato famine, bringing a huge influx of Irish people to Ireland (possibly including Sarah). The overcrowding caused epidemics of cholera and dysentery in Liverpool. Perhaps it was this, and the loss of so many children, that led the family to emigrate to America in early 1851.

In April 1851, Edward (39, Merchant), Sarah (34), Emma (14), Fanny (3), and Mary (1) all travelled to Boston, USA, on a trading barque called the *Inca*. Numerous ads had appeared in Liverpool papers in the preceding months, among whole pages of ship ads offering travel and shipping from Liverpool to cities all over the world. A newspaper ad from 1852 showed that the Inca left on the 29th of every month, and could take up to 600 tonnes of goods.

The Inca took the Saword family across the Atlantic to Boston, and then the ship travelled on (without them?) to Baltimore, San Francisco, and Latin America.

The family's trip to the US prompts a number of questions: The passenger list states that they belonged to the US, and that their last permanent residence was the US. Is it possible that Edward had already travelled there? (an Edward Saword is recorded in Iowa in 1838)? Or were they just eager to show that they considered themselves American citizens?

Also, where was 9-year old Charles? Did they leave him in a boarding school or with a family member?

Additionally, the arrival record states that Sarah was 'confined during the voyage'. Did she have (and lose) a baby on the voyage? Most of all, what were their plans and hopes and dreams for America? We'll probably never know the answers to these questions, but whatever they wanted to achieve in America, they soon had a change of heart, and were back in Britain by 1853!

From 1853, Charles, age ~ 12, worked as an apprentice in the Audit Department of the London & North Western Railway at Euston Station. However, at the end of 1856 he was dismissed. Next, in Feb 1857, Charles was indentured into the Merchant Navy for a period of 4 years, to serve on the *Gladiolus* at Aberdeen. However, in July the same year Charles deserted his apprenticeship on pay day!

Edward and Sarah had five more children by 1861 - Arthur Edwards (touchingly named after Edward's first wife Emma Edwards) b.1853, Alfred b.1855, Elizabeth (Eliza) b.1857, and twins William Gibson (named after his mother) and Walter b.1860. All of these children's births were registered in London, but in 1861 the family was living at Poulton Cum Seacombe, Cheshire. Edward was a General Agent and 12-year old Fanny, the oldest child, was a scholar. This large family had help from another Irish servant.

The two oldest children were no longer at home in 1861; Charles would get married later that year and **Emma married in 1865 in Jamaica**! It's possible she had never returned to England from the US.

Edward and Sarah had 3 more children in the 1860s - a second Henry b.1862, Florence b.1864, and Edward George b.1865 (all registered in London). Altogether, Edward had SEVENTEEN children - and 12 of them survived infancy. All nine of Edward and Sarah's children lived past childhood; however, Eliza was paralysed from infancy and she suffered from epilepsy. Two of her half siblings had died as babies from convulsions; maybe Eliza had survived the same infant convulsions (an inherited condition?) but been left permanently disabled.

By 1869, Edward had a large family in London, but he clearly had itchy feet and heard the call of the sea again (or had a business opportunity he couldn't refuse) because in 1869 he travelled to India. His son in law wrote to his family about Edward's trip, in August that year.

'We heard from Emma's father since I wrote to you before. He has arrived in India quite safe after an absence of only 83 days, so that in that 83 days he travelled by sea and land about 36,000 miles, and he expects in 2 years to be making £1,000 a year.'

However, in fact, by the time this letter was written, Edward had already returned to England! He travelled from Calcutta on the *Nyanza*, arriving in Southampton on 6 May 1869. Perhaps his business plans fell through, or perhaps he was taken ill; when the 1871 census was taken he was a patient at St Mark's Hospital, near Harrow - a '*Hospital for Fistula and other Diseases of the Rectum*' (and still a specialist bowel hospital today).

In spite of his dreams of emigrating to the US as a 'merchant', and his plans to get rich in India, his occupation given in hospital was still simply 'bookkeeper'.

Meanwhile, his heroic wife Sarah managed the family and the home alone. In 1871 she was 39, and living at Union Rd, Hackney, with 9 children aged 5-20 (two working). As if that weren't enough, she had to care for her 13-year-old paralysed daughter Eliza, and her 89-year-old mother in law Sarah. Her step-son, Charles, lived right next door, but he already had five children of his own as well. Neither of them had any live-in servants to help reduce the burden, so it seems that they were not as comfortably off as before.

In 1876, Eliza, Edward and Sarah's disabled daughter, died. She was 17, and had suffered from gangrene for two weeks. Edward was present at her death at home in South Hackney. At that time he was an East India Agent. That's the last record we have of him. In 1881, Sarah reported that she was a widow. However, we have no evidence of Edward's death, and as we will see in the next generation, people did not always tell census takers the truth!

Sarah continued to live in Hackney, and in 1881 she was still head of the household, which included a new daughter in law and a granddaughter. She then moved to Hornsey by 1891 - with her son Walter at the head of the household, along with her sons Henry and Edward. Walter and Edward were both married by 1895, so she may have lived with one of her married children in her final years, until 1900, when she passed away at age 70. I think she had a very hard life and I can only hope it included some happy times.

Charles Edward Saword (1841-unknown)
& Emma Read (1837-1920)

Charles was the oldest surviving son of 17 children! He was 24 when his youngest half-sibling was born. When Charles was 8, his mother died, and at age 9 or 10, the family emigrated to the USA without him; his whereabouts then are a mystery. Perhaps Charles stayed with his grandmother Sarah while he attended school.

It wasn't much of a childhood; Charles was working as a clerk at the age of 12, and indentured into the navy at 16, though that didn't last.

According to his grandson Alfred, Charles may have spent some of his early life in Saxtead, Suffolk.

Alf wrote that Charles *'was an amateur artist and I have seen a picture he painted of his country cottage. Later he went to London.'*

Charles was living with his grandmother Sarah Saword in 1861 - the 19-year old Insurance Clerk lodged with the 77-year old on Tottenham Court Road.

Four months later, in July 1861, **Charles married Emma Read** in St Pancras. Emma, four years older than Charles, came from Bedfield, Suffolk - less than 3 miles from Saxtead - and may have been working in London as a domestic servant, so Charles could have met her in Suffolk or London (and indeed she may have moved to London when Charles did).

Emma was the daughter of an agricultural labourer. She was also illiterate when she married - making her a surprising 'lower class' choice for Charles. According to their grandson, Alfred, the family did not approve! Nevertheless, the Reads were a family on the make; Emma's brothers George and Alfred had left rural Suffolk behind to become Constables with the new Thames Police in London.

Between 1861 and 1871 Charles and Emma had 7 children - **Frederick Charles Edward** b.1862 in Bedfield, and then **Emma Elizabeth** b.1864, Arthur b.1865, Alfred Herbert b.1866, James Edward b.1867, Charlotte b.1868, and Jane Louisa b.1870 - all in London.

Sadly, Jane died when she was just a baby, and Alfred died at 16 mths of broncho-pneumonia, on Christmas Eve (his father was present); he was buried on New Year's Eve.

Charles's sister **Emma**, the same age as his wife Emma, married in 1865 in the Cathedral in Spanish Town, Jamaica! Her husband was **Bolton Beanland**, a navy man who was on duty in Jamaica, and who like Emma came from the north of England.

We don't know what took Emma to Jamaica, but after marrying, Bolton and Emma returned to the UK, and had their first child, Harriet, in the garrison in Chester Castle.

Soon after that, Bolton was posted to Gibraltar, taking his young family, and his brother Abraham Emmett Beanland with him. They decided to settle in Gibraltar; Bolton was able to buy his way out of his military service and in 1873 Bolton and Emma established a stationery business on The Rock, supplying all kinds of goods to a wide variety of customers, ranging from sailors to local dignitaries.

We know from Emma's letters that she was close to Charles and their younger sister Fanny, and they often exchanged photographs of themselves, but there are also mentions in her letters of their younger half-siblings, which showed that they stayed connected to the larger family as well. For example, in 1869, Bolton compares his own brother, 'Emmett', to two of Emma's hard-working younger brothers (Arthur and Alfred):

'What a difference in him and two brothers of Emma's, one is 16 and the other is 14 years old. They have been getting £50 a year each for two or three years now, and last Christmas they got £10 as a Christmas gift from their employers.'

In 1871, back in London, Charles and Emma had settled at 26 Union Rd, South Hackney (now Bradstock Rd). Charles was a Merchant's Clerk and Emma a 'Merchant's Clerk's Wife'.

Next door, at 25 Union Rd, were Charles's step-mother Sarah (listed as head of the family, since her husband was in hospital), grandmother Sarah, and Charles's half-siblings - that's 18 Sawords in 2 houses! Charles's family shared their part of no. 26 with a widowed nurse from Manchester.

Her relationship to the family is given as nurse rather than lodger, so she presumably helped care for Charles's children, and maybe even the Saword children next door (including his disabled half-sister Eliza).

Another family - the Leipps - also lived in the house - a widow, her 12-year old son (a tea-dealer's office boy) and 6-year old daughter. It sounds cramped, and many of the neighbours' children were working to support their families, but this was a relatively comfortable street of clerks and tradespeople, even a piano teacher, in the outskirts of Hackney - close to Victoria Park and cricket ground.

Charles's oldest half-siblings were now old enough to work. Arthur and Alfred had already worked for several years; at 18 and 16 they were an East Indian Colonial Broker (or broker's employees), and a West Indian Merchant. Mary, at 20, had no occupation - compared with her 24-year-old neighbour who worked as a dressmaker. Presumably her brothers earned enough to maintain the family. However, since they had no live-in servants, except a nurse, Mary and her mother would have been kept very busy with domestic duties.

Charles and Emma had three more children in the 1870s - Clara b.1871, Sarah Cecile b.1872 and Sidney Herbert b.1874. Clara died as a baby.

Then, in 1872, Charles's 90-year old grandmother Sarah, who lived next door, passed away.

In 1874, Charles received some tragic news from his sister Emma in Gibraltar. Her husband Bolton had **died of consumption at age 34**, leaving her alone with five children, the youngest a newborn.

Emma soon wrote to Charles to ask if he would be willing to send his eldest son, Frederick, to help her in the shop. She assures him that she would '*treat him as my own*' and points out that Charles was in an office at the same age.

Charles continued to help Abraham and Emma by providing the goods they needed to sell in the shop. Charles also movingly sent Emma a brooch in which she could keep a lock of her husband's hair.

However, Emma had to write again to persuade him to send Fred to help her, this time suggesting that he might take Spanish lessons with Emma's son, and offering to pay his passage.

It's mere speculation on my part to wonder if Charles hesitated to send his young son out to work and far away from home, knowing well how that felt from his own experiences.

However, by 1874, Fred had travelled to Gibraltar to help his aunt. Emma wrote to Charles (refer to p.76) to reassure him that '*Fred has got over his homesickness*' and '*is very sharp in the shop*'. In the same letter, Emma asks Charles to thank their sister Fanny for her photograph (that is the last record of Fanny, who would have been about 25).

We actually know from Harriett's memoirs (p.103) that Fred left a few months later quite suddenly in the night.

'We knew we had an Uncle Charles, Aunt Emma and lots of cousins in London, and we had two photos on the sitting room mantel piece showing a thin gentleman with whiskers, and a thin child with long thin legs on his knee; and the other showing a stout lady holding a baby on her lap; these we knew were Uncle Charles and Aunt Emma.'

Unfortunately, Harriett adds, *'I don't think anyone was sorry when he left, but in justice to the lad I think he was lonely and home-sick, he had no companion of his own age to associate with & no doubt hated the shop and mean dark little house we lived in, and at the same time was too young to appreciate the beauty and romantic history and associations of Gibraltar.'*

Overall, I imagine it must have been quite an adventure for a 12-year old boy.

Emma's letters from 1874-1876 seem to show that the shop was increasingly successful, but then tragedy struck again, and she too died, leaving five orphans in the care of her brother in law. Charles continued to support the family.

In 1878 the youngest, Emily, age 6, came from Gibraltar to the **Sailors' Orphan Girls' School and Home in Hampstead**, where she would be close to her uncle and aunt Saword, and would spend the summer with them in London. Contact between Emma's children and the Sawords in England continued for many years.

Most of Charles's half-siblings also had their own families:

Mary married George Wright. They had no children. Mary was widowed in 1910, and in 1911 she was living with her brother Alfred. Mary was buried in her mother Sarah's grave.

Arthur Edwards, a bookkeeper and manager of a handmade paper mill in Hampshire, married Margaret Farmer, a widow (born Margaret Fairservice - daughter of a medical optician). Margaret's son became Arthur's step-son, and they also had a daughter. For many years, Arthur served with the Queen's Westminsters - a volunteer infantry regiment of the Territorial Army.

By 1911, Arthur was Manager-Director of Eynsford Paper Mill in Eynsford, Kent, a water-powered mill that had been established in 1648, one of the oldest paper mills in the country.

Arthur died in 1936 at his home in Eynsford - 'Ackender' - and many Saword siblings, nieces and nephews attended his funeral, as well as colleagues from the mill.

As a side note, one of those colleagues was another former manager of the mill, Miss Winifred Bird, who had started as a secretary, trained as a chemist, and became the '*only woman paper maker in the world*', traveling to New York in 1932 to show '*Americans [the] value of handmade paper*'!

Alfred, a bank clerk and accountant, married Gertrude Victoria Sharman. He and his family lived with his mother in 1881, and his widowed sister Mary in 1911. Alfred and Gertrude lived in London and had seven children, including a son and five daughters (one child did not survive). Sadly, four of his daughters, who were of marriageable age around WW1, never married - perhaps they lost boyfriends or fiancés in the war. Alfred's son Alfred followed in the Saword footsteps as a Commercial Clerk. Alfred senior died in 1931.

William Gibson, a commercial traveller in 1881, married Minnie James, a dressmaker. They lived in Wales and had 3 children. In 1891 Minnie and her children lived with Minnie's mother in Glamorgan, so presumably William was traveling on business.

In 1892, William travelled from Antwerp to New York. His Ellis Island immigration record shows that he had no calling at that time and planned to settle in Detroit, Michigan. However, William must have returned to England by 1895, as his next child was born that year. (making him yet another Saword who emigrated to America and came back!) William's daughter Violet emigrated to New Zealand. His son Percy was a Sapper with the Royal Engineers in WW1 and served with the Metropolitan Police from 1921-1946.

Walter, William's twin, was also a commercial traveller in 1881 and later a shipping clerk. In 1891 he was still single at 30, and the head of a household that included his younger brothers Edward and Henry, and his mother. At 35, he married Annie/Anna Elizabeth Thorpe; they lived in London and had 2 children. In the late 1920s, Walter, then in his late 60s, made trips to Gibraltar and Tangiers. *Was he visiting his half-sister's family in Gibraltar?* Walter died in 1940.

Henry was another commercial traveller in 1881. However, it seems he had originally wanted a career in the military. In 1877, as a new volunteer recruit in the London Rifle Brigade (aged about 15), Private Saword took part in a prize-meeting of the N (Tower Ward) company at the shooting range in Rainham (now a nature reserve), and was awarded a Cup, value £2. The Lord Mayor gave a speech at the prize presentation, and the Lady Mayoress distributed the prizes. In 1880, age 18, Henry served with the Royal Marines in Portsmouth but was discharged the same year. In 1891 Henry, still living at home with his brothers Walter and Edward and his mother, was a warehouseman - which could have been anything from fairly menial work to management. After 1891 we lose track of Henry.

Florence married Richard Wood, a Cabinet Maker. Florence's father was the very unusually named Esculapius/Æsculapius Simon Jude Wood. Esculapius/Æsculapius was the Greek God of Medicine, and Jude was the patron saint of lost causes, so perhaps Esculapius was a miracle baby, saved by medicine. His name was included in a mocking 1868 newspaper article called 'Queer Yorkshire Baptismal Names'! Esculapius had a job to fix lightning conductors to the tops of buildings, and in 1869 a newspaper reported on the '*extraordinary climbing and scaling exploits performed by a man belonging to Bradford, who rejoices in the possession of a string of extraordinary Christian names*'. In 1869 he and his name made the papers again, when a violent thug was restrained '*only with the help of a man bearing the classico-medical name Æsculapius Wood.*'

Finally, Edward George, known as George, was a wine merchant with his own business - Edward George & Co Wine Shippers. He married Clara Mary E Yeoman and they had 3 children (2 survived).

In 1897, when his first child was a toddler, he travelled on the Orient Line - either to Italy or Australia (Italy is more likely, but Australian wines were starting to win awards in the late 19th C so Australia is not impossible).

The family lived in Somerset in 1901 but was mostly based in London. In 1910, the address of George's company was 43 to 45 Great Tower St, very close to the Tower of London. The following year, George's much older half-brother Charles qualified to be on the City of London electoral register due to owning property at that same address. Either George leased the property from Charles, or they were in business together. In 1934, George had an adjudication with the High Court of Justice, and in 1938 he filed for bankruptcy. He died 2 years later.

Either Edward's wife Clara or daughter Clara performed in a fundraising concert for the Home of the Concert Artists Association in 1926 - reported in *The Stage*. Edward and Clara's son George Stanley ('Stanley') also had a theatrical streak. At his school's annual swimming contest in St Pancras Public Baths, 1910, Stanley won a fancy dress pole walking contest. He 'made a very fine lady in blue with hair of a golden hue, and wearing a short skirt.' A few years later Britain was at war, and George was busy with much more serious things, as a corporal with the King's Royal Rifle Corps' Military Foot Police.

Returning to Charles Edward Saword - in the 1990s, his grandson **Alfred Saword** wrote that his grandfather, Charles, had emigrated late in life:

'I know [Charles] also had income from the ownership of land and property. When the last of his children had grown up and left home, he

gave one large plot of land to his son Fred, another plot to my father [James], left his house and other sources of income to his wife and sailed for Australia. Nothing further was heard from him.'

However, in truth, Charles did not leave the country; rather, he left his wife!

In 1878, Charles had a baby with another woman, Jane.

Charles was listed as the father on the birth certificate of Florence Louisa Saword, and was the informant who registered the birth. His address was given as 81, Chilton St, Rotherhithe, Surrey (Jane's home?). Jane had given her name as Jane Saword, formerly Stovell.

Charles and Jane's relationship was not a one-off affair, but a long term partnership.

Like Emma, Jane was from a working class family.

Jane Stovell was born in Effingham, near Dorking, Surrey, in about 1844, to Thomas Stovell, a blacksmith, and Elizabeth. After her mother died when Jane was 17, her father remarried a woman only 4 years older than Jane, and he continued having children with his new wife into his late 70s! Jane's older brother Thomas was a publican who went bankrupt, and in 1888 he shot himself.

Between 1878 and 1901, Charles's two families lived north and south of the river, and we only have tantalising snapshots from the census returns.

The 1881 census show Charles and Emma still living together at 26 Union Road with six children (the whereabouts of Jane and Florence that year is unknown).

In 1882, Charles and Emma had one more child - eight years after the last one had been born. Sadly, baby Jane only lived for one hour. She had a 'foramen ovale persistent', known now as a PFO - a heart defect that is actually present in ¼ of the adult population. In Jane's case, it was evidently severe enough that she did not survive. It must have been very sad for her father to register her birth and death at the same time.

In 1891, Charles and Emma lived in Gascoyne Rd, very near Union Rd, with four of their children and son in law, whereas Jane 'Saword' and Florence lived in Camberwell, and Jane reported that she was married.

Jane may have had more children with Charles; the 1911 census notes that she had four children who died, but oddly did not mention a living child, even though Florence lived to old age.

In 1899, Charles witnessed his daughter Florence's marriage in Camberwell, to Charles Thomas Gibbons, a hosier who lived on the same street as his bride. (the other witness was the unusually named Wafforne Pearce Piper, who simply went by 'Pearce Piper'!).

Finally, by 1901 Jane and Charles (then a South American Merchant's Clerk) lived together in Camberwell as husband and wife.

It's unlikely that Charles and Emma got a divorce. However, Charles probably gave her enough money to live on comfortably.

In 1901, she lived in Tottenham with her adult daughters Emma and Sarah. Emma senior lived 'on her own means' (i.e. she was financially independent) and she claimed to be a 'widow' (perhaps something she had learned from her in laws 20 years earlier?). Her daughters worked from home as a dressmaker and embroiderer on their own accounts, and may have earned enough to support their mother, but Charles was a man who had supported his late sister's family in Gibraltar, and I like to think he would have taken care of his own wife and children too.

In 1911, Emma was living with her daughter Charlotte in Stoke Newington. However, she was probably financially independent.

Alf wrote,

'All I can say from my own knowledge is that [Charles] appeared to have left his wife well provided for. When she visited us in Southend-on-Sea ... she had her own house, was well dressed and quite cheerful. Her husband had not left until all children had grown up and were self-supporting. She had a reputation for being "difficult" and even her brother George Read agreed with that.'

In 1911, Jane ('Mrs J Saword') was living alone in Brockley, near Camberwell, with three lodgers. The census says she is a widow, but no death record for Charles can be found. Given that he was a South American Merchant's Clerk, he may have died abroad.

There is no sign of Charles in the 1911 census; however, an electoral register that year showed that he owned property in the City of London but lived in "Elmcroft", a house in Buckhurst Hill, Essex, quite far from Brockley.

Adding to the mystery, when Jane travelled alone from Quebec to Liverpool in August 1911, after attending her brother's funeral in Canada, her occupation in the passenger manifest was 'Wife'.

Whatever happened to Charles, we know that Emma passed away in 1920 (aged 82) and Jane in 1928 (aged 84). Emma was living with her daughter, Charlotte's, family in Southend-on-Sea, Essex. She died from an intracapsular fracture of femur (hip fracture).

Jane lived in South Norwood, and she died in Bedford from acute bronchitis, with her daughter Florence Louisa in attendance (she also left her possessions to Florence). Both Emma AND Jane were recorded as **'Widow of Charles Edward Saword, Shipping Clerk'**!

We'll probably never know more about these complicated relationships, and how many family members knew the truth, or simply believed that Charles had gone 'Down Under', never to be heard from again!

James Edward Saword (1867-1944)
& Mary Jane (Jennie) Read (1870-1959)

James was the third son of Charles Edward and Emma, and the fourth of their seven children.

He grew up in Hackney, and in 1881, age 13, he was still at school, although his three older siblings were all working already - 18-year old Frederick. (who had helped his aunt Emma in Gibraltar) was a jeweller's clerk, Emma, 16, was an apprentice, and Arthur, 15, was living in Harwich with his uncle and aunt Frederick and Jane Read. Frederick, his mother's brother, was a bootmaker, and Arthur was a tailor apprentice. Presumably within a couple of years James would have started his career as well.

Frederick, Arthur, and James all married within two years - Frederick to Alice Maud Benfield, Arthur to Elizabeth Jane Wilding, and James, in December 1888, to his first cousin, Mary Jane Read, who went by 'Jennie' (she didn't like her real name).

James's father Charles was a witness at the marriage.

Jennie was the daughter of George Read, an older brother of Emma Read - James Saword's mother. George Read was by then a Detective Inspector, and retired just 20 days after his daughter's wedding. Cousin marriage wasn't unusual, and was especially popular with the middle and upper classes; Charles Darwin married his first cousin Emma Wedgwood, and

270

even Queen Victoria and Prince Albert were first cousins. However, there was growing concern about it by the late 19th century. Nevertheless, James and Jennie's 55-year marriage seems to have been a stable one.

Their first child, Daisy Ethel, was born in 1890. In 1891, James, a Clerk to an Electric Engineer, Jennie, and 10-mth old Daisy lived in Thornton Heath (Croydon). Their 2nd child, Frederick James, died as a newborn in 1892, but by 1901 they had added 3 more children to the family: Sidney James b.1894, Algernon Leslie b.1896, and Edith Olive b.1898. The family moved to Essex in around 1897, to a big house in Hadleigh, South End. After Jennie's father George retired, his wife Mary Ann had become very frail, and James and Jennie moved in with them so they could help out.

In 1901, James and Jennie were living close to Jennie's parents in Prittlewell, Southend-on-Sea. James was a Builder's Clerk's Agent to a Brickmaker.

James's sister Charlotte, an embroideress, married George Daniel Greenwood in 1890. George was an umbrella salesman, but he was also a music hall performer billed as 'Gus Daniels'! As newly-weds they lived with Charlotte's parents Charles and Emma. Their first child, the theatrically named Lorenzo, tragically died as an infant in 1892 after receiving his smallpox vaccination. Their next child, Archibald (Archie) was born in 1895.

George was often on the road performing, and in 1901 and 1911 he was not at home when the census was taken. There are dozens of ads and reviews for Gus Daniels' performances in the British newspaper archives between ~1895-1905 from all parts of the UK. George performed with many different artists at each show, from contortionists to 'negro comedians', so must have met countless colourful characters. He usually performed alone, but one review from 1898 praised his performance of the sketch, '**The Demon of the Cellar**' with Ernest Lepard. Ernest directed five silent comedies in 1913.

George was a '*descriptive vocalist*' or '*character vocalist*' with a tenor voice. Descriptive singers told dramatic or comic stories through song, often with the assistance of painted backcloths, extras, and elaborate props. Charles Chaplin, the father of silent movie star Charlie Chaplin, was working as a descriptive vocalist in the same time period and they even performed at the same venue - the Alhambra Theatre of Varieties in Belfast (Charles senior and junior were close in age to George and his son Archie).

Like George, Charles lived in London but also performed in the provinces, and even in America. By the end of the 19th century, descriptive singing, usually associated with 'extravagant makeup and songs to match', was not as popular as it had been in the past. Additionally, Music Hall was heavily infused with alcohol, since performers were frequently required to encourage customers to buy drinks. As a result, Charles Chaplin became an alcoholic, and died from related diseases in 1901 at only 38.

Thankfully, George did not go down the same route. Instead, he and Charlotte moved out of London after 1911 and for a while lived next door to James and Jennie. George even did some clerical work for his brother in law. Archie was almost the same age as his cousin Algy, and they were close. The two boys' bedrooms shared a wall, and they drilled a hole, placed a bicycle tube through the wall, and used it as a speaking tube!

In spite of George's retiring from the stage, George and Charlotte continued to be a charismatic couple; Archie's son remembers that his grandma (Charlotte) was 'a very correct lady yet allowed him to do things that his other Nan didn't. In later years [Charlotte and George] 'put up' some who came to perform at the local Theatre (the Palace Theatre). One was Robertson Hare. He also used to perform at the seafront here in Southend-on-Sea.' Robertson Hare was a comic character actor of stage and screen (including >40 films) from before WW1 through to the 1960s.

By 1905 all of James's sisters and brothers were married:

Sarah, an embroideress like Charlotte, married Robert Henry Greenwood, a younger brother of Charlotte's husband George. Robert was a bookkeeper rather than an entertainer. Robert and Sarah had 2 daughters.

Sidney, an electrician, married Eliza Lethaby.

Lastly, at the age of 40, James's older sister Emma married George Longcroft, a merchant/representative for a German pharmaceutical firm. They had no children, but still employed a live-in domestic servant.

The first decade of the 20th century brought two more children for James and Jennie - Edward George b.1905, and lastly Alfred Charles b.1906 - as well as commercial success for James, who rose from being a worker to an employer.

Part of this success may have been due to an inheritance from his father Charles - who left him a plot of land before his 'emigration to Australia'. **It's unclear at what point Charles went off the radar. I can't help wondering how he said his goodbyes.**

In 1906, James was an agent for a Southend-on-Sea timber merchant, Stammers & Stammers. That year he gave evidence in the trial of a builder's manager (clerk) for Holding & Holding, who was forging cheques and embezzling the company.

In 1908, Sidney and Algernon (aged 14 and 12) were in court charged with letting off fireworks in the streets! They were cautioned and discharged.

Sometime before 1911, James's father in law George Read sold the house in Hadleigh, and bought 2 adjacent homes on Bournemouth Rd - one for himself and his wife, and one for James and Jennie. He named his house Alpha Villa, and the other 'Saxted Villa' - presumably a reference to James's father Charles.

In the 1911 census, James's family lived in Saxted - 53 Bournemouth Rd. He was a Builder's Merchant. However, although not formerly trained in architecture, James was also recorded as the 'architect' for many building projects in Southend-on-Sea from 1901-1912.

James's children were also embarking on their own careers - Daisy (20) was a dressmaker, Sidney (17) a clerk, and Algernon ('Algy'; 15) was following in his father's footsteps as an architect's pupil. Algy was artistic, a useful skill for an architect, but he also left behind some quirky cartoons.

Things seemed to be going very well for the Saword family.

However, in 1912, James - like his grandfather Edward 60 years earlier - decided to up sticks and emigrate to North America!

According to Alfred, James sold the plot of land he'd inherited from his father to his brother Fred. Jennie's half-sister had recently been widowed, and was happy to move in with her father and step-mother. This meant that James and Jennie were released from the responsibility of caring for her parents. Saxted Villa was rented out.

Then, James left for Canada, followed by Algernon (who travelled from Southampton to Quebec, in July, on the Cunard SS Ascania). Finally, the rest of the family followed, making a new home in Winnipeg, the capital of Manitoba province in Canada.

Jim Blanchard, author of '**Winnipeg 1912**', describes a boom period in the city:
'At the beginning of the last century, no city on the continent was growing faster or was more aggressive than Winnipeg. No year in the city's history epitomized this energy more than 1912, when Winnipeg was on the crest of a period of unprecedented prosperity. In just forty years, it had grown from a village on the banks of the Red River to become the third largest city in Canada. In the previous decade alone, its population had tripled to nearly 170,000 and it now dominated the economy and society of western Canada. As Canada's most cosmopolitan and ethnically diverse centre, with most of its population under the age of forty, it was also the country's liveliest city, full of bustle and optimism.'

The family photograph album shows them enjoying winter fun in Winnipeg, including tobogganing. However, they apparently found the winters very hard; on average, January days in Winnipeg don't get above -10 Celsius.

Then, in 1914, Britain declared war on Germany, and Canada was automatically at war as well. Sidney and Algy were both old enough to enlist.

However, as Alf tells us, they were *'very different. Sid became religious when in his teens, and joined the Plymouth Brethren. Algy liked the outdoor life, first in the Scouts, then the Canadian Territorials, and finally volunteered for war at the age of 18.'*

Sidney later wrote that he chose to be a **conscientious objector**. However, Algernon signed up in 1914 and joined the 90th Winnipeg Rifles in the Canadian Expeditionary Force (CEF). He spent Christmas 1914 back in England; The Winnipeg Rifles trained on Salisbury Plain and Algy's battalion even had a church service at Stonehenge! Algy was deployed to Europe in 1915 as a Signaller, a very dangerous position. Between April and July, back in Winnipeg, Algy was reported to be a prisoner of war or wounded. He had in fact been wounded (by chlorine gas) and taken prisoner in Ypres, Belgium, but then died on 24 April, at the age of 19.

In 1916, there was a census in Manitoba. The Saword family lived on Benning St, Winnipeg. They were Baptists. James was a Clerk for Whole Sale Provision, Daisy still a dressmaker, Sidney a stenographer for CPR (Canadian Pacific Railway), and Edith a saleswoman at Eatons.(Eatons department store in downtown Winnipeg opened in 1905, and was one of the world's largest department stores; by 1919 it covered 21 acres and employed 8000 people.).

Surprisingly, and poignantly, Algernon was listed on the census. Algy was noted as performing military service but was also an architect at Clemens. (Paul Clemens was an Icelandic architect who designed numerous unremarkable structures in the Winnipeg building boom from 1908-1914). In fact, Algy was not confirmed dead until as late as November 1916.

After Algernon's death was confirmed, the family, except Sidney, chose to return to England, travelling 3rd class on the *Andania* from New York to Plymouth in 1916. They were headed back to Bournemouth Rd, Southend, but they could not evict the tenant due to war regulations. James and Jennie possibly rented a different house in Southend, but sent their sons Edward ('Ted') and Alf to board with James's youngest brother, Sidney.

Sidney and Eliza had no children, and lived in Westcliff, close to Charlotte Greenwood. (Alf never met entertainer George; he thought Charlotte was a widow!) In 1917, James was employed on government contracts in Kent, so the family moved to Ramsgate, Kent.

On the day they moved, Emma Saword came to visit her son James, brother George, and niece Jennie. She would have been 80. Alfred, who was then about 10, remembered it well more than 70 years later

James's war work included building aerodromes and rest camps at Dymnchurch, Hythe, and Folkestone.

Back in Winnipeg, Sidney, a rate clerk, was drafted into the CEF - 1st Depot Battalion. He was discharged in December 1918 (after the war) due to being a railroad employee.

Some of James and Jennie's nephews also fought in the war. Archie, the son of George and Charlotte, was an electrician in the RAF. Edwin, the son of Arthur and Elizabeth, fought in the London regiment, and was promoted to second Lt. in 1918.

They both survived, but Ralph, the son of Fred and Alice, fought with the Royal Fusiliers and was killed in France in 1917. The year after the war, James and Jennie's daughter Daisy married Albert Langley. He had served all through the war, being wounded three times! Edith ('Edie') married Douglas Woodcock in 1920 - he was probably a veteran as well.

The 20s and early 30s brought some hardships for many of the Sawords. James may have lost a large amount of his money in about 1920.

His granddaughter Diane says,
'My father didn't talk to me about him and he died before I was born. Mum used to say that Alf was very cautious about investing money because his father had lost a lot, I think in the 1920s financial crash. I know they lived in a big, probably 4 storey house in a (Georgian?) crescent (I was shown the outside of it), in Broadstairs at one stage and my father went to a private school, but had to leave at 14 and start work - going to night class (where he met my mum, Ida Martin), to get further qualifications.'

At the same night class, Alfred's brother Ted met his future wife, Ida's friend Maray Swaffer, known as May. The couples would be married almost exactly a year apart, in Ramsgate, in 1928 (Ted & May) and 1929 (Alf & Ida).

James's daughter Daisy had three children from 1920-30. Tragically, her middle child, Ronald, died age 6 in 1932, and the youngest, Mary contracted meningitis the same year, age 2, and was left disabled.

According to Diane,
'When two year old Mary was taken into hospital, Daisy and Jennie went to visit her and found that her bed had been wheeled out onto a cold balcony and it looked as if she was being left to die; Jennie wasn't having any of that and took her back home.'
(In spite of this, Mary lived a long life, until 2005).

James's eldest brother, Fred, had started his working life helping his **aunt Emma in Gibraltar**. It was the beginning of a long and creative career! After returning from Gibraltar he was a jeweller's clerk, but by the late 1880s he ran a garden nursery and seed business in Thornton Heath, Croydon. In 1920, he was a '*Gibraltar Merchant*', in business as '**Stone & Saword**'. From about 1925, he ran Saword & Co, a retailer of cloth caps, including army caps, in Fitzrovia. Meanwhile, he kept a small farm at his home - 'The Hut' - in the village of Woldingham, near Caterham in Surrey - a few miles from the home of Charles Darwin. This was the land he had been given by his father Charles (and, later, brother James).

Alfred recalled visiting his uncle Fred, in about 1926,
'My father and mother, with brother Ted and his girlfriend in father's car, and myself following on a motorbike with Ida riding pillion, went for a day's trip to visit uncle Fred. He had built a large house on the land. It was surrounded by lovely countryside and had several acres of land, part of which was orchard, with a row of beehives, and part was pasture on which he had 3 pedigree Jersey cows. There was also a kitchen garden. We had a lovely cream and fruit tea, and afterwards went on to what had been my father's plot on the other side of the road.'

James's plot was being used as extra pasture for Fred's cows. I wonder if James regretted selling his share before going to Canada!

However, in 1929, Fred, trading as Saword & Co, **declared bankruptcy**.

Arthur, who was out of contact with his brother James's family, had led quite a different life to those of Fred or James. As a teenager he had been a tailor's apprentice but in 1891, a newlywed, he was an Assurance Agent for Prudential, though living in a mostly working class neighbourhood. Prudential grew rapidly at that time and by 1900 they insured ⅓ of the UK population. However, clearly something went wrong for Arthur and Elizabeth, because in 1901 he was a packer for an electric light company, in a neighbourhood surrounded by boilers and stokers, factory workers, and other labourers.

By 1911 things had somewhat improved; Arthur was an electrician for Hackney Borough, and his son Edwin was a clerk. Edwin survived the war and has descendants in New Zealand. The youngest daughter, Ethel, was a keen musician, winning medals for pianoforte and elocution. Her Hungarian music teacher became her husband, and he has the longest name on my family tree - 'Jules L C de Merey, formerly known as Merey De Kaposmere Et Kisdovoran, Gyula Lipot Karoly Vilmos Oliver'!

Sarah and Robert Greenwood's older daughter Ruth became a missionary. In 1930, she was in South America, probably Peru, and in 1936 Burma. Ruth became ill with appendicitis in Burma, and unfortunately died during surgery. Her body had to be brought down a mountain. There is a memorial to her in St Peter's, Harold Wood, Essex.

James's son, Sidney (Ruth's cousin), was also a missionary. After WW1,

Sidney remained in Canada, and married a nurse, Eleanor Scott. They travelled frequently as missionaries, and eventually raised their family in Venezuela.

In 1975, Sidney published his autobiography, *Fifty Years With the Gospel in Venezuela*. Sidney and Eleanor have numerous descendants in Venezuela, El Salvador, and Canada, many of whom continue to work as missionaries.

Charles's son, Sidney Saword, the missionary, with his wife Eleanor, and children Margaret Jean, Ruth, Eunice, James, and Sidney (Jack) - in about 1938-9

James & Jennie celebrated their Golden Wedding in 1938, on the brink of WW2. They lived in another house named 'Saxted', in Broadstairs, Kent.

James & Jennie Saword's Golden Wedding, 1938

That same year, Alfred and Ida moved their family from Ramsgate to **Bolton, Lancashire**, where Alf was employed as Chief Sanitary Inspector. Later in the war, they moved again to Hull, where Alf was appointed Chief Sanitary Inspector and Chief Housing Inspector.

The Second World War brought more hard times for the Sawords.
James had lost a son and nephew in the first world war, and he lost another of his sons, Ted, in WW2.

Ted, a manager of a furniture and travel agent in Mumbles, Glamorgan, was a Company Quartermaster (CQMS) with the 308 Reserve Motor Transport Company of the Royal Army Service Corps (RASC). He served in France and Egypt before being deployed to Greece.
During Operation Demon, on 26/27 April 1941, the Royal and Merchant Navy attempted to evacuate British Commonwealth troops from mainland Greece. However, during the withdrawal from Navplion, the Dutch troopship Slamat was bombed and caught fire.
After orders to abandon ship, the survivors were picked up by HMS Diamond and, later, by HMS Wryneck.
As the two destroyers tried to catch up with the convoy they were both bombed and sunk in close proximity.
Forty-nine survivors were picked up by HMS Griffin at around 02:00 the next day and another seventeen men eventually made it to Crete in one of Wryneck's whalers.
Ted survived the two sinkings, but despite being a champion swimmer, he was later reported missing.
[With thanks to Brian Crabb, author of the upcoming book Operation Demon, http://briancrabbmaritimebooks.co.uk]

Two years later, his widow, May, made national news with her struggle to be recognised as a 'war widow' - and receive adequate compensation - because her husband was '*still missing*' and had not '*officially been presumed dead*', in spite of a letter from the War Office informing her that '*in view of the long lapse in time during which no news has been received from your husband ... it is feared there can be very little hope that he can be still alive.*'
This infuriating red tape left her with three young children to care for under serious financial pressure.

During the war, Ramsgate became a danger zone because of a possible

German invasion, and was made an evacuation area. Also, Emma's home in London was suffering from constant air raids. Elderly people and children received a government allowance for evacuating.

Fred was on his own after his wife Alice died in 1940, so it makes sense that Emma and Jennie, as well as Daisy and her disabled daughter Mary, all went to stay with Fred, whose house was much further from the coast. James and Daisy's husband had stayed home due to work commitments.

Alf wrote that:

'Daisy's husband had stayed there all the time as he could not afford to lose his job as a compositor on the local newspaper.' With his experience in WW1 *'he was used to such conditions'* and *'the government had provided strong shelters in the back gardens of all houses in danger areas.'*

However, the evacuees weren't as safe in rural Surrey as they thought...

Alfred recounted a frightening episode, in 1944:

'One night a stray bomber dropped a stick of bombs across the house (a "stick" being 3 or 4 bombs released one after the other, to fall in a line about 100 yards or so apart).

None made a direct hit but the first was a short distance from the front of the house, shattering all the windows and blowing open the door.

The next, a second later, shattered the back windows and slammed shut the door. All the family had taken shelter under table and all escaped with only minor scratches from flying glass and plaster.

My parents then returned home for the rest of the war.... with a battery of anti-aircraft guns opposite their houses.'

Emma died later that year, and Fred died in 1945. Unfortunately, due to age and probably the extreme stress of the times, James and all but one of his siblings (and most of their spouses) died between 1935 and 1945. James himself died in 1944. Arthur was the only sibling to outlive the war; he passed away in 1954.

However, Jennie - Diane's **'Grandma Saword'** - lived until 1959 in a bungalow called ... Saxted!

Her daughter, Diane's Aunt Daisy, lived in an adjoining bungalow, and Jennie helped care for her granddaughter Mary.

Diane visited them each year until Jennie died in Thanet, at the age of 90.

Jennie had also inherited the house in Ramsgate that her son Alfred's family had once lived in, and she left half of that to Daisy, *'in recognition of the fact that Daisy had lived next door to her for 30 years and been a great help to her throughout her adult life.'*

The rest was shared equally between the family, Ted's share being divided between his children.

Alfred & Ida Saword

Alfred and Ida Saword had four children.

Tragically, their only son, David, who worked as a policeman in Hong Kong, died there in his early 20s, in 1967.

**James's son, Alfred, and Ida
with Janet, Rosemary, David, and Diane – 1955**

Alf & Ida's grandchildren still have the Saword spirit of travel and adventure, and have put down roots in France and Chile.

As for my husband and myself, we emigrated to California, where we lived for 16 years, but like so many of the Sawords who went to the Americas before us, we have returned to England!

REFERENCES

I made many discoveries online. My searches revealed information on all the following:

Anglo-Ashanti Wars

The Third Anglo-Ashanti War, also known as the "First Ashanti Expedition", lasted from 1873 to 1874.

On 27th September, 1873 a team of Royal Engineers landed at Cape Coast Castle. Their job was to expand the single file track that led to Coomassie, 160 miles (260km) away into a road that was suitable for troop movements. By 29th January, 1874, the road was more than half completed and they were close to Ashanti outposts.

The Battle of Amoaful was fought on 31 January. A road was cut to the village and the Black Watch led the way, forming square in the clearing with the Rifle Brigade, whilst flanking columns moved around the village. With the pipes playing 'The Campbells Are Coming' the Black Watch charged with bayonets and the shocked Ashantis fled. The flank columns were slow moving in the jungle and the Ashantis moved around them, in their normal horseshoe formation and attacked the camp 2 miles (3.2km) to the rear, the Royal Engineers defended themselves until relieved by the Rifle Brigade. Although there was another small battle, two days later, the Battle of Ordashu, the action had been decisive and the route to Kumasi was open. There were 3 killed and 165 wounded Europeans, 1 killed and 29 African troops wounded. The Asantahene, the ruler of the Ashanti, after being threatened with being chased further north, signed a harsh British treaty, the Treaty of Fomena in July, 1874, to end the war.

Darwin's Teaching of Women's Inferiority

It is known less widely that many evolutionists, including Charles Darwin, also taught that women are biologically inferior to men.

Educational Reform in Germany: 1865-1914

Franco-Prussian War

German Empire (1871-1918)

German S.S. "Elbe"

From Log Cabin to White House

Publisher: Hodder & Stroughton

Humboldt's Travels in America

HMS Northumberland

Irish Presbyterian Kirk

Burnley Listed Buildings
Kirk Church, Lancashire

Sailors' Orphan Girls' School and Home – Hampstead:

Rosslyn Hill, 1878

Retracing our steps through Church Row on our way towards Rosslyn Hill—which is a continuation of the High Street towards London—we notice on our right, at the corner of Greenhill Road and Church Lane, a large and handsome brick building, with slightly projecting wings, gables, and a cupola turret.

This is the Sailors' Orphan Girls' School and Home, which was originally established in 1829, in Frognal House, on the west side of the parish church. The present building was erected in 1869, from the designs of Mr. Ellis.

The objects of the institution are the "maintenance, clothing, and education of orphan daughters of sailors and marines, and the providing of a home for them after leaving, when out of situations." The number of inmates is about one hundred, and the children look healthy and cheerful. Its annual income averages about £2,000. This institution was opened by Prince Arthur, now Duke of Connaught, in whose honour the road between it and the Greenhill is named Prince Arthur's Road.

Poppy Water

In the article, Benjamin Breen tried to recreate "poppy water" as described in the 19th Century and found it gave "A noticeable glow of wellbeing set in around half an hour after drinking less than half the concoction, attributable to the traces of opiates in poppy seeds".

Shoeburyness

In the wake of Crimea, the Royal Artillery School of Gunnery was established at Shoeburyness in 1859, with Horseshoe Barracks and various other amenities being added not long afterwards. Over the years that followed Shoeburyness was integral to the development of new and improved artillery weapons.

Syrup Of Ipecac

Ipecac was used in cough mixtures as an expectorant or an emetic from the 18th until the early 20th Century.

Use Of Ipecac For Medicinal Purposes

Ipecac has been widely used in syrup form as a potent and effective emetic. Ipecac powder had been used to induce sweating at the onset of influenza, and small amounts of the extract have been incorporated into cough syrups as expectorants. Emetine, derived from the root, has been used for more than a century to treat dysentery.

Sir Ughtred & Earl Spencer

ABOUT THE AUTHOR

V.J. Beanland (Vanessa Wester) was born and raised in Gibraltar.

With a degree in Accountancy & Law, she initially worked for two leading accountancy firms, before she changed career and qualified as a secondary school mathematics teacher.

For many years, she devoted her time to the upbringing of her children, whilst giving up a lot of her time to help voluntary organisations.

In 2010, Vanessa embarked on a new career and launched into the world of fiction and publishing via Smashwords, Amazon and Createspace. Over the space of four years, she wrote and published four books – Hybrid, Complications, Return, and Emily. In addition, she compiled an anthology called First Date (Love & Regrets), and then published six anthologies to raise money for fantastic causes, such as Cancer Research and the British Heart Foundation.

In 2017, Vanessa published 'Journey to Gibraltar', under her maiden name V.J. Beanland, as an eBook to mark 150 years of the first arrival of a Beanland on the Rock of Gibraltar. But, knowing that her father wanted a physical copy, she updated the original and this version was born.

Reading and writing will always be her greatest indulgence. The day she decided to start writing her ideas down, she found another way to lose herself in a book, whilst finding an outlet for her imagination. It is the best way she can think of to escape from everyday life.

Vanessa is currently working with teenagers again on the Isle of Wight, and thoroughly enjoys being back in the world of secondary education.

Find out more about her via www.vanessawesterwriter.blogspot.com

Printed in Great Britain
by Amazon

48075410R00162